Lianne Holten

Mothers, Medicine and Morality in Rural Mali

MANDE WORLDS

edited by

Jan Jansen,
Mohamed Saidou N'Daou,
Dorothea Schulz,
and Stephen Wooten

vol. 6

LIT

Lianne Holten

Mothers, Medicine and Morality in Rural Mali

An ethnographic study of therapy management of pregnancy and children's illness episodes

LIT

Cover photograph by Agnès Pataux © 2009
Fanta Kante with her grandson Fajugu Kante in Farabako,
published with permission.

Bibliographic information published by the Deutsche Nationalbibliothek
The Deutsche Nationalbibliothek lists this publication in the Deutsche Nationalbibliografie; detailed bibliographic data are available in the Internet at http://dnb.d-nb.de.

ISBN 978-3-643-90301-3

A catalogue record for this book is available from the British Library

Klosbachstr. 107
CH-8032 Zürich
Tel. +41 (0) 44-251 75 05
Fax +41 (0) 44-251 75 06
E-Mail: zuerich@lit-verlag.ch
http://www.lit-verlag.ch

LIT VERLAG Dr. W. Hopf
Berlin 2013
Fresnostr. 2
D-48159 Münster
Tel. +49 (0) 2 51-620 320
Fax +49 (0) 2 51-23 19 72
E-Mail: lit@lit-verlag.de
http://www.lit-verlag.de

Distribution:
In Germany: LIT Verlag Fresnostr. 2, D-48159 Münster
Tel. +49 (0) 2 51-620 32 22, Fax +49 (0) 2 51-922 60 99, E-mail: vertrieb@lit-verlag.de

In Austria: Medienlogistik Pichler-ÖBZ, e-mail: mlo@medien-logistik.at
In Switzerland: B + M Buch- und Medienvertrieb, e-mail: order@buch-medien.ch
In the UK: Global Book Marketing, e-mail: mo@centralbooks.com
In North America: International Specialized Book Services, e-mail: orders@isbs.com

For Traina Kante, I wish her well

Fanta Kante with her grandson Fajugu Kante in Farabako, published with permission.

In the series Mande Worlds have appeared:

Vol. 1. Stephen Wooten (ed.) *Wari Matters: Ethnographic Explorations of Money in the Mande World* (2005)
Vol. 2. Stephen Belcher, Jan Jansen & Mohamed N'Daou (eds.) *Mande Mansa: Essays in Honor of David C. Conrad* (2008)
Vol. 3. Amber B. Gemmeke *Marabout Women in Dakar: Creating Trust in a Rural Urban Space* (2008)
Vol. 4. Molly Roth *Ma parole s'achète: Money, Identity and Meaning in Malian Jeliya* (2008)
Vol. 5. Sabine Luning *Les nouvelles choses – rites et politique dans la chefferie de Maane (Burkina Faso), 1960-2000* (2010)
Vol. 6. Lianne Holten *Mothers, Medicine and Morality in Rural Mali An ethnographic study of therapy management of pregnancy and children's illness episodes* (2012)

TABLE OF CONTENTS

ACKNOWLEDGEMENTS ix

1. INTRODUCTION: THERAPY MANAGEMENT OF PREGNANCY AND CHILDREN'S ILLNESSES IN FARABAKO 1
Biomedicine in the middle of nowhere 1
A research trajectory from mortality to morality 4
Pregnancy strategies and obstetrical outcome 6
Illness narratives of therapy management 9
Household dynamics of health 11
Local discourse on health and health care 11
Shame as a factor in therapy management 12
Respondent's feedback: 'Do not forget poverty' 12
Moralities in health as a main focus 13
Research questions 14
Theoretical orientation 15
Structure of the book 17

2. THE VILLAGE OF FARABAKO 21
An historical sketch 21
Agriculture in a 'forgotten zone' 23
Mande personhood: Pervasive hierarchy 25
A village of brothers 27
Spirits, power objects and Allah 29
Social change: Participating in the money economy 32
Conclusion 34

3. HEALTH CARE OPTIONS IN FARABAKO 35
Musokɔrɔbaw: The power of words 35
Somaw: With the help of the fetish 40
Herbalists: In the name of Allah 43
Biomedical health care 44
Social change: Health as an individual responsibility 46
Conclusion 47

4. THE VULNERABILITY CONTEXT OF CHILD MORBIDITY AND MORTALITY 49
A typical illness episode 49
Vulnerability context 50
Exposure to physical risk 51
- *Living conditions* 51
- *Food insecurity* 53
- *Endemic infectious diseases* 54
- *No (biomedical) prenatal care* 55
- *Teenage pregnancy* 56
- *Female circumcision* 57
(In)Capacity to cope with health adversity 59
- *Schooling/biomedical knowledge* 59
- *Limited reproductive choice* 60
- *Social capital* 61
Potentiality: The social risk of shame 64
Identity construction as a 'gelling point' 65
Passivity as agency 66
Conclusion 67

5. THE MORALITY AND ETHICS OF SHAME 69
Shame and honour 69
Shame as a technology of the self 71
Shame as the performance of ethics 72
Maloya: Shame in Farabako 75
- *Institutional shame* 75
- *Embodied shame* 76
- *Public discourse of shame in Farabako* 77
Prohibitions: 'Having shame' 77
Gossip: Feeling ashamed 80
Shaming: Making someone feel shameless 82
Ethical moments: The social risk of being considered shameless 83
- *Binetu's story: A respectful widow* 84
- *Nakani's story: An abortion gone wrong* 84
- *Narama's story: Asking for help, or not* 87
Inhabiting a moral discourse 88
Conclusion 90

6. THE MATERNITY CLINIC AS A ZONE OF AWKWARD ENGAGEMENT 93
Perceptions and practices of obstetric care 95
- *Perceptions of reproductive risk* 95
- *Medicine use* 97
- *Monitoring the foetus* 98
- *Managing obstetric complications* 99
Prenatal care in a landscape of shame 100
Perceptions of good medical practice 102
- *The secrecy and danger of knowledge* 102
- *Characteristics of a good healer* 104
- *Lack of privacy and autonomy* 107
Social and economic conditions under which midwives work 109
The ethical dilemmas of a new biomedical practice 109
Conclusion 112

7. ILLNESS NARRATIVES OF THERAPY MANAGEMENT: THE MULTIPLE SOCIAL REALITIES OF ILLNESS 115
Methodology 115
Illness narratives as performative representations 116
Varying accounts of Baba's illness episode: A case study of household therapy management 118
- *Father Kanda's account* 118
- *Mother Fatumata's account* 118
- *'Grandmother' Dusuba's account* 120
- *Context in which the narrative was told* 121
Conflicting stories 125
- *Symptoms and diagnoses* 125
- *Treatment* 125
- *Duration of illness* 126
Health surveys: The child gets lost in the telling 127
- *Positioning within medical pluralism and status within the household* 127
- *Contesting/affirming ideal gender roles* 128
- *Gendered knowledge: 'Women know nothing'* 128
- *Gendered diagnoses: diagnose and treat that which you know* 131
Fitting narratives into biomedical discourse 131
Conclusion 132

8. THERAPY MANAGEMENT OF MALNUTRITION: A SHAMEFUL ILLNESS OR A PROBLEM OF FOOD? 135
Biomedical and public health discourse on malnutrition 136
- *Proximate causes and prevalence of malnutrition* 136
- *Intermediate factors contributing to malnutrition* 138
- *Macro level management of malnutrition* 140
Case study Bobo: A local approach to malnutrition 141
Sede 145
- *Becoming pregnant too soon* 145
- *Lack of reproductive choice* 145
- *A shameful diagnosis* 147
- *Dangerously hot belly* 148
- *Treatment of* sede 149
Case study Samba: A biomedical approach to malnutrition 150
The complex of factors leading to 'passivity' 153
- *Women have little social power* 154
- *Children's entitlement to food* 154
- *Local theories on illness; sede is not about food* 155
- *Nutritional health education does not work* 156
- *Contraceptives are the only method of prevention* 157
Conclusion 157

9. MOTHERS ACCEPTING SUFFERING TO MAINTAIN THE MARRIAGE ALLIANCE: THE DARK SIDE OF SOCIAL CAPITAL 159
My methodological approach 159
Narrative construction of the self 160
Story lines in Farabako 160
Aminata's story 162
The suffering of insecurity 167
Patriarchal blackmail 172
Conflict and conflict resolution: Keeping the social fabric intact 174
- *Conflicts with husbands* 174
- *Conflicts with co-wives* 175
Gender-based violence, social ties and insecurity 176
The agency of lament 178
Conclusion 179

10. MEDICAL ETHNOGRAPHY AS AN ETHICAL TRAJECTORY 181
A moral anthropology 181
An anthropology of morals 182
Towards a feminist anthropology of moralities 184
The morality of biomedicine in friction 185
The language of representation 188
Conclusion 189

11. THE LANGUAGE AND LOGIC OF WELL-BEING 191
Non-action in therapy management 191
Ontological insecurity 195
The embodiment of inequality 196
The intersubjective logic of shame 198
Recommendations: Beyond culture 199
Suggestions for midwifery practice and further research 200
Conclusion 202

REFERENCES 203

GLOSSARY OF BAMBARA WORDS 211

SAMENVATTING: MOEDERS, GENEESKUNDE EN MORALITEIT IN RURAAL MALI 214

APPENDIX 1 218
Methodology Overview 218
- *1st Fieldwork period* 218
- *2nd Fieldwork period* 219
- *3rd Fieldwork period* 220
- *4th Fieldwork period* 220
- *5th Fieldwork period* 221

APPENDIX 2 222
Table 1. Explanation of terms for free-listing children's illnesses in Farabako 222
Table 2. Free-listing of children's illnesses in Bamako 226

APPENDIX 3 227
Women's social networks in Farabako 227

APPENDIX 4 229
Map of Mali 229

APPENDIX 5 230
Table 3. Household Therapy Management of Children's Illness Episodes 230

LIST OF FIGURES

Figure 1. Household members of infant Baba's therapy management group 119
Figure 2. Multiple representations of one illness episode 121
Figure 3. Family tree of Madi Kante, his wives and children 163
Figure 4. A mother's vulnerability context: factors influencing non-action in therapy management 194

ACKNOWLEDGEMENTS

This book could not have been written without the help of many people who I would like to thank (more or less chronologically).

First, I would like to thank Gijs Klumper for having had the insight to suggest that I study anthropology at forty. It was a good idea and one that has opened my mind and enriched my life. I am also indebted to Jan Jansen for giving me a way to combine my work as a midwife with ethnographic research. However, most of all, I thank him for introducing me to Farabako, a village that I have fallen in love with. I owe a great deal to Annemiek Richters. I feel privileged to have been able to work with her. I greatly respect her drive to aid women all over the world. I thank her for taking me on as an independent scholar and giving me the freedom to conduct this research as I envisioned, often nudging me in interesting directions. Her help, especially during the writing phase of this research, has been invaluable. I thank Annemiek for preventing me from relativizing everything 'to pieces' and for having confidence in me.

I am deeply grateful to all of the villagers of Farabako. They welcomed me with drums, dancing, singing and high hopes. I thank them for trusting me to deliver their babies and treat their sick children and for taking me into their confidence and finding time to talk with me. I am very much indebted to Madi Keita, the head of the village (*dugutigi*), for his hospitality and facilitation of my project to set up a maternity clinic in Farabako.

My special thanks go out to the family of Namagan Kante with whom I lived for eight months; I will never forget their hospitality. I believe that Namagan and I have truly become friends and I will not forget our late night ritual of drinking *peyibafura* ('Dutch medicine' i.e. Dutch gin) together by the light of a single flashlight while trying to communicate in the local language. Namagan's first wife Nasira was my *jatigimuso* (my hostess); she cooked for me, she washed my clothes, brought me water to wash with twice a day and swept my floor. She never let me help her, despite my many efforts. I thank her for taking such good care of me. Her daughters Mariamu and especially little Fanta kept me company and tried to teach me *Maninkakan*. Her son, Musa, teased me about being afraid of mice while occasionally removing dead mice from under my bed. I want to thank Namagan and Nasira for naming their baby after my father. I also want to thank Namagan's second wife Trayina, his third wife Sali and his wife in levirate Kuda for all the personal talks and gossip that we had. My thanks go out to other family members who supported me in manifold ways: Kali Kante, Brehima Kante, Kanda Kante, Jankiné Kante and Sògòba Kante. I never feel alone when I am in Farabako.

This book could not have been written if not for my research assistant Abdulaye Traore. Abdulaye arranged meetings with respondents, translated for me and brought me wherever I wanted to go on his motorbike. He was my key informant. Abdulaye even endured jokes and insults from the village men for carrying my bag (which he insisted on). He calls me ma mère because I have helped his family from time to time.

I would not have been able to set up the maternity clinic without the help of Jeneba Kante, and Kamisajè Kulibali the local midwives. Jeneba became a good friend; her curiosity and my curiosity made for interesting times in the clinic. We seem to have the same sense of humour and working with her was a pleasure. I will not forget evenings sitting outside in front of her house and shelling peanuts by the light of the fire while relaxing after a hard day's work.

With great respect I thank the *musokɔrɔbaw* of Farabako: Baraka Kante, Fanta Kante, Fanta Keita (*dugutigimuso*), Fanta Keita (Suko), Jeneba Kamara, Kinyèba Fofana and Nandabi Danyogo for sharing their medical knowledge with me. My distinct appreciation also goes to the *somaw* of Farabako: Bala Kante, Musa Kante, Namagan Kante and Samba Kante (now deceased). I also thank Fawulen Keita for sharing his knowledge of medicinal plants with me.

I owe a great deal to Mahamadou Faganda Keita, my colleague, friend and research assistant. Mahamadou guided me through the do's and don'ts of Malinke daily life in Farabako, and the chaos of Bamako. I thank him for translating sensitive questions, even though they were sometimes embarrassing and shameful for him, because he understood their importance for my research.

Special thanks go to Djibi Keita, 'my' taxi driver in Bamako, whose dependability, generous laugh and beautiful family I will not forget. I am also grateful to Ablo Sangare, for getting me to Farabako safely in his four-wheel drive with the music of Bob Marley blaring. It was always reassuring to know that Daouda Diawara was in Siby, looking out for my best interests. In Bamako, the hospitality of Saskia Brand, Moussa Fofana, René de la Ruelle and Annemie de Winne, and Brahima Camara and his wife Salimata Camara helped to make my stay a pleasant one. I thank my female respondents in Bamako for sharing information and confidences with me.

It was very special to have my daughter Claudia and her friend, Merel Joosten, accompany me to Farabako as research assistants in 2012. I am grateful that I can share my memories of Farabako with them. I also want to express my gratitude to Agnès Pataux for travelling with me. I value our long philosophical talks and the striking photographs she took.

My sincerest thanks go to the friends in the Netherlands who supported me and pulled me through the past year: Anita (tears, late night talks and cultural distractions), Guido (beauty treatments, good food and relational analysis), Piet and Julia (sushi and support) and Beau (music, movies and popcorn). I also thank the staff of Café Kalkhoven, especially the bar man, Richard, for the beer, the dancing and the occasional cigarette. I am particularly grateful to my son Michiel for his support and understanding.

The fieldwork on which this study is based was sponsored by Leiden University Fund (LUF)/Van Walsem and Stichting SMART. The writing phase of this research was sponsored by the Amsterdam Institute of Social Science Research (AISSR). I am grateful for the help of Machiel Roest and Diederik Klumper with French translations and to Julia Challinor for her precise and rapid editing.

Finally, and most importantly, I would like to explicitly acknowledge the indispensable contribution that the women of Farabako have made to the realisation of this book. My thanks go to:

> Alamoko Kante, Badjo Kamara, Bamagan Kante (I), Bamagan Kante (II), Binètu Keita, Bugudi Keita, Jeneba Traore, Dusu Traore, Fadima Kante, Fadima Kante, Fanta Kante, Fanta Keita, Faramata Fofana, Fatuma Keita, Hawa Kante, Jeneba Traore, Kajatu Keita, Kajatu Keita, Kamisa Fofana, Kamisajè Kulibali, Kani Keita, Kaninba Kante, Kanku Kante, Kanku Keita, Kinyèba Bagayogo, Kinyèba Kamara, Kinyèné Kamara, Kinyèba Fofana, Kinyèba Kulibali, Korotun Keita, Kuria Bagayogo, Fatumata Kuda Kante, Kumba Sinayogo, Lolo Kante, Maimuna Konate, Maimuna Sinayogo, Mané Kante, Masitan Keita, Masuruni Danyogo, Naida Kante, Nakani Kante, Nakuria Kamisoko, Nanjakale Traore, Nantakadi Kamara, Nantènè Kante, Nantènè Traore, Narama Keita, Nasira Kulibali, Nasira Fofana, Nasira Kante, Nasira Koita, Nene Bagayogo, Nene Keita, Numuntènè Kante, Numusira Kante, Rokia Keita, Sabiyanjè Keita, Salimata Sinaba, Sika Kante, Sise Keita, Sitan Kante, Sitan Keita, Sitan Traore, Sobaraka Fofana, Sògòba Kante, Soloba Kante, and Traina Kante.

My sincerest apologies if I have forgotten anyone.

Lianne Holten, aka 'Dusuba Kante'
Oegstgeest, November 2012

1. INTRODUCTION: THERAPY MANAGEMENT OF PREGNANCY AND CHILDREN'S ILLNESSES IN FARABAKO

Miles away from the last village, and crossing a third riverbed, I couldn't help but wonder what I had gotten myself into. I was on my way to Farabako, a small geographically isolated village in the Mande Mountains of southwest Mali. The gravel road had ended an hour ago; a dirt track led up into the hills through a dusty dry landscape of shrubs, termite hills and leafless *sɛnɛ* trees with their red flowers. The riverbed crossings were small oases with palm trees, lush green foliage and iridescent blue birds. It was January, the dry season, and the water level was low enough to cross by four-wheel drive. The most striking feature of this journey was not the scenery, but rather my feeling of being in the middle of nowhere. The bumpy track finally led to a village of mud houses bathed in a golden light from the afternoon sun. Standing a bit apart at the entrance of the village was the pink building that with my help was to become a maternity clinic.

Biomedicine in the middle of nowhere

It was precisely because the village was in the middle of nowhere that I, as a midwife, had been asked to set up a maternity clinic in Farabako. In the rainy season, when the rivers overflow, the villagers are cut off from biomedical health care facilities in the region. Even in the dry season these facilities are difficult to access. Government institutions and non-governmental organizations do not reach Farabako.

It was a coincidence that I had ended up in Farabako. I went there for the first time in 2007, at the invitation of the anthropologist Jan Jansen, who had been doing research on oral tradition and divination in the area for more than ten years (e.g. Jansen 2009, 2011; Jansen and Diarra 2006). When the wife of one of his informants lost yet another baby during a difficult delivery, the men of the village asked for help finding funding for a maternity clinic, which they hoped would reduce the high child mortality rate in the village. They were convinced that they would be able to manage the clinic themselves. Jansen agreed and secured financial support from two Dutch charitable organizations.[1] Two women, Jeneba Kante and Kamisajè Kulibali, were chosen by the villag-

[1] At Jansen's request, a Dutch foundation Wereldwijs [Worldwise] from Tilburg financed a six-month apprenticeship for two Farabako women at one of Bamako's bigger maternity clinics. The construction of the maternity clinic in Farabako was financed by a gift of 5,000 euros from Mies Louwman, an elderly Dutch lady who had approached Jan Jansen for a meaningful small project in Mali. The equipment for the clinic was financed by a donation from a Dutch civil initiative (Derde Wereld Groep Soest).

Midwives Jeneba Kante, Lianne Holten and Kamisajè Kulibali in front of the maternity clinic in Farabako

ers to go to the capital, Bamako, for a six-month course in midwifery, which they completed. Meanwhile, the men of the village built a three-room clinic. At the time, I was not only a practicing midwife, but also an anthropology student interested in studying pregnancy strategies in a low-income country. Jansen, one of my anthropology professors, proposed that I do my anthropological fieldwork in Farabako and start the clinic. I agreed, and in January 2007, I arrived in Farabako to equip the clinic, train the midwives and simultaneously start my ethnographic research. I had brought with me all the instruments and materials I found necessary to perform prenatal examinations and deliveries. I also brought drugs to stock the small pharmacy in the clinic. But most importantly, I came equipped with a Dutch biomedical model of midwifery care.

Biomedicine is the term commonly used to designate the medical discourse and practice that has dominated the West and travelled to the rest of the world. Most practitioners of biomedicine consider it to be objectively based on a naturalistic view of the human body, perfected over time by means of rational and scientifically based research and training. Because of this view, biomedicine is widely thought to be a stock of knowledge and practices that offers the best possible means of treating disease[2] and relieving suffering worldwide. It is this perspective and the attendant assumptions that medical anthropologists have sought to challenge.[3]

In hindsight, it would have been preferable to have done medical anthropological research before setting up the maternity clinic, to determine if a maternity clinic was necessary and feasible in such a small village. There are only approximately 400 inhabitants in Farabako. But as it was, I was faced with a *fait accompli*—the clinic had been built and so I came to initiate biomedical obstetric care in Farabako. At the time, I did not doubt that this was the appropriate action. The maternal and child mortality rates in Mali are among the highest in the world[4] and coming from a country with one of the lowest mortality rates, I felt this was an injustice that needed to be remedied. I hoped I could contribute, if only in a small way, to improving the health situation in Farabako.

My goal was in line with Millennium Development Goals (MDGs) number 4 and 5. MDG 4 is to reduce the mortality rate of children under five by two thirds by 2015. To reach this goal, improved immunization coverage and special efforts to fight pneumonia, diarrhoea and malaria, while bolstering nutrition, are needed. MDG 5 is to reduce the maternal mortality ratio by three quarters and achieve universal access to reproductive health for women by 2015. The World Health Organization recognizes that in addition to a range of interventions before, during and after pregnancy, a key strategy to reduce maternal and neonatal deaths is to ensure that all births are attended by a skilled health worker. Yet in rural Mali, only 38% of births are attended by skilled health personnel. With the two MDGs in mind, I went to Farabako thinking I could help by setting up a maternity clinic and training two local midwives to administer a biomedical model of obstetric care. Although initially, my approach was clinical obstetric health care focused on treating individual patients, I gradually changed to a more public health approach and focused on social determinants of health.

Biomedicine moves across the globe as 'an inextricable mix of things (e.g., medicines, medical devices, machines), techniques (e.g. medical procedures),

---

[2] I use the term disease to mean a condition defined in (Western) terms of pathophysiology. I use the term illness to mean the subjective experience of disease as affected by interpersonal, sociocultural and economic factors. These terms have been criticized as being too focused on the individual patient; the term sickness has been suggested as superior for capturing the social aspect of disease. I use the concept of therapy management to this end (Nichter 2002).

[3] For example, Lock (2002) in her cross-cultural study of brain death, shows how biomedicine is not a uniform body of knowledge and practice. The same biomedical diagnosis of brain death was given in other cultural settings, yet different morally laden responses to the diagnosis and treatments followed due to differing ideas on life and death and personhood. Lock argues that biomedicine is shaped by (local) values; it is not the epistemologically free endeavour that it claims to be (2001: 487).

[4] The maternal mortality ratio is 540 (per 100,000 live births) in Mali, 480 as the WHO African regional average, 210 as a global average and 9 in the Netherlands. The under-five mortality rate is 234 (per 1,000 live births) in rural Mali, 178 in Mali as a whole, 119 for the WHO African regional average, 57 as a global average and 4 in the Netherlands (WHO for 2010).

and bundles of shared understandings and epistemological practices' (Janes and Corbett 2009: 168). It is often portrayed as universally applicable and superior to 'traditional' medicine. Biomedicine can travel in development projects, such as setting up a maternity clinic; however, the flow of biomedicine is not without restraint. The people of Farabako were not simply a blank slate waiting to receive the 'truth' of imagined universally applicable biomedicine. As in many countries in the South, in Mali biomedicine has not been successful in setting the terms of health care; it is not the only form of health care and it does not always work smoothly. 'Global' biomedicine interacts with local communities, 'where it is transformed and transforms, through being adopted, used and resisted' (Janes and Corbett 2009: 177). The process of interaction between biomedical discourse and local medical discourse will be described throughout this book.

A research trajectory from mortality to morality

At the time, I believed that if I understood the health beliefs and therapy management of pregnant women and mothers, then I could use this knowledge to better implement Western biomedical health care. So, while setting up the maternity clinic, I simultaneously did ethnographic research on the therapy management of pregnancy and children's illnesses.

The concept of therapy management was first used by Janzen (1978) in his *Quest for Therapy Management in Lower Zaire*. Therapy management refers to the diagnosis of illness, the selection and evaluation of treatment, as well as support for the afflicted (1978: xviii). A 'therapy management group' is a set of individuals who take charge of therapy management with or on behalf of the sufferer. Therapy management is a concept that goes beyond individual health care seeking and pays attention to the social dynamics of the household, extended kin groups and other relevant social networks. Studies of therapy management devote attention to the relationships between cultural assumptions and values, social roles and institutions, power relations and economic circumstances that influence the ways in which people respond to illness in context over time (Janzen 1987; Nichter 2002). The study of therapy management provides insights into decision-making and priority setting within households, for example, how gender and generational relations influence issues of entitlement to resources and health care. It involves not only looking at what people do, and the reasons for their actions, but also considering what they are unable to do, and what underlies apparent passivity, acceptance or fatalism (Nichter 2002: 101).[5]

[5] Another much-used notion in medical anthropology is the 'hierarchy of resort', introduced by Romanucci-Ross (1969). Similar to therapy management, it is a concept used to analyse the various steps taken in health seeking behavior in a particular case and in a particular setting. However, the notion of a 'hierarchy' suggests a tree and branches whose logic is followed in sequential steps of the therapeutic process. In therapy management in Farabako, successive episodes of a therapeutic process were not as clearly determined by prior logics as 'hierarchy of resort' would suggest, but are open to *ad hoc* questions and issues that arise in the midst of a case.

My aim in studying therapy management was to learn why maternal and child mortality was so high in Farabako. By understanding the variety of contextual factors that determined how therapy was managed, I hoped to be able to improve health care in Farabako.

I used a grounded theory approach (Charmaz 2006) to try to understand the social and cultural processes that influenced the household therapy management of pregnancy and children's illnesses. The grounded theory method explicitly unites data collection with data analysis; respondents' concerns shape the direction and form of the research, rather than preconceived concepts and hypotheses. Between 2007 and 2012, I visited Farabako five times for fieldwork. I spent one to three months there at a time for a total of eight months in the field. The data analysis of each fieldwork period generated new insights, new theoretical concepts to explain them, as well as new questions. I returned to the field each time to corroborate previous findings, investigate new insights and address the newly risen questions. The advantage of doing fieldwork in this manner was that I was able to selectively choose whom to interview and what to observe next according to themes that emerged from analysis of data from earlier fieldwork periods. For example, in the data analysis of the first fieldwork period, shame emerged as a theme that was relevant for my respondents. I had not anticipated this. Away from the field, I had looked for theoretical concepts to understand shame. Back in the field, I returned with new questions and ideas about whom I should interview and what questions I should ask to specific people to gain a deeper understanding of shame. I continued interviewing respondents until I reached data saturation (theoretical sampling).

Another advantage of returning to the village intermittently over a period of five years was that I was able to evaluate the work at the maternity clinic over time. The disadvantage of this method was that I was only able to observe village life during the dry season from October to May; in the rainy season, the village is not accessible due to road flooding. On the other hand, the advantage of being in Farabako only in the dry season was that I could leave the village in case of illness or personal emergency.

During each visit to Farabako, I lived in the compound of my host Namagan Kante with his first wife Nasira Kante, his co-wives, cousins, nephews and children. Namagan is an important local medical expert (*soma*) specializing in sand divination. During my fieldwork periods there were frequently guests staying in his compound, as well as patients and visitors. Participant observation in the household was an important research tool.

I was lucky to have the same two assistants during all fieldwork periods: Abdulaye Traore and Mahamadou Faganda Keita. Abdulaye is an inhabitant of Farabako and knows all the ins-and-outs of the village. Abdulaye is originally from Bamako and attended school there. He moved to Farabako at the request of Namagan's father and married Namagan's sister. After five years of working together, we became an efficient team. In the evening I would tell him who I wanted to talk to the next day, and he would arrange it. Accordingly, we were often able to do three in-depth interviews per day. Abdulaye also helped translate for me in the clinic. My *Maninkakan*, the language spoken in Farabako, was sufficient to do an examination of a pregnant woman or a sick child, but I often needed his help to explain a treatment or give advice to a patient. Mahamadou, my other assistant, has a MA in anthropology from the University of Bamako. He wrote his MA thesis on women's marriage songs and he has conducted research on divination and sacrifices in the goldmines near Farabako (see Keita 2010). Mahamadou now works as a high school teacher and independent scholar in Bamako. He was well respected in Farabako and had good rapport with the villagers. Each fieldwork period, he would come for a few weeks to help me with interviews. I used his help when conducting interviews of a sensitive nature, when I suspected that women would speak more openly in front of a translator who was an outsider. Mahamadou also transcribed and translated my taped interviews. I have often been asked if a female interpreter would not have been better. It has been my experience that in an interview setting, women often had more difficulty speaking freely in front of other women, especially if they were older, than in front of my male translators. Furthermore, no woman in the village spoke enough French to translate for me.

Jeneba Kante, one of the two midwives I began training during my first visit to Farabako, was a wonderful colleague. Using her limited French and my limited *Maninkakan*, we were able to communicate and work together in the clinic: primarily, doing deliveries, conducting antenatal check-ups, and treating sick children. Participant observation, more precisely 'observant participation' (cf. Wacquant 2006) in the maternity clinic was a valuable research tool.

In the next six sections from *Pregnancy strategies and obstetrical outcome* through *Respondent's feedback: 'Do not forget poverty'*, I describe how in five fieldwork periods, my research evolved from a focus on maternal mortality to child mortality and eventually to morality as a factor in the therapy management of particular children's illness episodes. Throughout these sections, I indicate how the research methodology (grounded theory) was adapted to generate answers to the new questions generated by each change of focus. The details of the methodology used in each fieldwork period are presented in Appendix 1. In the remaining sections, I describe the main focus of the book, present my research questions and give an overview of my theoretical orientation. I conclude with an outline of the book.

Pregnancy strategies and obstetrical outcome

During my first fieldwork period, three months in 2007,[6] my aim was to explore the magnitude of maternal and child mortality in Farabako and the

---

[6] This first fieldwork period was during my MA studies in anthropology and the subsequent four fieldwork periods were during my PhD research follow-up.

The first women to utilize the maternity clinic in 2007

strategies women used to deliver a healthy baby in a context where biomedical health care was difficult to access. To do this, I conducted reproductive life history interviews, asking my respondents questions about their pregnancies, deliveries and the care of their new-born babies and young children. The interviews gave me information on health care options available in Farabako and on local mother and child care; both were important to understand therapy management.

In this first fieldwork period, I was able to interview 53 women who represented approximately 75% of the adult female population of Farabako. The women were a representative sample of the village. These 53 women had been pregnant a total of 293 times. How had their pregnancies and births been experienced? Were there any complications? Did they seek prenatal care or did they take medication? Where did they deliver and who helped them? These were some of the questions I asked. The interviews took 1-2 hours and were held either in the maternity clinic or at the women's homes. I posed my questions in *Maninka*. Abdulaye Traore, my assistant, helped me to understand the answers.

The data of the 53 reproductive life histories was coded and analysed in SPSS using Categorical Principal Components Analysis (CATPCA),[7] a multivariate analysis. I was looking for women who had had a positive obstetrical outcome, and wanted to know if this group was statistically correlated to

[7] CATPCA analyses objects (respondents) and variables (answers to survey questions) simultaneously. It is therefore possible to identify groups of respondents who have answered the survey in a similar fashion.

agency variables such as 'prenatal care', 'medication during pregnancy', and 'delivery by midwife or doctor'. This sample was a quite homogenous group; in the statistical analysis most women had had uncomplicated home births and been assisted by the *musokɔrɔbaw* (elder women specialized in attending births and treating children's illnesses).

The majority of women did not seek prenatal care. In addition, when their children fell ill these women did not always seek (bio)medical help, as the following story illustrates:

> Fatuma Traore does not know how old she is but, because she has had seven children and is now pregnant with her eighth, I estimate she must be in her thirties. Four of her seven children have died. In her first pregnancy she was ill with malaria. As for all her earlier pregnancies, she had no prenatal care, neither traditional nor biomedical.[8] She used no modern or traditional medicine, only a *tafo* (a string prepared with incantations by an elder woman, a *musokɔrɔba,* to protect the pregnancy). One week after an uncomplicated home delivery, her first baby died of 'a fever'. She had not sought medical attention of any kind for the baby. During her second pregnancy Fatuma took *misɛmani*, a drug used to induce an abortion. She did this because she 'was young and did not like Farabako'. The *misɛmani* gave her pains but the pregnancy stayed intact and she delivered a healthy baby girl. Her third child died at three years of age. The little girl had been ill with a skin disease for a year before she died. A local medical expert (*soma*) had been consulted and he had given the child *maninkafura* (Malinke [*Maninka*] medicine) to no avail. The child had not been taken to a doctor. Around this same time her fourth child also died. Fatuma does not know why this baby girl died, she had only been sick for a day. The next two pregnancies were without incident, and again without prenatal care. The home deliveries were attended by elder female family members (*musokɔrɔbaw*), and went well, although baby number six did not cry until she was doused with cold water over which incantations had been said. Fatuma's last baby was the first boy; he was born after an uncomplicated pregnancy and birth. Sadly, at eight months he fell ill with *kɔnɔ*[9] (an illness with symptoms of fever and convulsions that was explained to me as a kind of witch that transforms itself into a bird in order to eat children). After the baby boy was ill for one day, a family mem-

[8] I use the term 'traditional health care' to mean local (indigenous) medical discourse. I use the term 'traditional medicine' to mean medicine that was prepared from local medicinal plants. My respondents called this *maninkafura* (Malinke medicine). I use the term 'biomedical' to mean Western (cosmopolitan) medical discourse. I use the term 'modern medicine' to mean Western drugs that can be bought in a pharmacy or from drugsellers. My respondents called this '*faramasifura*' (pharmacy medicine). Although the terms 'traditional' and 'modern' are problematic, I use them here for their legibility.

[9] Bailleul (2000) translates *kɔnɔ as*: convulsions caused by infections such as malaria or tetanus and attributed to an evil-doing bird.

ber took him on the back of a motorcycle to the doctor, but sadly the baby died the next day. (Based on reproductive life history Fatuma Traore, 2007)

During the interviews it became clear that my respondents could only remember one woman (living in Farabako) who had died during the delivery of her child (approximately 1 in 65).[10] At the time of the interviews, half of the women were still young and most will probably have more babies, so it is possible that this number will increase. My sample of 53 women was too small to extrapolate, but it seems fair to conclude that maternal mortality is not higher in Farabako than in the rest of Sub Sahara Africa where the lifetime risk of maternal mortality is 1 in 28 women (WHO for 2010).

Whereas maternal mortality was lower than expected in Farabako, I was shocked by the significant number of children who had died. Of 263 children born to my 53 informants, 40% (106) had died before reaching the age of ten. If we compare this to World Health Organization statistics for Mali, the perinatal and under-five mortality rates in Farabako are relatively high; too many children die.[11]

What behaviour by women during pregnancy, birth and directly after birth led to a good obstetrical outcome? In the statistical analysis, there was no correlation between prenatal care and the number of neonatal deaths; obstetrical outcome was not better for the group that sought medical help. The women showed very little (what I called) action and those who did, did not have a better outcome. I initially found that health seeking 'strategy' was not an appropriate concept for studying health in Farabako, as women seldom sought health care (indigenous or biomedical) (Holten 2010). When interviewing mothers, they often told me that they had 'done nothing' when they or one of their children had become ill. This seeming passivity in the face of mortality became the focus of my subsequent research when I approached passivity as agency within the therapy management of children's illnesses.

Illness narratives of therapy management

Having understood that not maternal mortality, but rather child mortality was the pressing problem in Farabako, my research focus changed from the therapy management of pregnancy to therapy management of children's illnesses. I returned to Farabako for my second fieldwork period, in January 2009, to research factors contributing to high child mortality. Initially, I needed to

---

[10] Of the 400 inhabitants of Farabako in 2007, 65 were adult women.

[11] Perinatal mortality in Mali is 50 per 1000 live births; in Farabako it is approximately 120 per 1,000 births (31 of the 263 births were stillborn or died in the first week). In Mali the under-five mortality rate is 178 deaths per 1,000 live births and in rural Mali the rate is 234 (WHO for 2010). Of my respondents' children, 81 children had died before they reached the age of 5 years. Eighty-one of the 245 live births equalled 33%, thus, approximately 330 children died per 1,000 live births. This Farabako sample is too small to extrapolate, but does indicate that the perinatal and under-five mortality rate is high in Farabako.

understand the illness categories of children's illnesses used in Farabako. I asked women, men, and local medical experts (*musokɔrɔbaw* and *somaw*) to list the names of all the children's illness they knew (see Appendix 2).

Once I understood enough vocabulary used when speaking of children's illnesses, I conducted semi-structured interviews on therapy management. I asked 24 mothers to recount one of their children's illness episodes. In these illness narratives, mothers told me how the course of the illness had progressed. They spoke of symptoms and diagnoses, medication, who did what and when, and which members of the therapy group paid for treatment. One of my goals was to learn what kinds of illnesses the children in Farabako suffered from. Therefore, after listening to the illness narratives, I conducted a survey based on the WHO verbal autopsy list. A verbal autopsy includes lists of symptoms and is used in health surveys to try to determine the cause of morbidity and mortality in settings where there are no medical records (Soleman et al. 2006).

Part of understanding therapy management requires knowing how women use their social networks to seek health care. To explore this, I conducted name-generator and support-transaction interviews. In name-generator interviews, I asked the same 24 mothers to name the people who they could ask for help if they or their children became ill and who they had asked for financial aid, advice or practical support in the past year. In the support-transaction interviews, I asked the same respondents to name the people, who had been ill, who they themselves had recently helped. These interviews were inserted in a network analysis using Netdraw, thereby showing the ties between individuals and families in the context of therapy management (see Appendix 3). The main finding of this part of my analysis was that women had limited social capital (within and outside of the village) they could draw on if they or their child fell ill.

A recurring theme in the illness narratives and social-network interviews was a discourse of shame (*maloya*). This raised the question of how a discourse of shame factored into the process of therapy management. I conducted open interviews and focus group discussions on the subject of *maloya* with mothers, fathers, *musokɔrɔbaw* and *somaw*. I found that the moral discourse of shame sometimes made it difficult for women to access (biomedical) health care; they 'had shame'[12] in asking for (financial) help. For example, during a focus group discussion, the women told me the following:

> Women have shame in telling their husband that a child is ill, because he has nothing. There are women who do not have shame and directly ask their husbands for help when a child is ill, but some say nothing to their hus-

---

[12] I deliberately use the term 'had shame' or 'have shame' (rather than feeling shame) because when my respondents spoke of *maloya*, they spoke of 'having shame' (a good thing, virtuous) or 'feeling ashamed or being considered shameless' (a bad thing). More about this concept is presented in chapter 5.

> bands. (Jeneba Fofana, 48 yrs,[13] Focus group discussion January 2012)
> *Maloya* [shame] makes it difficult for women to take action. If a woman becomes pregnant too soon, and the child has *sede* [an illness category similar to the biomedical category of severe malnutrition LH] she will keep it a secret and often wait to ask for help until it is too late and the child is dying. *Maloya* is the reason they do not ask for help sooner. (Fanta Danyogo, 65 yrs, Focus group discussion January 2012)

One new insight during this second fieldwork period was that the social risk of being seen to be shameless mediated physical risk in therapy management. I also became aware that mothers were often not individually able to or primarily responsible for taking action when their child was ill. I needed the perspective of the fathers and mothers-in-law, as the mothers identified both as important members of a child's therapy management group.

Household dynamics of health

To understand therapy management and child mortality in Farabako, I needed to understand the rural household dynamics of health. I decided to contrast household therapy management in Farabako with households in the urban setting of Bamako, the capital city. I did this when I returned to Mali, from October through December 2009, for my third fieldwork period and conducted in-depth interviews, in Farabako (28) and Bamako (18). I spoke with mothers (18) (some for the second time), fathers (12), mothers-in-law (9) and healers involved in the treatment (7) of a child's illness episode. In total, I collected 70 illness narratives. I learned about gender relational power dynamics in therapy management from these interviews. The surveys and interviews gave me more information on the social realities than the physical aspects of health and illness. In the illness narratives, therapy group members presented themselves as good parents, good healers or good women and positioned themselves within medical pluralism.

Local discourse on health and health care

During the first three fieldwork periods, most of the interviews were semi-structured interviews and surveys. Yet, I realised that my biomedical assumptions on health and healing were, to a degree, determining the questions I asked. I chose the topics and I recorded the information according to what I found relevant. I was trying to fit my respondent's information into my biomedical categories. This approach limited my comprehensive understanding of the health situation in Farabako; what had been lacking so far, were the women's own words on health.

[13] Most women (especially those who had had no schooling) did not know how old they were; therefore, most of the ages throughout this book are estimates made at the time of the interview.

The focus of my fourth fieldwork period (February 2011) was the local discourse on health and health care in Farabako. It had become clear to me that in order to understand the choices made in therapy management, I needed to know what people considered to be a 'good healer' and what they considered to be good health.

To find answers to these questions, I did in-depth semi-structured interviews on local medical ethics with herbalists, *somaw* and *musokɔrɔbaw*. This was indispensable information for understanding the friction between local medical (ethical) discourse and biomedical (ethical) discourse, and to evaluate how and why biomedical health care facilities in the region were used (or not).

I conducted open interviews with ten women I knew well. I asked them to tell me their life history and about their health. I wanted to hear the words women used when speaking about their lives and their health. An important theme that emerged out of this data was that women suffered because they felt that they were not being taken care of; they felt insecure. Health was primarily spoken of as social, and not only physical well-being. Part of social well-being for the women of Farabako was to be considered a good woman who 'has shame' (*maloya*). The discourse of shame had been a recurring theme throughout each fieldwork period and needed further investigation.

Shame as a factor in therapy management

My goal during my last fieldwork period, in 2012, was to dive deeper into the discourse of shame (*maloya*), in order to reach saturation in my data and to validate that *maloya* was also an important theme for the women themselves. I needed to hear how the women of Farabako spoke of *maloya*. In open interviews, I asked ten mothers, 20-80 years old, to tell me what significance *maloya* had for them. These were very intimate interviews, conducted in my hut. My assistant Abdulaye Traore translated my interview question and then left us alone; I sat on my bed with the tape recorder and my respondent sat close to me talking into the microphone. Although I could not understand most of what they were saying, and the women knew this, they talked for quite some time about the importance of the discourse of shame in their lives. The analysis of these transcripts provided rich quotes and confirmed that my data had reached saturation. I had a great deal of data on the subject of shame and was no longer hearing new information. It became clear; in Farabako, the discourse of shame was a significant factor in therapy management.

Respondent's feedback: 'Do not forget poverty'

During a village meeting in 2012, with representatives of all the families of Farabako present, I asked permission to use the name Farabako and to use the photographs I had taken. Everyone was adamant that I use the real name of the village. Most villagers wanted me to use their real names. Yet due to the personal nature of some of my data, I have decided to change the names of my respondents. I have made a few exceptions; the *musokɔrɔbaw* felt very strongly that they wanted their real names in this book, and the *somaw* and midwives of Farabako have been written about before and therefore I use their real names (e.g. Jansen 2009, 2011, Holten 2010).

I conducted four feedback focus group discussions with the following groups: *musokɔrɔbaw*, young mothers, men in their forties and young fathers. I explained to these respondents what I was planning to write in this book. I asked them if they had feedback or suggestions on how to improve my work. I attempted to give my respondents the chance to object to what would be said about them. But I wonder if they felt they were in a position to object at all. Throughout my fieldwork, over five years, I worked day and night in the maternity clinic. I delivered their babies and treated their sick children. I even stitched the village chief's foot after a farming accident with a hoe. The villagers are happy with the small pharmacy I set up, where they can buy antibiotics if their child becomes ill. I am respected in the village for the health care work that I do when I am there. I am also an older woman and it would be disrespectful to disagree with me. This, and the fact that I am seen as Farabako's link to money from *Peyiba* (the Netherlands), makes it difficult for anyone in Farabako to openly disagree with me. The only issue the villagers told me needed more emphasis in my book was their extreme poverty. Poverty was the main cause of high child mortality, and poverty lay at the base of the shame and suffering the women had spoken about to me, as this quote illustrates:

> Shame (*maloya*) is a very serious matter. If, for example, my child becomes ill, and I tell his father this, I will feel ashamed if the father needs to tell me that he has no means to provide money for the care of the child. That brings *maloya* on to me because I have come to discover that my husband has no money. In life, when you can't get what you need that brings *maloya*. Life is very difficult here in Farabako, we earn nothing here in terms of money, there is only agricultural activity here and you earn nothing in agriculture. We have children whose needs we cannot satisfy with our means of farming, the harvests are no longer good and it shames us not to meet the needs of our children. (Fatumata Kante, 31 yrs, Open interview January 2012)

The feedback given to me by my respondents helped me to shape the final focus of my research, namely the link between poverty, the discourse of shame, suffering, and the powerlessness of mothers when confronted with health adversity.

Moralities in health as a main focus

This research trajectory of coming and going with new insights and foci has culminated in this ethnography of the therapy management of children's illnesses. I argue in this book that in Farabako, in the context of extreme poverty, the moral discourse of shame (*maloya*) is a significant factor in therapy management. I will show that a medical system is a social system rather than primarily a knowledge system. Because the medical system is a social system, we need insight into local moralities to understand child mortality. This ethnography illuminates the actual local moral content of therapy management of children's illnesses in a context of vulnerability, in which poverty is a key factor. This study looks at what is morally at stake concerning health for the women and their children in Farabako (cf. Kleinman 1999).

My work as a midwife in the maternity clinic gave me access to data that I would not have had if I had come to do anthropological research without a medical background and without being involved in providing biomedical care. Working as a midwife, I was often confronted with situations that were difficult for me to understand. My background as an anthropologist helped me to become aware of the (lack of) fit between my biomedical discourse and the local medical discourse. This awareness was a prerequisite for understanding how the new maternity clinic was perceived and used by the women of Farabako, as well as the newly trained midwives' problems providing a Western model of care. Both my anthropological questioning and self-awareness of my own biomedical assumptions helped me to realise a comprehensive understanding of health and health care in Farabako.

This ethnography looks at the 'moral reasoning' (cf. Mahmood 2005) of women and men in the context of health care in Farabako, *and* my moral reasoning as an anthropologist and midwife. I look at how the discourse of shame (*maloya*) factors into women's health care seeking for themselves and their young children, *and* the role of my Western biomedical (and bioethical) discourse while providing treatment. This book elucidates the process of negotiation between local and Western moral and medical discourses in and around the maternity clinic in Farabako.

But most of all, this book is about the women of Farabako—women living 'in the middle of nowhere'. Women doing their best to keep themselves and their children healthy in a context of scarcity—a scarcity of means, scarcity of health care facilities and a scarcity of agency in terms of the capacity to take action in the face of child mortality.

Research questions

My main objective was to understand how therapy management of pregnancy and children's illnesses is practiced in Farabako.

My presumption was that a focus on therapy management would help me to understand the factors leading to high child mortality and why mothers sometimes refrained from taking action when their children were seriously ill.

The four main questions and a set of sub-questions that evolved during the research trajectory were:

1. Which factors influence child morbidity and mortality in Farabako?
   a. How are children exposed to physical risks of disease and death?
   b. What is the capacity of mothers to cope with health adversity?
   c. What are the health care options for women and children in Farabako?
   d. What are the relational power dynamics in the rural household production of health and how are they gendered?
   e. What is the role of therapy management in child morbidity and mortality?
2. How is the diagnosis of illness, the selection and evaluation of treatment, as well as support for the afflicted managed in Farabako?
   a. What perceptions do women have of their own health?
   b. How do pregnant women secure a positive obstetrical outcome?
   c. What perceptions do therapy group members have of children's illnesses and how are they represented?
   d. What do therapy group members do when a child becomes ill?
   e. How do women use their social network when seeking health care?
   f. Why do mothers sometimes take no action when their children are ill?
3. How do local moralities factor into therapy management?
   a. How does the moral discourse of shame (*maloya*) factor into the therapy management of children's illnesses?
   b. How are biomedical and local medical discourses, specifically their moral dimensions, negotiated in the context of a biomedical health care project?
4. How did my Western, biomedical, feminist assumptions travel?

Theoretical orientation

Using a grounded theory approach, as I gained new insights during each fieldwork period, I needed new theoretical concepts to explain them. I have chosen to introduce and subsequently discuss the theoretical concepts throughout the book. I address the appropriate theoretical concept in each chapter for interpreting specific research findings. Below, I merely give an overview of my theoretical orientation.

I went into the field each time with theoretical knowledge gained from scholars working in Mali (e.g. Imperato 1977; Dettwyler 1994; Brand 2000; Jansen 2000, 2009; Schulz 2011). After my first fieldwork period, to contextualize therapy management and mother's responses to health adversity, I used the concepts of social and symbolic capital (Bourdieu 1986) and 'vulnerability context' (Watts and Bohle 1993; Delor and Hubert 2000) (chapter 3). When I found shame to be an important factor in the vulnerability context, I conceptualized shame in the broader context of morality using the framework for an anthropology of moralities as developed by Zigon (2007). I used Foucault's (1994a) concept of 'technologies of the self' and Mahmood's (2005) notion of 'inhabiting a discourse' to examine the role of local moralities in therapy management (chapter 4). By exploring the discourse of shame in relation to the practical engagements in which it is embedded, such as therapy management, I have come to understand the significance of subordination for the women of Farabako.

In attempting to implement biomedical midwifery care, I observed how local (medical) moralities were negotiated in the maternity clinic. Tsing's (2005) concept of 'friction' was useful to understand how biomedicine was made to fit the local context with specific moralities such as the discourse of shame (chapter 5). During interviews on the illness episodes of children it became clear that local moralities also played a role in the construction and representation of illness in Farabako. The work of Pool (1994) and Good and Good (1994), helped me to understand how meaning is produced through the inter-subjective experience of health and illness (chapter 6 and 7).

Following Hunt (2000), Lauritzen (2004), Gammeltoft (2006), and Squire et al. (2008), I approach illness narratives and life history narratives as embodied discourse and performances, hereby illuminating individual lives *and* broader social processes. When conducting a narrative analysis (Riessman 1993) on life history interviews, I focused on the narrative construction of the self. Women in Farabako described having a lack of security and spoke of the (physical and psychological) violence inflicted upon them. The concept of 'everyday violence' as used by Scheper-Hughes and Bourgois (2004), Farmer's (1997) concept of 'structural violence' and Richters' (1994) concept of gender-based violence on an interpersonal level are all concepts that were useful to understand women's lives and their role in therapy management. The women spoke of their health in terms of suffering rather than illness. Kleinman, Das and Lock's (1997) concept of 'social suffering' guided me in my analysis of health as a social, rather than physical, well-being in Farabako (chapter 8).

Scheper-Hughes (1995) and Fassin (2008) have influenced my reflection on the role of morality in ethnography (chapter 9). While writing this book, Fassin (2011) and Wilson and Brown (2009) guided me to find a language to represent the women of Farabako; I have chosen neither a language of compassion nor human rights, but rather a language of 'methodological relativism' (Jackson 2005).

Finally, Giddens' (1991) concept of 'ontological security', Fassin's (2003) 'embodiment of inequality' and Jackson's (2005) 'intersubjective logic' helped me to analyse the relationship between shame, suffering and a lack of security (chapter 10) and to understand the language of well-being (Mann 1997) in Farabako. Although I started with a participatory action research approach, attempting to improve the lives of women and children by implementing biomedical health care, my research became more focused on health as social well-being. It is only by understanding women's 'being in the world' that we understand their health (cf. Jackson 2005).

Structure of the book

The trajectory of this research, in which the focus moved from maternal and child mortality towards the importance of morality in health, can be followed in the structure of this book.

In chapters 2 and 3, I set the scene with a short historical and socio-economic sketch of the village of Farabako and I describe the health care options for the population before the maternity clinic opened in 2007. In all subsequent chapters, the recurring theme is local moralities as a determining factor in various aspects of therapy management.

In chapter 4, I focus on the 'vulnerability context' of child mortality in Farabako. Poverty, endemic diseases, lack of reproductive choice, and difficulty in accessing adequate biomedical health care are all factors that expose the children of Farabako to physical risk. Women's capacity to cope with this physical risk was restricted by their limited social capital and by the moral discourse of shame (*maloya*) that inhibited the women from asking for help. Embodying the moral discourse of shame was an act of identity construction to strengthen the women's symbolic capital. I describe how the women's responses to health adversity succeed in avoiding social risk, but are not (yet) adjusted to the new biomedical possibilities of avoiding their physical risk and that of their children.

In chapter 5, I focus on the concept of shame in more depth. I approach shame as an institutional morality, an embodied disposition and a public discourse. Social change, in the form of increasing individualism and the introduction of biomedicine in Farabako, has illuminated the women's need to ethically weigh their social risk of being called shameless. I give examples of 'ethical moments' in and around the maternity clinic, moments when, in the context of therapy management, something happened to force a woman to consciously reflect upon the proper ethical response. I examine the ways that women inhabit the moral discourse of shame. Submission to the discourse of shame can be a condition for achieving one's potentiality. In this sense, 'having shame' can be seen as a 'technology of the self' in becoming a 'good woman'.

In chapter 6, I demonstrate how the discourse of shame contributes to friction between the biomedical discourse and local medical (moral) discourses. I explore how assumptions that biomedicine and its moral discourse are universally applicable work out in the particular context of setting up the maternity clinic in Farabako. I argue that, from the perspective of a Dutch midwife, this clinic can be perceived as a zone of awkward engagement for the imagined universality of biomedicine within the local health and gender arena. A new form of biomedicine was made to fit the local context with specific moralities. I found that moral issues, such as what it means to be a 'good healer' and a 'good woman', were at the core of the friction from which this new biomedical practice was born. I describe the ethical dilemmas that arose in the new practice and the role of moral discourse in the use of, and access to, (bio)medical health care.

In chapter 7, I explore the influence of the local moral and gender discourse on illness representations in Farabako. I describe how, under the assumption that a health survey would provide the necessary information to understand high child mortality in Farabako, I set out to interview parents and other household members about their children's illness episodes. I often heard differing versions of the same illness event. The way parents spoke about their child's illness episode said more about how they wished to position themselves within medical pluralism and how they wanted to present themselves towards me (and my maternity clinic development project) than how the therapy management actually took place. As a consequence, I did not obtain the information I set out to acquire, namely information on clinical symptoms, diagnosis and treatment that would help to improve (biomedical) health care for children. The 'actual illness episode' of the child was often hidden in the illness narratives of the parents. On the other hand, these illness narratives did turn out to be a useful tool to gain insight into the multiple social realities of illness in Farabako, for example, gender constructions and relational power dynamics within the household in the context of therapy management.

In chapter 8, I show how moralities not only play a role in the representation of illness, but also in the construction of illness categories. I illustrate how an understanding of local medical and moral discourse is a prerequisite for understanding the therapy management of children's illnesses and I focus on the particular case of malnutrition. From a biomedical standpoint, severe malnutrition is caused by not eating enough food, or eating the wrong kind of food. However, from a local standpoint, malnutrition in Farabako is not primarily about food. It is a shameful illness caused by a lack of reproductive choice within a context of vulnerability. I show how biomedical and local medical discourse must be negotiated to find a common ground, an overlap, an aspect that fits both discourses; only when this is found, can (medical) intervention be acceptable in Farabako.

In chapter 9, I shed light on how the women of Farabako perceive their health and what they consider as necessary conditions to attain well-being. I consider well-being to be an important factor in therapy management. In life history interviews, when I asked women to tell me about their health, they did not primarily speak of their physical well-being, but rather they spoke of social well-being. The women told of not being taken care of and of the (physical and psychological) 'everyday violence' they endured to keep their social ties intact. For the women of Farabako, the security of being well taken care of is a prerequisite for physical and psychological well-being. Central to this chapter are the effects of the structural violence of poverty and patriarchy, and how the women express these effects when articulating and accepting suffering. Accepting suffering is a form of agency; it reasserts patriarchal ideology; but, at the same time, it can be part of the ethical project of working on becoming a good woman and a virtuous member of the community.

In chapter 10, I reflect on how I moved from a clinically applied medical anthropology approach (social science *in* medicine) to a critical medical anthropological approach (social science *of* medicine) during the research period. My focus went beyond health care seeking and health beliefs towards the respondents' and my (as a Western feminist anthropologist and biomedically trained midwife) moralities and ethics in the context of health care. My approach shifted from a moral anthropology towards an anthropology of morals; I describe how this was a necessary step to understand therapy management in Farabako.

In the final chapter, I describe the mechanisms and factors that rendered mothers in Farabako powerless to take action when they, or one of their children became ill. I then investigate the links between health, morality, gender and poverty. I do this by analysing the relationship between three significant themes presented and discussed in this book: not-being-taken-care-of, shame and suffering. I posit that women's suffering is an expression of the lack of ontological security in the context of vulnerability. Shame is an expression of the embodiment of structural inequality. By demonstrating shame, women in Farabako created a way of existing and co-existing within a context of patriarchy and vulnerability. In Farabako, shame works as an intersubjective logic in therapy management when managing the potentialities of child disease and death. I conclude by arguing that health care workers and policy makers must understand the language and the logic of patients' therapy management as a first step to make health care interventions successful.

Understanding the role of local moralities in health is crucial for implementing biomedical health care and lowering child mortality in out of the way places such as Farabako. This ethnography can contribute to developing a new language of health and well-being, not only for clinical care, but also for public health policy and programs. Feelings of insecurity and powerlessness as indicators of 'ill-being' must be considered when planning and implementing public health programs to reduce maternal and child mortality.

2. THE VILLAGE OF FARABAKO

Farabako is a small village in the Sobara region of southwest Mali, close to the Guinean border. The village is situated in the Mande Mountains, 120 kilometres from the capital, Bamako (see map Appendix 4). This chapter sets the scene with a short historical and socio-economic sketch of the village. It presents Farabako as rooted in a history of isolation: ignored by Mande rulers, French colonials and to some extent by present-day NGOs and the Malian government. The chapter continues with a description of the uncertainty of subsistence farming, the importance of hierarchy and kinship in social relations, and the integration of religion in all aspects of village life. The chapter concludes by referring to recent changes in the villagers' participation in a money economy that have profound implications for their day-to-day life, gender relations and therapy management in Farabako.

The inhabitants of Farabako are almost all ethnically Malinke (*Maninka*). They speak *Maninkakan*, a Mande language related to *Bamanakan* (Bambara), the *lingua franca* in the West African Sudan. Farabako lies in the Mande region, a geographic area that covers the southern part of Mali and reaches into Guinea, Côte d'Ivoire, Senegal and The Gambia. These populations share related languages and a similar cultural heritage. They all trace their history back to King Sunjata Keita, founder of the Mali Empire. Although the Mali Empire, which had its heyday in the thirteenth and fourteenth century, has ceased to exist, the stories of Sunjata are still heard through a large part of West Africa today. People consider Sunjata and his helpers to be their ancestors and almost every family has stories of how their ancestor helped or fought against Sunjata (Jansen 2001).[14]

An historical sketch

Historically, the Mande Mountains have been an inhospitable region that travellers avoided. Mungo Park, in his famous *Travels into the Interior of Africa*, described his travels from Bamako to the Atlantic coast via Siby and Narena

[14] I also heard these stories; for instance, my host in Farabako, Namagan Kante, often spoke of his ancestor Sumaoro Kanté. Sumaoro Kanté was Sunjata's main antagonist and a potent sorcerer and ruler. Namagan, my host in Farabako, compared himself to his ancestor and claimed (to tease me) to want one hundred wives, one more than Sumaoro Kanté had had; at the time Namagan had four wives, the most of any man in the village. The Sunjata epic as part of daily life became clear to me in the four-wheel drive on the way to Farabako. The driver, my translator and a man showing us the way to the village had never met each other before, yet they had an animated discussion about their shared ancestry with Sunjata, and thus, it was as if they were closely related by kinship.

(1795). He followed an old trade route, the Mandesira,[15] the 'road to Mande' thereby just skirting the Sobara region. Early in his career, in 1879, the future governor of the Soudan Français, Joseph Gallieni, also avoided the Mande Mountains when he was sent to scout a route to the Niger River necessary to open trade for European factory products. During the partition of Africa, in the 1880s and 1890s, the Sobara region was added to French colonial territory. The earliest written reports on the Sobara region date from this time.[16]

According to the oldest sources, the Sobara belonged to the Cercle de Niagassola in present-day Guinea. This region had little hinder of the wars that had taken place in the Mande area, against the armies of Segu, El Hadj Umar Tal and Samori, successively. In the nineteenth century the Sobara region did suffer from plundering by the Kangaba rulers, who had suzerain status in most parts of the Mande region, and who considered the Sobara region to be their granary.

The chieftaincy of the Sobara region has historically belonged to a member of the Keita family from the village of Sorokotoro. The French nominated the regional chief (*jamanatigi*) as 'chef de canton'. In approximately 1900, the Keita family from Sorokotoro had no adult male candidates, so the French appointed a Keita family member from a younger branch of the family, who was living in Nioumamakana. In this way, Nioumamakana developed into the administrative centre of the region and currently serves as the centre of a 'commune', the smallest unit of the decentralized administrative system that Mali initiated in 1990s (see Zobel 2006). Presently, Farabako falls under the commune of Nioumamakana.

Farabako is first named in a list of villages dating from 1891. This was probably the village that used to be located where Farabako is now, of which now only remnants of former furnaces remain. The present-day inhabitants have no historical link to the inhabitants who lived there in 1900. Present-day Farabako was not listed in the 1950 census (see Jansen and Diarra 2006: 25). The colonial official, who took the census, rightly noted that it was difficult to count the Sobara villages because within a few years new villages were created and others disappeared (sometimes temporarily) as people moved to areas with fertile ground. In the last ten years, the villages in the Sobara region have become more permanent, generally due to the availability of facilities such as water pumps and services such as schools and health clinics.

The Sobara has always been sparsely populated; in 1950 the census included only thirteen villages with 1,795 (tax paying) inhabitants. The colonial official who took the census wrote: '*La mortalité est effrayante*' (the mortality is

---

[15] For details on the population and habitation strategies along the Mandesira, see Jansen 2005.

[16] I base the following historical sketch on personal communication with Jan Jansen, who in the 1990s did extensive research in the Archives Nationales in Bamako. The National Archives has presently put an embargo on sources of historical information due to fears that they might be used in feuds or to historically substantiate land claims.

frightening) and adds: 'How could it be otherwise?' He goes on to say that the high mortality rate is caused by geographical isolation, lack of sanitation and endemic diseases (Jansen and Diarra 2006: 22). Those who did not die were often afflicted by blindness, syphilis or leprosy. The birth rate was high, there were few old people, and the average age was estimated to be 35-40 years. This illustrates how difficult and unpredictable life was in this inhospitable region. In the rainy season, the region was cut off from the rest of the world for several months as overflowing rivers and streams made it impossible to enter or leave the Sobara.

Farabako was originally a hamlet (*buguda*) of a Keita family from the neighbouring village of Dambele Makadjana (described as a '*village néant*' in a 1891 source) and a Kante family from the village of Sobara-Kenyèba. The two families lived there during the rainy season to be close to their fields. It is not clear when the villagers decided to live in Farabako year round, but it was probably in the 1960s or 70s. When Jansen started his fieldwork in 1999, the villagers had been living there permanently for several decades; but many people spoke of Farabako as not a real village. Now, since the arrival of the maternity clinic and a large garden for women, Farabako is considered a village (*dugu*). Currently, Farabako also has two *bugudaw* (hamlets) of its own: Kalifabugu and Kokoli. The two hamlets are located on opposite sides of a mountain ridge, fifteen kilometres and eight kilometres from Farabako, respectively.

Agriculture in a 'forgotten zone'

All the inhabitants of Farabako survive by farming activities. This region has a tropical savannah climate with distinct dry and rainy seasons. Contrary to what the name suggests, the Mande Mountains are barely high enough to be called mountains. The region consists of vast unfertile plains divided by hills up to 600 or 800 metres. Agriculture is possible on the hills where farmers are dependent on rainfall running down the hills over their fields. The villagers generally cultivate millet and peanuts. They start planting in May when the rainy season starts and harvest from October through December. Because the earth in this region is not fertile, staple crops such as millet and corn can be cultivated for a maximum of seven years after which the land must lay fallow for twenty years. Although Farabako is located in a relatively sparsely populated area and there is no scarcity of land to cultivate, the population of the Sobara is increasing (despite migration to Bamako) and thus land is no longer as abundant as in the past. This sometimes leads to tensions between villages, for instance contesting land that has lain fallow for many years.

The inhabitants of Farabako cultivate according to a system that is prevalent among agriculturalists in Africa. During the rainy season people live in hamlets (*bugudaw*) close to their fields, leaving a small portion of the population in the village. After the harvest, when the rain stops and the small streams dry up, the people leave their hamlets and return to the village where there is water year round. During the dry season, the villagers use the lull in farming activities to repair their houses and keep up their social networks. It is a time for collective rituals and festivities and for celebrating weddings. The women (and a few men) work in their gardens where vegetables and fruit are grown for household consumption and to sell at market.

The daily meal consists of millet or corn with a sauce of vegetables or ground peanuts. It is normal for men to contribute the grain and women to take care of the sauce. This traditional division of labour creates tension in many marriages, as there are recurrent 'struggles over the sauce price' (*nasɔngo kɛlɛ*) (Schulz 2011: 101). This is because the ingredients of the sauce have changed over the years, and are now only available by taking part in a money economy, a sector where women are less active in the Sobara region.

Many men, especially those who are the least well off, or after a particularly bad harvest, leave Farabako in search of money. Some go to the goldmines, which have been exploited in the Mande region since the Middle Ages, but is now especially popular due to the high price of gold on the world market. It is hard and dangerous work without any certainty of making money (Panella 2010). Some men try to make extra income by smuggling contraband (liquor and cigarettes) from neighbouring Guinea. Others try their luck in cities such as Bamako and Kayes. Despite these efforts, all inhabitants live on less than a dollar a day.[17] Also, when measured by indicators other than economic, Farabako is poor; there is a lack of (or limited access to) food, clean water, health care, education, jobs, and representation. The inhabitants live day-by-day with an uncertain future.

Farabako is geographically remote from major economic centres and is difficult to reach due to the absence of an appropriate infrastructure. As stated before, the village is quite isolated, even by local standards, since the dirt track leading to the village is washed away in the rainy season. Jansen and Diarra (2006) have called this region 'a forgotten zone'. The government rarely reaches Farabako. In colonial times, the French never penetrated the hills of the Sobara; the region was sparsely populated and difficult to traverse and the French were not inclined to travel through it to collect taxes. The French stopped 21 kilometres from Farabako at what became the village of Sandama. French sources called it 'la porte du Sobara'. In the 1930s, the French constructed a road between Bamako and Kouremale, but the side branch of this road did not reach Sandama until 1993. Road works in this region are relatively

---

[17] Men *reported* having an average personal income of 100 euros per year and women 3 euros per year. My respondents were reticent in talking about their finances and these figures are most probably lower than their actual incomes. Furthermore, Shipton (1990) has shown that the term *personal income* is problematic in the West African setting, as liquidity is often quickly converted into forms of wealth that shelter it from the daily demands of kin. But even after taking this into account, it seems fair to say that the inhabitants of Farabako are extremely poor.

Research assistant Abdulaye Traore on a road to Farabako in the dry season

difficult and expensive due to the bridges required to guarantee access in the rainy season. At present there is no road from Sandama to Farabako and Farabako is still routinely cut off from the outside world.

The villagers take the law into their own hands, as my host told me after he had punished an adulterer by whipping and banishing him: 'There is no police in Farabako'. There is no state health facility, school, or NGO in Farabako. Few, if any of the villagers have the birth certificate necessary to give them citizen's rights. Most adults in Farabako are illiterate, and only a few adults speak the official language of French. Only a third of the children walk the four kilometres to the elementary school in a neighbouring village (twice as many boys as girls attend school). The secondary school is twenty kilometres away and for a child to be able to go there, he or she must be able to stay with a foster family.

Mande personhood: Pervasive hierarchy

In Mande cosmology, social relations exist prior to the person. It is only by means of social relations that one can achieve personhood (Brand 2000: 15). Personhood is a concept that allows for the identification of the individual through his or her connection to the social world; an isolated individual has no social significance. To achieve personhood one first acquires a name, a patronymic (*jamu*) tracing back to the times of Sunjata. One's *jamu* indicates one's social category and determines the behavioural codes for interaction with other families. Next, personhood is connected to the stage in one's life cycle. Men and women must be circumcised, marry and have children and grandchildren to achieve full personhood. Finally, achieving personhood depends on demonstrating correct behaviour such as having shame (*maloya*) and showing respect (*bɔnya*). What is considered as correct behaviour varies according to social category and gender.

Mande society is divided into three social categories. The first category is so-called nobles (*hɔrɔnw*) and most are farmers. The second category is craftsmen/artisans (*ɲamakalaw*) and includes blacksmiths (*numuw*) and bards (*jeliw*). *Ɲamakalaw* transform nature into culture; blacksmith men turn iron ore into tools, blacksmith women turn clay into pots. Blacksmith men give young male children a position in society through circumcision and blacksmith women give young girls a position in society through excision. Blacksmith men are often experts of the supernatural (amulet making and divination). Bards create social identities for people by relating them to the past via their ancestors. *Ɲamakalaw* create a position in society for people by transforming them into social beings (Jansen 2000: 6-7). The third social category is slaves (*jɔnw*). Slavery has long been abolished, but the classification remains intact, although I have never heard a person being called a slave in public. In Farabako the Kante were blacksmiths and the Keita were nobles. Although the nobles in Farabako are ranked higher in the social hierarchy, they are, on average, poorer than the blacksmith families. In these hierarchically structured social relations there is mutual dependency. The bard (*jeli*) cannot exist without the noble (*hɔrɔn*) whose praise he sings and the noble would have no fame without the bard.

According to Brand (2000), hierarchy is an important principal underlying the dynamics of Mande social relations:

> Every relation is hierarchical: total equality is not only inconceivable, it is undesirable for the inhabitants of Mande. Whenever a situation of equality between persons seems to be teetering on the brink of becoming concrete, use is made of one of the many social mechanisms to create hierarchy (Brand 2000: 19).

Social mechanisms that create hierarchy are age, gender, kinship and social category, and age is the most important (in many contexts). One must respect one's elder even if that person is only a year, or in the case of twins, only minutes older. Not only age, but social trajectory also plays a role; a mother has more status than a young girl and a post-menopausal woman (*musokɔrɔba*) has more status than a woman of childbearing years. Young women are subordinate to men, but not always; younger brothers for instance should respect and obey their older sisters. This hierarchy demands relationships of respect. A relationship of respect (*bɔnya*) is, for instance, present between a father and son, and between a mother-in-law and daughter-in-law. These relationships are all characterised by a mutual distance, a certain degree of avoidance that serves to avoid conflict. To show respect, one must demonstrate correct behaviour; one must express the correct greeting, not speak unless spoken to and accept authority. Demonstrating *maloya* (shame) is one way of showing respect (more on this in the following chapters). Relationships governed by respect often have an intrinsic rivalry (for resources) and are therefore strained.

In contrast to relationships of respect, joking relationships are relaxed; almost anything can be said without fear of being considered shameless (*malobali*). Joking relationships (*nimɔgɔya*) exist, for example, between affines of the same or younger generation, and between grandparents and grandchildren (Brand 2000: 76). Another form of joking relationship (*senankunya*) exists between members of various families (for example, between the Traore and the Kone), ethnic groups (like the Bozo and the Dogon) or social categories (Mande blacksmiths/potters are *senankunw* of the Fulbe herders). Conflict with one's *senankun* is inconceivable; therefore, they are often asked to act as mediators.

Complementarity and flexibility are two other important principles underlying Mande social relations. Hierarchy is contextual. In one situation a woman can be seen as a sister or mother and thus demand loyalty, while in another she is a wife subordinate to her husband. Hierarchy may be dominated by criteria other than gender; a woman may be a noble, a *senankun*, a sibling, a family member, or a stranger before she is a woman and how she is treated varies accordingly (Brand 2000: 20). This gives hierarchy certain ambivalence; no one is truly dominant at all times.

A village of brothers

Farabako is patrilineal, virilocal, and exogamous; it is a village of brothers and their wives and children. Typically, three generations live together in one compound including a man, his wives and children, his parents, his father's co-wives and their sons, and his father's brothers and their sons and their grandchildren. The man's 'sisters' (including half-sisters and female cousins) will have been married elsewhere.

After arriving in Farabako, in 2007, my first step was to take a census of the village; there were a total of 356 men, women and children present in the village at that time. But, this number changed constantly during the time I was in Farabako as people were often on the move. Women went to the village of their birth to stay with their mother for a while (especially when they were having marital troubles). Men, women and children went to work in the goldmines in Guinea or the markets in the capital, Bamako, when they needed money. Women moved temporarily to one of the two hamlets in the hills belonging to Farabako to cultivate the land. And everyone seemed to go at one time or another to pay their respects and make an offering for a deceased family member in another village.

While taking the census, I constructed genealogies for all Farabako households. The family trees turned out to be essential for determining who was who, as uncles were called 'father', all co-wives were called 'mother', cousins were called 'sister' or 'brother', and all distant family members were called 'cousin', 'aunt' or 'uncle'.[18] In large polygamous families with up to thirty children, a family tree was indispensable for understanding the relationships among various members of a therapy management group for a sick child—in particular, who were the biological parents and who was the head of the family.

The village had fifteen extended family households (*gwa*): seven Kante, six Keita, one Kulibali, and one Traore. Most of these kinship groups are large (on average 32 members) and polygamous with many children. The village is headed by the *dugutigi*, the oldest member of the (Keita) founding family. The *dugutigi* decides on matters pertaining to land use, among other issues. He does this with the help of a council of elders, which has representatives from each extended household.

Men in Farabako want many wives in order to have many children, who they need to work the fields. My male respondents told me that there are more men here than women, and thus it is difficult to find marriageable women in the region. Men in Farabako do not want to marry women from Bamako because 'they cannot work'. There are general rules traced back to the Sunjata period about who may marry whom. *Numuw* (blacksmiths), like the Kante, can only marry other *numuw*. For example, my host Namagan is a Famusala Kante (the Famusala lineage is only found in Farabako and Guinea). He married Nasira Kante, of the *Numu Bambala* lineage (this lineage is found in neighbouring villages on the Mali side of the border). People of the Keita family are *hɔrɔnw* (nobles) and can only marry other *hɔrɔnw*.

Each man and woman has his or her own hut. Young children sleep with their mothers. When they reach puberty, girls often sleep with their grandmothers and boys sleep together with other boys of approximately the same age. When daughters marry, they must leave Farabako. Thus, the men stay in Farabako and their wives come from outside. This means that the wives are strangers and have no kin of their own in Farabako, only affines until they give birth to children of their own. A woman represents the interests of another group of patrilineal kin (*bonda*), namely that of her parents. This is a constant source of tension for married women. In the span of a lifetime, as a woman ages, she will increasingly belong to her husband's *bonda*, as her interests eventually lie with her sons (cf. Grosz-Ngaté 1989).

Badenya (lit. mother childness) is a relational term signifying a harmony amongst members of extended families (Bird and Kendall 1980: 15). Cohesion and consensus, community values that are highly appreciated in Mande, find expression in the concept of *badenya*. *Badenya* represents loyalty and trust that

[18] The kinship terminology is Iroquois; a father's brothers are considered fathers and a father's brother's children are considered siblings.

is presumed to exist among siblings of the same mother and father (see Brand 2000: 27). *Badenya* is a harmony norm; there should be solidarity among members of an extended family. There should be mutual assistance and pity (*hinɛ*) in times of difficulty, such as health adversity. My respondents complained that *badenya* is diminishing due to increasing individualism.

> *Badenya* is typified by mutual respect between the elders and the youth but now we see that this *badenya* is losing value. There is no longer any solidarity between families; it is especially individualism that prevails amongst the youth of today. (Nene Kante, 50 yrs, January 2012)

Spirits, power objects and Allah

Religion in Farabako is integrated into all aspects of life, including medical treatments. I couldn't tell you what religion looks like in Farabako, because it is not institutionalized. For a few years, Farabako has had a small mud building that serves as a mosque, but during my stay it was almost always locked. I only saw it open on Muslim holidays. There were few inhabitants who openly professed their Muslim faith (to me). The members of the Keita family made more use of the mosque than did the members of the Kante family. In Farabako there is a mix of Islam and animism; the people believe in Allah, good and bad spirits that can lodge in nature (*jinɛw*) and power objects (*basiw*).

A djinn (*jinɛ*) is an invisible being that can possess people. *Jinɛw* can take on human and animal forms to influence men to do good or evil. They punish those who are indebted to them but do not follow their many rules. The *jinɛw* must be appeased by bringing them offers, performing rituals and observing taboos. According to Abdulaye Traore, there are many *jinɛw* in Farabako:

> If you work together with a *jinɛ* you can become rich. It is a force that is very strong. If a *jinɛ* loves you, you can work together, but it is dangerous; if you speak of this collaboration with others you will die immediately or you will become mute. If you don't keep your promise to the *jinɛ* it is also very dangerous. (February 2007)

A *jinɛ* was described to me as a force that enters someone; one knows this by dreams. I was told that there are also female *jinɛw*. It is said that if a man has a child with a female *jinɛ* he will not be able to have children with his wife. The children from a *jinɛ* relationship are invisible to others. Only the father and the *jinɛ*-mother can see them. These invisible children are said to work with their father in his fields.[19]

---

[19] Geschiere (1997) argues that the invisible is used as an explanation for success. In Cameroon, among the Maka, new wealth was attributed to witches turning their victims into zombies and then putting them to work on invisible plantations.

There is said to be an enormous serpent-*jinɛ* that lives in a cave in the mountain close to the village; I was told that 'he can give you gold'. I was allowed to visit two *jinɛw* dwellings (*jinɛyɔrɔ*) where one can give sacrifices (for example, a white sheep). Both were caves next to small waterfalls and off limits for women.

Whereas men can 'have' a *jinɛ* that helps them to gain material wealth, *jinɛw* are often spoken of as dangerous for women. For women, the time that they wash themselves in the evening is the time they are the most susceptible to *jinɛw*; it is the time *jinɛw* are most likely to enter them.

> You feel it even if you don't see it. Washing in the dark is too dangerous. The *jinɛ* can have sex with you and then you will have a baby with deformities. (Dusuba Sinayogo, 50 yrs, March 2007)

Having sex with a *jinɛ* was the only cause of congenital defects that my respondents named. They told me that women should not be out in the bush (*kungo*), the area outside of the village, between one and two in the afternoon as it is very hot and there are many *jinɛw* about at that time. I was told of a woman who had 'had a *jinɛ*'; this *jinɛ* was said to have had sex with her in her dreams. The woman went to a *soma* to have the *jinɛ* exorcised. Having said this, I did observe that women often washed after dark generally out of necessity. Once a woman had given all her family members water to wash, and it was finally their turn, the sun had gone down.

There is one *jinɛ* that women can turn to for help: Moribayasa. Moribayasa seems to be a different category of *jinɛ*; he (Moribayasa is a male *jinɛ*) is not dangerous. One of the oldest women in Farabako told me that if a woman wants a child she asks 'Moribayasa please give me a child'. When the woman becomes pregnant she must go to the baobab tree, just outside of the village next to the stream where the women do their washing and where Moribayasa lives. There, the woman must make an offering of kola nuts, corn or beans (or some other foodstuff) to thank him. Women can ask Moribayasa for other things as well, for example they can ask for a good harvest.

Baraka Kante, an esteemed elder woman of the village, told me that once when she was stranded on the road from Guinea back to Farabako, she had asked Moribayasa for a motorcycle to appear to give her a lift, and one did. Baraka assured me that Moribayasa was so powerful that even when I was back in the Netherlands I could ask the *jinɛ* to help me, but then I must not forget to perform a sacrifice for him on my return to Farabako. At the time of my interview with Baraka, six young women were sitting around us. I asked these young women if they ever asked for anything from Moribayasa and they all said 'no never'.

The *somaw* are the ritual leaders in Farabako (see Jansen 2009, 2011). The *somaw* in Farabako are all men of the blacksmith category and members of the

Soma Samba Kante performing a sacrifice for his family's basiw *(power objects)*

Kante family. The *somaw* have altars of power objects (*basiw*, singular *basi*), also called fetishes,[20] in their houses. A *basi* is a man-made object believed to have supernatural powers. The *basiw* that I, as a woman, was allowed to see, were black objects made of animal horns and (for me) unidentifiable materials covered in dried blood. The *somaw* give sacrifices of blood (food) and alcohol (drink) to their *basiw*. In return their *basiw* work for them, doing good, for example in healing, but they can also do harm.

The only power object that a woman can have that is not secret, is a *sinsin*, a fetish of twins. Women have a *sinsin* power object if they are a twin or if they have delivered twins. The *sinsin* is made of half of a calabash with two small pieces of wood smeared in chicken or goat's blood and fastened to its centre. The *sinsin* hangs above the door of the woman's room. If a family member is in labour, then the woman will place it on the ground, otherwise, it is said, the

[20] See Pietz (1988) for an account of the origin of the term fetish, first coined by Portuguese traders in the fifteenth century, and later used as an overarching explanation of the 'unenlightened' strangeness of African societies (1988: 116).

woman will not deliver. Every time the owner of a *sinsin* undertakes something, she can take it down from the wall and sprinkle water over it and ask for help; for instance for luck, a good harvest or a good trip to Bamako. If her wish comes true, then on her return the woman must again sprinkle water over the *sinsin* and give an offering of a kola nut. According to Baraka Kante, if she forgets to do this then, that night, she might dream of a fire in front of her hut.

In health matters, sacrifices can be made to *jinɛw* and power objects to secure their help. Sacrifices are sometimes also made for the health of an extended family and even for the village as a whole. When the maternity clinic opened in 2007, a cow was sacrificed during the opening festivities to bring good luck to the enterprise.[21]

Social change: Participating in the money economy

Farabako is mostly self-sufficient. Up until the 1960s, villagers worked collectively on the land, whereas presently, every family produces food for their own consumption. Therefore, money is not openly present in everyday life; there is no intensive money economy in the village. For a few years, there has been one small shop that sells sugar, tea, rice, batteries, cigarettes and candy. Women selling their produce or prepared food in Farabako have prices so low (for example 20 FCFA, 4 euro cents, for a fried beignet) that one can hardly speak of taking part in the market economy. It was explained to me that money was not seen as an individual, personal possession; if you had money you had to share it. If a villager made a bit of money, he or she would be obliged to give some to those who asked. One way of avoiding this was to buy a cow (see also Shipton 1990). One of my female respondents, Sitan Kante, made a substantial amount of money working in the goldmines. Knowing that she would have to give money to her husband (who had not been lucky in the mines himself) if he asked, she bought a cow (100,000 FCFA, approx. 150 euros) to safeguard her small fortune, a classic move in the Mande Mountains.

In Farabako wealth is expressed in cows, but things are changing. In 2009, gold was found in Dagala, a mining site five kilometres from Farabako and led to a gold rush. Historically, gold mining has always been a possible dry season activity for inhabitants of Farabako (see also Jansen 2010). But, the fact that the mining site was at walking distance from the village meant that all the inhabitants of Farabako, men, women and children went to the goldmines to try their luck. As a result, many villagers neglected their gardens and fields that year and those that did not find gold or make money with other activities at the gold mines went hungry. The men worked in the pits. The women pulverized and washed the rock and they cooked for the miners. A market selling every possible consumer good and produce sprouted at the mining site. Even a motorcycle

---

[21] The sacrifice and ensuing feast served to inform people from neighbouring villages about the health care project and invite them to consider using the clinic.

Soma Namagan Kante performing a sand divination

seller opened shop. Buses coming from the capital and from Guinea brought goods and foreign workers. All kinds of income-generating activities became possible. For example, the *somaw* did divinations to determine the best place to dig a pit and the best way to appease the *jinɛw* that roamed the mines.

Rather than diminishing with modernization, sand divination is now often used by people searching for successful participation in the modern market economy (Jansen 2009). Namagan Kante, an expert in this field, assured me (also before the goldrush) that he has more work now than ever.

> There are more social problems such as rivalry between men for jobs. There is not more *boni* ['magic'] these days, but there is more need of sand divination and medicines. (Namagan Kante, 43yrs, March 2007)

Despite the fact that most villagers did *not* find a substantial amount of gold, as a result of the gold rush, there was more money in the village. This was visible in 2012, since three men of the Kante family (all *somaw*) had satellite televisions (powered by solar panels). Consumerism is also more visible now than a few years ago, as one young father put it:

> For men, life has become more difficult. Before all men were equal and they worked together. If there was a good harvest of millet it went to the

> family. Now men are looking for money only for themselves. Men have more problems now; they want a motorcycle, and once they have one, they want a television. (Madu Keita, 25 yrs, January 2012)

With the arrival of money in Farabako, more money is needed. With the arrival of biomedicine in the form of the maternity clinic, money is needed. But men and women lack work opportunities outside of subsistence farming. Women have limited or no independent income. Men's growing inability to provide for their families leads to a pervasive atmosphere of disappointment and resentment that contributes to women's growing sense of vulnerability in Farabako (cf. Schulz 2011 for Bamako).

Conclusion

Farabako is a relatively young village situated in the geographically isolated, and historically 'forgotten zone', of the Sobara region. Life in Farabako is one of poverty and uncertainty; income-generating activities are limited. The position of women is especially difficult; they come from outside of the village and marry into Farabako as strangers without kin. Women have little or no independent income, but money is now needed where it was not before: for example for the daily meal and to access biomedical health care. High child mortality is found at the intersection of historical, socio-cultural and economic processes on the one hand, and the physical environment on the other. In chapter 4, I use the concept of 'vulnerability context' in studying this intersection, but first I turn to the health care options available to women in Farabako.

3. HEALTH CARE OPTIONS IN FARABAKO

To understand the choices made in household therapy management, it is necessary to understand which health care options are available. In Farabako, the health care context is medical pluralism. This chapter gives an overview of the various medical experts who practice in Farabako. I describe how the medical experts are positioned in the village, their methods of diagnosis and treatment, and how they acquired their knowledge. While the local medical experts are rooted in their respective healing traditions, biomedical health care is relatively new in Farabako.

Musokɔrɔbaw: The power of words

Every extended household in Farabako has elder women (*musokɔrɔbaw*) with special knowledge of medicinal plants. As explained earlier, *musokɔrɔbaw*[22] are the elder women of the village who attend births and treat young children.

From left to right: Fanta Kante Nasira Fofana, Maimuna Konate, Fanta Keita, Kanku Kante, Kinyèba Fofana, Jeneba Kamara, Baraka Kante and Nandabi Danyògò, musokɔrɔbaw *of Farabako*

[22] I use the term *musokɔrɔbaw* (singular *musokɔrɔba)* rather than 'traditional birth attendant' (TBA). For me, the term TBA has a negative connotation; in medical anthropological literature TBA's are sometimes portrayed as being unskilled. I found the *musokɔrɔbaw* to be skilled health care workers. The term 'traditional' is also problematic here in that the body of knowledge of these older women is not fixed, but ever changing in these 'modern' times. I do use the term 'traditional medicine' to mean indigenous remedies as distinct from 'modern medicine' by which I mean biomedical drugs bought in a pharmacy or on the street from drug sellers.

Musokɔrɔbaw have personal secret knowledge (*dalilu*)[23] of the incantations (*kilisiw*) necessary to prepare certain traditional medicines. If a woman is to become a *musokɔrɔba*, she must be post-menopausal and her mother must be deceased. Knowledge of pregnancy and birth is thought to be dangerous; it can cause a miscarriage or premature birth, and for this reason only post-menopausal women have this knowledge.

When I told Kinyèba Keita and Jeneba Kamara, two highly esteemed *musokɔrɔbaw*, that I was interested in learning about the incantations they used during deliveries, they agreed to an interview. When I arrived, it was made clear to me that knowledge is only passed down from one individual to the next in private; sharing knowledge is a one-on-one activity. Thus, Kinyèba left me alone with Jeneba in her hut. Jeneba wanted 2,000 FCFA (approximately 3 euros) for her personal secret knowledge (*dalilu*), because she had paid when she had acquired it from another *musokɔrɔba.* I had a private interview with Kinyèba on another day and she gave me other *kilisiw* (incantations) for free. No two *kilisiw* that I heard from various *musokɔrɔbaw* during my stay were the same.

When I asked Abdulaye Traore who the most powerful *musokɔrɔba* in the village was, he immediately said: 'Baraka Kante, because she has a lot of gris-gris and her grandmother used to be able to transform herself into a panther'. Baraka was in her seventies and as a *musokɔrɔba* she has helped many women during their deliveries. Baraka is a Kante, the family most renowned for traditional healing in Farabako. The next section is a compilation of several informal talks I had with Baraka in her hut during stiflingly hot afternoons and evenings.

Baraka had heard that I was interested in the incantations (*kilisiw*) that the *musokɔrɔbaw* use to help women during labour. She wanted to give me *kilisiw*, but first she sent the six young women away who had been sitting in front of her hut, as it could be dangerous for them if they happened to be pregnant at the time. Hearing incantations can cause a miscarriage. Baraka, like the other *musokɔrɔbaw*, believes that incantations are beneficial for an easy delivery; they speed up labour. Incantations are only used when labour has already started; they are not used to induce labour. The incantations are said, or rather spit, into water. The saliva is the medium through which the words enter the water. This practice is called *jimakuma* ('talking with water'). The woman in labour must drink this water after which the incantations will be repeated by the *musokɔrɔba* three times over her back and three times over her abdomen.[24]

---

[23] In Mande there are various categories of secret knowledge: public secrets that are shameful to say out loud (*gundo*) and secrets that are personal possessions (*dalilu*) (personal communication Jan Jansen).

[24] To have an easy delivery is spoken of as 'delivering like a dog'.

Incantations to speed up a delivery

Tu bisimilayi	Greetings to the fetish
Wulu dogo	Hide the dog
Wululajɛla dogo ju-a-mina-a	Hide those who hunt with the dog, those who have caught him
Bila, a mina, a bila	Release, catch him, release him
Tu bisimilayi	Greetings to the fetish
Wulu bilali	The letting free of the dog
Wulu bilali	The letting free of the dog

Incantations always begin with *tu bisimilayi*, a greeting to the fetish; in the case of incantations, saliva is the fetish as it is the medium through which the words enter the body. But Baraka says that this is different from asking something of a fetish (power object, *basi*); if you start the incantation without greeting the fetish it will still work. 'It is the power of the words, not the power of the fetish that makes it work'.[25] There are special incantations to stop premature labour, to alleviate abdominal pain and to deliver twins.

Baraka also uses incantations when she makes a cotton cord *(tafo)* that some pregnant women wear around their abdomen to protect against premature labour. She takes a cotton cord and measures the woman's abdomen; she then makes knots in the cord. Baraka says incantations over each knot in the cord and the same incantations are said over water that the woman must drink:

Incantations used in making a tafo:

Tu bisimilayi	Greetings to the fetish
Ni lafiu ma wuli	If the black of night does not dissipate
Kɔnɔ kana wuli	The bird should not take flight
Kɔnɔ kana wuli	The bird should not take flight
Ni tilen ma wuli	If the sun has not risen
Kɔnɔ kana wuli	The bird should not take flight
Kɔnɔ kana wuli	The bird should not take flight

Baraka then lays the cord on the ground and the woman picks it up and ties it around her waist. She does not hand the *tafo* to the woman directly because this could cause Baraka to have abdominal pains herself. During labour, shortly before the baby is born, the *tafo* is cut and another set of incantations are said.

When Baraka's (classificatory) daughter Fadima went into labour, Baraka called me to come and help deliver the baby. This was an honour and I went to

[25] See Traoré (2000) for an in depth study of the prestige that the *Maninka* attribute to the spoken word.

Musokɔrɔba *Baraka Kante with her* sinsin *power object*

her hut immediately. Fadima had recently come back to the village to deliver the baby at her mother's compound. She had not come for any prenatal check-ups. In between the contractions I tried to find out more about Fadima. This was her second pregnancy; her first child had died when he was one year old. When I asked her how many months pregnant she was; she said 'I forgot'. She wanted to deliver in the maternity clinic, so the three of us walked there. Before leaving, Baraka took her *sinsin* fetish off the wall and laid it on the ground to enable her daughter to deliver. When we arrived at the clinic, I asked Baraka to stay and help. By then the two midwives, Jeneba Kante and Kamisajè Kulibali had also arrived. The first stage of labour took a very long time and all through the night the midwives, two *musokɔrɔbaw* and I all took turns rubbing Fadima's back and comforting her. At the beginning of Fadima's labour, Baraka prepared *jimakuma* (literally 'speech water') by saying these incantations (*kilisiw*) three times over a cup of water:

Incantations for jimakuma:

Tu bisimilayi	Greetings to the fetish
Cɛkɔrɔnin ye nogo dɔn	The old man has let the dirt (sperm) enter
Musokɔrɔba ye nogo bɔ	The old woman has let the dirt exit

The water had been pulled out of a well in a calabash, swiftly in one go. Drinking this water is said to speed up delivery. Fadima had to drink all the water at once, after which Baraka said the same incantations directly onto Fadima's belly three times, and then on her back three times. Next, Baraka tapped several times on the floor where during a home birth the child would have been born.[26] Together with the midwives, I examined Fadima and listened to the baby's heartbeat. Fadima was in a lot of pain and cried out like a child who needed to be consoled. While Fadima was on her hands and knees, one midwife took her head in her lap while the other midwife rubbed her back. After several hours, Baraka asked Fadima if she had been unfaithful to her husband. Adultery is a possible cause of protracted labour; only after the woman has confessed can the baby be born.[27] Fadima said that she had not been unfaithful. After a few more hours, Baraka and I simultaneously found that the labour was taking too long and something needed to be done. I gave Fadima a painkiller to relax her a bit, and Baraka gave her traditional medicine (*surumugu*, 'suru poweder') to speed up the contractions. Baraka did not tell Fadima what the medicine was for and Fadima did not ask. One or both of the treatments seem to have helped, because an hour later a healthy baby boy was born. The first thing Fadima asked was, 'is it dead?'

Musokɔrɔbaw are also specialized in the treatment of babies and young children. According to Baraka, there are special incantations to protect a baby once it is born. The *musokɔrɔbaw* prepare the leaves from a *sɛnɛ* tree with incantations to wash the baby with for protection from '*kɔnɔ*'. I was told that *kɔnɔ* is a serious illness and many babies die of it; there are evil people who can transform themselves into birds that fly at night and eat children. The symptoms of *kɔnɔ* are convulsions and eye rolling. *Kɔnɔ* was described to me, by the *musokɔrɔbaw*, as an illness with symptoms similar to those of the biomedical illness categories of cerebral malaria and other severe infections such as teta-

[26] Similarly, Allen (2002: 202) describes how a traditional birth attendant (TBA) in West Central Tanzania prepared an herbal tea drink in a case of protracted labour. The woman in labour drank from a cup held by the TBA, the TBA then let go of the cup and the cup tumbled down the length of the pregnant belly to the floor. The TBA picked it up and tapped it three times on each side of the belly, held it up once more to the woman's breastbone and let it fall again onto the floor. Symbolizing how the baby should be born—straight out of the womb without any problems.

[27] In West Central Tanzania the term *usangalija* is used to denote protracted labour due to a 'mixing of men' (adultery during pregnancy). One of the symptoms of this condition is that the baby moves up the birth canal instead of down during labour. Traditional medicine and confession are the cure (Allen 2002).

nus.[28] Babies must drink the plant mixture and be washed in it; baby girls must be washed four times, baby boys three times. The *musokɔrɔbaw* also massage the baby while saying the incantations, they continue this until the baby urinates or defecates; at that point the illness is thought to have left the body.

Somaw: With the help of the fetish

In the Kante family, men with expert medical knowledge are called *somaw*. They use power objects, (*basiw*), sand divination and their extensive knowledge of the medicinal properties of plants to diagnose and treat illness.[29] In the Keita family, some of the older generation of men who have medicinal knowledge call themselves hunters (*dɔnsow*).[30] The *dɔnsow* have knowledge of the supernatural and the magical, similar to the *somaw*. The *dɔnsow* and the *somaw* often perform together.

Musa Kante is a highly esteemed *soma* and the son of the famous *soma* Farabako *Jigin*. When a patient comes to Musa, he asks about the complaint and its duration. He usually does not perform a physical examination, and never performs one if the patient is a woman. If it is not a serious illness, Musa gives the patient traditional medicine. For serious illness, Musa first goes into the bush where there is a secret *basi* that only initiates may see. He throws two halves of a kola nut in front of the *basi*; if they both fall ‘open’ or if they both fall ‘closed’ it means that he can treat the patient. If one falls open and the other closed (during three throws) this means that Musa cannot cure this patient and he will send him to a healer in another village. He determines who is the best healer by asking the *basi*. If the *basi* agrees that Musa can treat the patient, a sand divination follows to determine the cause and treatment of the illness, which sacrifice must be made and which medicinal plants should be used. A usual sacrifice is a goat and two chickens. Once the patient is healed and returns to their village, a sheep must also be sacrificed. If money is a problem and the patient’s family cannot buy a goat, Musa will use the sand to transform the goat into a chicken. The goat and the chicken embody the illness and when they are offered as a sacrifice, the evil that caused the illness will be undone. Sand divination is used to determine the cause and treatment of illness, but also to foretell the future, determine the culprit of a crime or the cause of social problems (see also Jansen 2009, 2011).

When asked which illnesses they can cure, the *somaw* were confident they could cure most illnesses, including malaria and infertility in particular. On the other hand, they were adamant that they could not cure HIV/AIDS, epilepsy or mental illness. The *somaw* treat mostly adults; children are more often treated

---

[28] Bailleul (2000) translates *kɔnɔ* as a symptom: convulsions caused by infections such as malaria or tetanus and attributed to an evil-doing bird. However, my respondents spoke of *kɔnɔ* as an illness; this was unusual because normally they spoke in terms of symptoms.

[29] See Jansen (2009, 2011) on *somaw* in Farabako.

[30] See Camara (2011) for a description of the origins and present-day meanings given to hunters.

Soma *Musa Kante with ceremonial spear and headdress with power objects*

by the *musokɔrɔbaw*. The *somaw* I spoke with had difficulty answering my questions about causes and symptoms of illness. Questions about causes usually provoked answers about symptoms and questions about symptoms yielded answers such as; 'because of my training and expertise I recognize the illness.'

Somaw spoke of 'natural illnesses', such as a backache, which can be treated with traditional medicine made from plants and bark. In such illnesses, natural forces are unleashed due to an imbalance of, for example, hot and cold. This imbalance can be either within the body or in the social arena, which roughly corresponds to Foster's (1976) concept of naturalistic aetiology. In Farabako, behaving badly towards another person is seen as a cause of illness; to be cured, the patient must apologize.

Somaw also spoke of illnesses in which the sick person was a victim, when the object of aggression or punishment was directed only at them. This corresponds to Foster's category of personalistic aetiology. Such illnesses are caused by the intervention of an animate force (sensate agent). This force can be a human (a witch or sorcerer) or a non-human agent (*jinɛ*).[31] For example, a person can become ill by walking where a serpent-*jinɛ* has just been. In these cases, making a sacrifice is the cure. A person can also become ill due to *boni korote* ('magical poison throwing'). This illness is caused by a *jinɛ*'s curse or by a person doing evil. This illness is manifested by psychological symptoms or physical symptoms such as wounds, swelling or blindness. Exorcism is the cure.

The causes of illness are not simultaneously seen as causes of death. Death is not caused by illness; God causes death. One can become ill from natural causes but one dies because it is God's will. As the *soma* Musa Kante put it: 'If it is your last day, then you will die.'

Traditional medicine is made of plants and tree leaves, roots and bark. The *soma*'s apprentices collect these. They are pound into a powder or boiled in water. There are distinct medicines for each illness and these medicines have a specific dosage (sometimes measured using half a peanut shell). If the treatment does not work, after a time, the *soma* will consult the sand again and if necessary change the treatment. The *somaw* told me that treatment with traditional medicine could take a long time and involve the use of a wide variety of plants and trees.

Because of their training, knowledge of illness and plants and initiation in metaphysical knowledge, the *somaw* are able to treat supernatural illnesses with natural medicine. They have medicines to protect people from disease, *jinɛw* in the bush and also to protect against boni koroté (see Jansen 2011). Musa Kante explained that the *somaw* can recognize and cure *boni korote* because they can also cause it. The *somaw* can curse people, and even kill people by 'giving that person's name to their *basi*'. If a man buys a certain kind of *basi* from a *soma*, he can harm others with it. Women cannot do this themselves; 'they must pay men to do evil for them'. Musa Kante prefers not to sell *basiw* to men from Farabako to avoid problems.

The *somaw* recognize the power of words, as the *musokɔrɔbaw* do, and this is evident in their use of incantations. *Somaw*, like *musokɔrɔbaw*, use incantations when preparing a *tafo*, the cord worn around the waist, used by pregnant women to ward off abdominal pain. Incantations are also used by the *somaw* when preparing traditional medicine to speed up a delivery (*jimakuma*). Although, I must say that I find the incantations used by the *soma* Namagan Kante to be slightly less poetic than those used by the *musokɔrɔbaw*.

If, by accident, this incantation is said when a pregnant woman is not in labour she will start having contractions and may miscarry.

---

[31] Imperato (1977), in his study of the Bambara, makes a distinction between conscious human agents (sorcerers) and unconscious human agents (witches). He also makes a distinction between jinn in a corporeal form such as a snake and jinn that possess a person. In Farabako witches were considered to be conscious of their acts.

Incantations used for jimakuma:

Tu bisimilayi	Greetings to the fetish
Bakɔrɔ yɛlɛnna bamuso kan	The billy goat mounted the nanny goat
O jiginna	She who has delivered
Toro yɛlɛnna misimuso kan	The bull mounted the cow
O jiginna	She who has delivered
Dudukɔdɔ yɛlɛnna syɛmuso kan	The rooster mounted the chicken
O jiginna	She who has delivered
Sagajigi yɛlɛnna sagamuso kan	The ram mounted the sheep
O jiginna	She who has delivered
Karsa (togo) o jiginna	(the name of the woman) has delivered

The *somaw* also make amulets for children to bring luck and protect them from illness or bad spirits. These amulets are called *sɛbɛn* (lit. writing). Signs, the same as those used during sand divination are written on paper. These papers, together with plants, are wrapped in a small piece of animal skin that is tied around the child's neck, wrist or waist.

Although the *somaw* make amulets to protect children, it is the older women in the village who treat children when they are ill. One young mother told me:

> People do not normally consult the *somaw* when their children are ill; most go to the *musokɔrɔbaw*. You go to the *somaw* when someone wants to do you harm. It does not happen often that someone wants to harm a small child. (Nantɛnɛ Kante, 23 yrs, 2009)

Herbalists: In the name of Allah

Herbalists (*furatigiw*) are men, often of a younger generation, who possess medicinal knowledge, and who are not *somaw* or *dɔnsow*. They do not (openly) make use of power objects (*basiw*) in their treatments. They do openly profess their Muslim faith.

In November 2009, I accompanied the herbalist Fawulen Keita when he went to look for medicinal plants in the bush. Along the way, he explained to me that he uses the leaves of the *sɛnɛ* tree in his treatment for *mimi* (an illness of the throat). Fawulen says incantations (*kilisiw*) over the leaves and then boils them in water. The patient must then inhale the steam from this concoction. A man from another village sold this knowledge to Fawulen in exchange for a goat.

Incantations for mimi

Tu bisimilaye	Greetings to the fetish
Sukɛlu fifa	A male sorcerer's evil will go with the wind
Sumusolu fifa	A female sorcerer's evil will go with the wind
Ne ko Allah	I say God
Ne ko Alakira	I say His Prophet

Fawulen explained that he can only treat people who are ill with the help of God, and only if he shows respect to God. As we walked further, Fawulen showed me the root of the binbiligele[32] tree and the leaves of the female jamagara tree that he uses to treat dysentery and abdominal pain. He acquired this knowledge from a stranger who gave it to him as thanks for his hospitality. We didn't have to walk far before Fawulen pointed out a kuntaninobo, which is a climbing plant used to treat the childhood illness of *kɔnɔ*. Fawulen acquired this knowledge from a man from another village who had successfully treated a child with *kɔnɔ* when visiting Farabako. Fawulen had paid the man a goat for this knowledge.

Incantations for kɔnɔ

So ni ɲama	House protected against evil
Konko ni ɲama	Forest protected against evil
Kɔnɔ ni ɲama	Birds protected against evil
Sɔgɔ ni ɲama	Wild animals protected against evil
Ne ko fifa	I say (this evil will) go with the wind
O ka taa wula la	This wind must go in the bush (and let the house alone)

In this incantation, Fawulen tells me he is asking respect of the house, forest, birds and animals.[33] He continues to show me other plants and explains that his mother and brother had also given him knowledge of certain plants and methods of treatment (for free). When I asked if Fawulen had incantations for malaria (*sumaya*), he said no, only plants. He explained that some plants need incantations to be effective and other plants are effective without incantations.

Biomedical health care

Until 2004, there were no biomedical health facilities in the Sobara region. The closest health facility for prenatal care was in Siby, a small town 70 kilometres from Farabako. Now there are two health clinics staffed with a doctor and a

---

[32] I was able to corroborate the spelling of some, but not all of the names of plants and trees.

[33] Translation by Abdulaye Traore.

Herbalist Fawulen Keita gathering medicinal plants

midwife, one in the village of Sandama and one in Nioumamakana. Both clinics are twenty kilometres away; it takes at least one hour by motorcycle over rough terrain, crossing several river beddings, to get there. This is only possible in the dry season, since during the rainy season the rivers are impassable. Not all families own a motorcycle or have the money to pay for petrol. Money for petrol (*esansiwari*) costs between 500 and 1,000 FCFA (0.75-1.5 euros) per litre; this is more than most men's average daily wage. A *sotrama* (the almost always dilapidated green mini buses that are seen all over Mali) used to stop in Farabako on Mondays only, but they stopped coming in 2006 because of the bad roads. It takes a day (or two if they have to walk) for a woman to go to a health clinic for a prenatal check-up or for a consultation for a sick child. This is time that most women cannot be away from home.

If people do manage to make it to a health clinic, they cannot be sure that they will find the only doctor on staff in residence. If he is in residence, the doctor has limited capacities for treating sick children and obstetrical complications. The cost of a consultation and the medication prescribed by the doctor is often prohibitive. The pharmacy is not always well stocked. For blood transfusions, instrumental delivery and caesarean section a referral to the capital Bamako is necessary, fifty kilometres away from Siby. There is no ambulance service in the Sobara.

In February 2007, the maternity clinic opened its doors. There were two midwives working in the clinic doing antenatal consultations and delivering babies, and a young man with knowledge of Western medicine working in the clinic's small pharmacy.

Travelling drug salesmen sell their ware in surrounding villages on market days and they occasionally visit Farabako. They sell (dubious) Western medicine; it is not clear if the medicine is real or fake. I have seen drug sellers sell Nivaquine® as a treatment for malaria, while mosquitoes in the region are said to be resistant to Nivaquine®. They also sell painkillers and amphetamines as medicine for 'fatigue', which many young men working in the field or goldmines are eager to buy. Drug sellers are popular. This is true despite the fact that villagers realise that their ware is not always to be trusted, because their prices are well below a pharmacy's prices, and people can buy one or two tablets at a time, rather than a whole course of treatment.

Social change: Health as an individual responsibility

Medical treatment provided by the *musokɔrɔbaw*, *somaw*, and *furatigi* is always given for free. If a patient recovers, he or she may give a gift (for example, a chicken) to the healer as thanks. Recently biomedical treatment has become available to the villagers of Farabako, but money is needed to access it. As we have seen in the previous chapter, social change, in the form of participation in the money economy, has been problematic in Farabako due to extreme poverty.

In the past, the head of the extended family (*dutigi*) was formally responsible for the health of his family. If a child was ill, the mother would tell the *dutigi* and he would arrange for the necessary means (financial or otherwise) for treatment. Until his death in 2009, Bala Kante was the *dutigi* of the Kante family, one of the two largest families in Farabako. Bala was a *soma*; he was known for his knowledge of children's illnesses. Bala was seventy-eight and bedridden at the time of my interview with him. I asked Bala how health care in Farabako had changed over the years.[34] He told me that in the past, everyone had knowledge of traditional medicine for all common illnesses. Now they do not. The head of the family (*dutigi*) used to be responsible for the family's health, and people would tell him if a child was ill. Bala often did divinations to see what he should sacrifice for the good health of the family. In the past, all family members gave the head of the family money and he used this for all problems, marriages, funerals and illness. According to Bala, this began to change in the 1960s, when materialism and individualization became more prominent in Farabako. People started wanting things for themselves and there

[34] Bala was used to talking in this vein (see Jansen and Diarra 2006). His stories were quite easy to follow and temporally in line with my linear idea of time. His style of narration was possibly influenced by his stay in Bamako in the 1950s and 1960s. After this interview, Bala did a divination for me (without my asking). Instead of using sand, Bala made marks on paper. This paper was folded into a small wad that was then covered in leather. Bala told me that this amulet would protect me against betrayal. Sadly, Bala died only a month later.

was diversification of work. From this time on, people no longer worked exclusively in the fields. People no longer had the same goals and no one wanted to work collectively anymore. Bala went on to say:

> Now, the father is responsible if the child becomes ill, then the mother, then the father's brother. People have less confidence in traditional medicine than they used to and this knowledge is getting lost. Everyone now wants to go to the pharmacy and this costs money. The head of the [extended] family can no longer arrange this. In the past, it happened that three years would go by without a child dying. (Bala Kante, 78 yrs, December 2009)

Means and medical knowledge have become less centralized now, in the context of individualization and extreme poverty; the *dutigi* no longer makes all medical decisions. Currently, every household looks out for itself, but, not every household has the money or (biomedical) knowledge of children's diseases necessary to take (biomedically) adequate action when a child is ill.

Conclusion

The *musokɔrɔbaw*, *somaw* and herbalists all have extensive knowledge of medicinal plants, and all affirm the importance of the power of words in the treatment of illnesses. While the *musokɔrɔbaw* rely mainly on the power of words in their incantations, the *somaw* and the herbalists also call in the help of a fetish and Allah, respectively. Each type of healer has his or her specialities. The *musokɔrɔbaw* are specialised in attending births and treating young children. The *somaw* are specialised in sand divinations and treatment of illnesses caused by social problems and the supernatural. And the herbalists are specialised in treatments for specific illnesses. The medical knowledge of these different types of healers, however, is not standardised, it is personal and individual.

Biomedical care was difficult to access before the opening of the maternity clinic. The health care situation is changing in Farabako; biomedical care is now available in the village and health is no longer seen as a collective responsibility, but more as an individual enterprise. Pregnant women and mothers must manoeuvre in this context of medical pluralism and social change when seeking health care for themselves and their children.

4. THE VULNERABILITY CONTEXT OF CHILD MORBIDITY AND MORTALITY

After having explored the health care options available in Farabako, this chapter turns to factors that influence child morbidity and mortality. To understand therapy management of children's illnesses, we need to know all health care options, the factors that put children at risk for disease and death, as well as how mothers and significant others are able (or unable) to cope with these risks.

In Mali, the under-five mortality rate is 178 per 1,000 live births, however, in the rural areas the rate is higher at 234 per 1,000 (WHO for 2010). By the time they reach menopause, the women of Farabako have borne an average of eight children, and 3-4 will have died in utero, during labour or in childhood. The results of the reproductive life history survey I conducted indicate that the under-five mortality rate in Farabako is higher than the national rural figures.[35]

In this chapter, I focus on children's risks for disease and death while exploring the vulnerability context in which these risks are embedded. I start by presenting a typical child's illness episode extracted from my interviews with mothers, fathers and mothers-in-laws on the household therapy management of illness episodes of their children under five years old.[36] After introducing the concept of vulnerability context, I present the various factors for the context of childhood disease and death: the specific physical risks that children in Farabako are exposed to, the various capacities and incapacities of mothers to cope with their child's exposure to the risk of death or disease, and the social risk of shame that the mothers face when their child is sick. I analyse the intersection of these factors in terms of identity construction and the role identity construction plays in mothers' seeming passivity in the face of child mortality.

A typical illness episode

A typical illness episode described to me was as follows. On day one, the mother saw that her child was ill and gave it traditional medicine that she, her husband, or her mother-in-law had prepared. If, after approximately three days, this treatment was found to have been ineffective, another course of treatment was sought. Most often, a *musokɔrɔba* and/or a *soma* or herbalist was consulted. If this treatment was also deemed ineffective, it was up to the husband to buy *faramasifura* (Western medicine) and/or to take the child to the doctor

[35] In my survey, 66 children <5yrs died per 245 live births which represented 27%; in other words, approximately 270 per 1,000 live births. This sample is too small to extrapolate, but does indicate that the under-five mortality rate is high in Farabako

[36] Based on 70 illness narratives and verbal autopsies.

at the health clinic (although, in cases of serious illnesses this was often too late). If the husband had no money (and this was often true), he would attempt to draw on his social network. If this approach was not successful, the husband would 'leave it at that'—it was out of his hands (and in God's). If the husband was not at home, the mother was not always able to draw on her own (limited) social capital to manage the illness of her child.

During the illness narratives of their sick children, mothers often told me that they had not taken their child to a doctor, nor had they asked family, friends, or neighbours for (financial) help to access biomedical care. In light of the high under-five mortality rates, parents' failure to use available health care facilities for their sick children has often been called 'irrational health behaviour', and has been assumed to be dictated by passivity and fatalism (Nichter 2002: 101). In this way, the victim is often blamed for a failing health care system. However, studies have shown that this seemingly 'irrational behaviour' is the outcome of a rational weighing of social and physical risks within the household (Tolhurst et al. 2008; Tolhurst and Nyonator 2006; Adams et al. 2002; Nichter 2002; Finerman 1995; Castle 1993, 1994; Dettwyler 1994; Scheper-Hughes 1992).

In the literature on health-seeking behaviour and child survival, there has been a move from individual (physical) risk models to an emphasis on the social relations that influence health care decision-making at the household level. But in emphasising the social element of health care decision-making one must not lose sight of the physical and environmental aspects of illness. High child mortality is found at the intersection of socio-cultural and economic processes, on the one hand, and physical exposure to health risks on the other. The concept of a vulnerability context captures this intersection.

Vulnerability context

In their work on famine, Watts and Bohle (1993) use the term 'vulnerability' to explain why some people are more likely to experience hunger than others. Poor people are usually the most vulnerable, but, in addition to income there are other factors that co-determine whether an individual will go hungry. The same can be said of health adversity, the poor are more vulnerable, but a lack of financial means is only part of the problem. Vulnerability is determined by the risks of exposure to crisis situations, by the risk of having inadequate capacities to cope with these situations, and by the risk of potentially serious consequences of these crises (Watts and Bohle 1993: 118). The point where these three factors, exposure to (physical) risk, incapacity to cope, and potentiality of serious consequences intersect can be called a 'space of vulnerability' or 'vulnerability context'. This approach moves beyond individual risk factors (such as income and age) to emphasise the relational, contextual and processual aspects of risk for childhood disease and death. By using this approach, I hope to avoid the pitfall of considering vulnerability to be an essential characteristic of the individual that remains stable over time. Rather, I show the potential changeable nature of vulnerability over time on an individual level as well as on a social network level.

Exposure to physical risk

In Farabako, as in most of rural Mali, unsanitary living conditions, food insecurity, endemic infectious diseases, lack of prenatal care, teenage pregnancy and female circumcision expose the unborn and children to disease and risk of death.

Living conditions

Farabako consists of fifteen households (*gwa*). Most of these kinship groups are large, with an average of 24 members, and are polygamous with many children. The largest household is headed by my host, Namagan Kante, and has 57 people: 22 adults and 35 children. The smallest household in Farabako has six members. The houses are made of mud with either thatched or corrugated sheet iron roofs and are grouped closely together. There is no electricity or running water in Farabako. Water is hauled from wells. The inhabitants complain that the water is not safe to drink and that this dangerous for their health. In Mali, 44% of the population has access to safe drinking water (UN 2011). The unsafe water in Farabako plays an important role in the high incidence of intestinal infections in children such as dysentery.

Water is carried from the well several times a day

The villagers live in close contact with animals; chickens, sheep, goats and cows walk in and out of the compound. Cooking is done outside on open fires. The chickens pick at any grain of rice or millet that is spilled on the ground. Goats come and eat peels and lick the cooking pots clean after every meal. Animal dung is collected and used as fertilizer for vegetable gardens. In Farabako, dung is not associated with disease, as it is for me. Small children were not discouraged from playing on the ground among the goat droppings. All children come into contact with animal droppings, which expose them to intestinal parasites (worms) and bacteria such as tetanus.

In Farabako, to go to the latrine, one takes a plastic kettle of water along to wash with after defecating; only the left hand is used for this purpose. No soap is used to wash hands after defecating and as many as thirty people use the

Children live in close proximity to animals

same plastic kettle for this purpose. The kettle is also used for washing before daily prayers. Children sometimes drink from the plastic kettle, putting the spout (that had recently been somewhere else) into their mouth. The plastic kettle is washed once a week with soap. Small children are washed once a day with soap by their mothers or older sisters. Children wash their hands before every meal, but often all in the same large tin can or using the plastic kettle, without soap. The children eat only with their right hand, but it is my contention that despite the practice of separate hands for separate purposes, because they use the dual-purpose plastic kettle and seldom use soap, children (and adults) are exposed to intestinal parasites and bacteria that can cause diarrhoea.

Small children in Farabako play with knives, walk right next to open wells and sit close to open fires, all with a minimum of parental supervision. Generally, children's activities go well and they learn to be careful. But accidents do happen. I treated one child who had blinded himself by falling on a knife and two children with second-degree burns. One child had fallen in the cooking fire and the other had pulled a pot of boiling millet over himself. Luckily, all three children survived these mishaps. Snakebite is another real danger in Farabako, as snakes are present in the fields and sometimes in homes. Most snakes are not lethal, but I have heard stories of small children dying of snakebite.

In sum, contaminated water, living in close contact with animals, accidents and (from my point of view) a lack of hygiene expose children to health risks.

Food insecurity

All inhabitants live from farming activities; the men and women cultivate mostly millet and peanuts on their fields. The women each have their own vegetable garden, where they cultivate vegetables such as onions, lettuce, and tomatoes, and fruit such as mangoes, bananas and papaya. The food is needed for household consumption, but women must sell some of their peanut harvest to generate income needed to buy items such as salt, sugar, rice, coffee, clothes, shoes or batteries for their flashlights. Most years, the food reserves run out before the next harvest is in. Every year, the villagers worry about going hungry. In the months before the next harvest, there are food shortages and their diet is not varied. On average, once in every seven years there is a real famine. This is visible in their bodies. When I was in Farabako before the harvest in November, the villagers were emaciated. When I was in Farabako in January, the inhabitants looked less thin and healthier.

In Mali, 34% of the population is at risk for hunger (Butt et al. 2005).[37] This lack of food security can lead to malnutrition and stunted growth in children, which in turn makes children susceptible to disease. Globally, malnutrition is

---

[37] Risk of hunger (ROH) is an indicator that shows the percentage of a population that is malnourished in a country or a region. The computation of ROH requires estimates of availability of food, population, nutritional requirements, and a measure of the inequality of access to food (Butt et al. 2005).

directly or indirectly responsible for 35% of deaths for children under five (WHO for 2006). In Farabako, 13% of the children under five years old suffer from severe malnutrition (wasting) due to unbalanced diet, intestinal parasites and early weaning (more on this subject in chapter 8). While most healthy children can fight infection with their natural defences, children whose immune systems are weakened by malnutrition or undernourishment are at higher risk of developing infections such as pneumonia.

Endemic infectious diseases

Pneumonia is a common cause of child death in West Africa and in Mali, 14% of the under-five deaths are caused by pneumonia (WHO for 2010). Pneumonia can be treated with appropriate antibiotics, preferably prescribed by a doctor, but access to biomedical health care facilities is difficult, costly and time consuming. Immunization and adequate nutrition is the most effective way to prevent pneumonia. Few children in Farabako were vaccinated against common children's diseases and in 2010 a measles epidemic hit Farabako and several children died. Since then, the doctor from the neighbouring village of Nioumamakana comes once a year to vaccinate the children of Farabako against common children's diseases such as measles (for free). Because families often go to live temporarily in small hamlets (*bugudaw*) close to their fields, and the vaccination campaign did not reach those areas, not all children have been vaccinated.

Malaria is endemic in the region and accounts for 21% of the under-five death in Mali (WHO for 2010). The children of Farabako have malaria several times a year. The majority of my respondents told me that they did not know the cause of malaria. The link between mosquitoes and malaria was not apparent and therefore, only few children slept under a mosquito net. Malaria is also dangerous for a child before birth. While the average adult person of an endemic region possesses some immunity to the parasite, pregnancy causes complications that leave the woman and foetus extremely vulnerable. The parasite interferes with the transmission of vital substances through the placenta, often resulting in stillbirth, spontaneous abortion, or dangerously low birth weight.

When I asked women during reproductive life history interviews, 'Were you ill during the pregnancy?' they often answered, 'No'. But when I asked 'did you have malaria?' they said 'Yes'. The women seldom volunteered the information that they had had malaria as if it was a way of life that was so common as to be not worth mentioning. Also, the term *sumaya* (literally 'cold'), the *Maninka* term for malaria that I used, may have been confusing to them. When I asked a traditional healer Musa Kante what *sumaya* was, he told me that *sumaya* is ten distinct diseases. He went on to name the ten 'diseases' that I recognized as individual symptoms of malaria, such as fever, headache, tiredness, dizziness, coughing, vomiting, stomachache and jaundice. This was consistent with the way women told me they had been ill; they named the symptom not the disease. For example, they would say 'yes, I was ill in that pregnancy, I had headaches' instead of saying 'I had malaria', which they often only admitted after probing. Malaria was by far the most prevalent complication during pregnancy, as 60% of the women reported having had malaria during one or more of their pregnancies. However, since the women tended to speak of diseases in terms of symptoms, and I asked questions in terms of diseases, I firmly believe that the instances of (what I called) malaria were under reported. To complicate matters further, malaria can also be asymptomatic. In the 52 cases of women who reported having had malaria during their pregnancies, only during seven of the pregnancies did they seek treatment in medical health facilities.

No (biomedical) prenatal care

Malaria prophylaxis is an important part of prenatal care in this region; it can prevent severe maternal anaemia, preterm labour and low birth weight. Yet only fourteen (26%) of the women interviewed had received some form of (biomedical) prenatal care at one time or another. Prenatal care ranged from one visit to a doctor, who happened to be in the village during a vaccination campaign, to five consultations with a midwife in a maternity clinic in the capital Bamako. The women had not sought prenatal care in all their pregnancies, in fact in only 7% of all the pregnancies did they do so. The main reason for women to seek prenatal care was because they were ill with malaria (seven women) or because they had had a stillbirth in a previous pregnancy (three women). Only two women went for regular check-ups; one was a woman who happened to be living in Bamako near a maternity clinic at the time she was pregnant. The other was the only young woman with seven years of schooling who lived in Farabako. She went for prenatal check-ups at the health clinic twenty kilometres away in Sandama, because she thought it was the right and 'modern' thing to do. Only five women actively sought prenatal care for prevention of obstetrical complications. For the other women, it was convenient (the doctor just happened by) or for the treatment (not prevention) of malaria. All in all, very few women, also by Malian standards,[38] had any form of prenatal care and this exposed their unborn children to the risk of malaria.

Because pre-existing problems, and not problem prevention, were the main reason to seek medical care, it is not surprising that in this sample prenatal care did not lead to a decrease in infant mortality. One would expect prenatal care to lead to a lower perinatal mortality, but this was not the case. Of the children born to mothers who had had some prenatal care, the number of children dying around the time of birth was only slightly lower (10.5%) than in the group of unchecked pregnancies (12.7%).

---

[38] According to the WHO (WHO for 2006), in Mali, 70% of pregnant women were attended by a skilled health provider at least once.

Teenage pregnancy

In the reproductive life history interviews, in 2007, it became clear that many first-born children had died. In 2012, a second round of interviews confirmed this. I found that 47 of the 71 (66%) of the women interviewed reported that their first child had died. All my respondents had delivered their first baby before the age of eighteen. Teenage pregnancies in Mali have been associated with lack of prenatal health care, lower birth weights and higher child mortality (LeGrand and Mbacké 1993). Biological factors such as a prolonged labour due to an undeveloped pelvis, as well as the higher risk associated with all first pregnancies (such as a higher risk of contracting malaria), could account for at least part of this high first-born mortality. Of the 47 first-borns who had died, ten had been born prematurely (21%)[39] and eight were stillborn (17%). Twenty-three first-borns died from infectious diseases, and four died from malnutrition, before the age of five. Two children died between five and ten years of age. When I asked my respondents why they thought so many first-born children died, they did not speak of diseases such as malaria, they spoke of God, contraceptives and their uterus being ‘too weak’.

My respondents typically replied to my questions about their explanation for the cause of their first child’s death in this fashion:

> I do not know why I delivered too soon or why many first children are born too soon. Yes, I have noticed that many first children die, but this is not something that I can understand. (Jeneba Fofana, 48 yrs, January 2012)

> It is God. If a child is born that does not love life, it will return to God. (Sitan Fofana, 45 yrs, January 2012)

I was not asking relevant questions; the *cause* of first-born children’s death was God, the *why* was therefore not in their power to fathom. My female respondents did speak of becoming pregnant too young. Some women told me that they had married soon after developing breasts or directly after their menarche. Women often did not know how old they were, but it was clear that they had married young; they estimated their age to have been between ten and sixteen years old (average age thirteen years). They became mothers between the ages of twelve and sixteen. My female respondents spoke of their uterus not being strong enough.

---

[39] Because women normally did not know how many months pregnant they were at the time of delivery, it is impossible to know if their baby was born too soon (preterm labour) or if their baby was too small (small for gestational age). Many babies who are small for gestational age have been subjected to intrauterine growth restriction (IUGR). IUGR refers to a condition in which a foetus is unable to achieve its genetically determined potential size. These foetuses are at risk for poor outcomes.

> The cause is God. Many children die if their mother is eleven or twelve years old and their uterus is not strong. Fourteen or fifteen is a better age… if God wills it. (Numusira Kante, 25 yrs, January 2012)

Sali Keita was married at fourteen and delivered her stillborn baby at fifteen. When I asked her what would be a good age to get married, she answered; 'Women do not have the right to decide about this.' The women spoke of having no say in when they could marry. In Farabako, it is the right of the elder men of a girl's father's family to decide when she should marry. When I asked Madi Keita, a young father, what is a good age for a girl to marry, he answered that in his own opinion, 17-18 years old is a good age, but that it is his older brother who will decide when his daughter is to marry. My respondents also spoke of the necessity of having many children.

> Women cannot marry later; it is the right of the man to decide when. Men are against contraceptives because they want many children and do not know the pain of labour. Women also want many children, seven or eight, because many children die. (Dusuba Sinayogo, 55 yrs, January 2012)

In Mali as a whole, the adolescent birth rate has decreased slightly from 198 per 1,000 births in 1994 to 190 per 1,000 births in 2004. However, Dusuba Sinayogo, an older female respondent, explained to me that teenage pregnancy is not something of the past in Farabako; girls are becoming pregnant sooner now than before. In her youth, girls had their first children at fifteen to seventeen years, but now girls are becoming pregnant at age twelve or thirteen. Her explanation was that girls are now sexually active at an earlier age and are not guarded as strongly by their family as they had been in the past.

First time deliveries are normally more lengthy and difficult than subsequent deliveries; it is the first time that a child passes through the birth canal. But a first time delivery of a teenage girl has an increased risk of low birth weight, preterm labour and neonatal death and the added complication of the pelvis not being fully grown. Another reason that first time deliveries are difficult for the mother and child in Farabako is that all girls have been circumcised.

Female circumcision

All the women in Farabako had been circumcised,[40] and found my question, 'Have you been you circumcised?', very silly. Female genital cutting (FGC)

---

[40] I consciously struggled with which words to use here. As a Western midwife with feminist convictions, I am against any form of female genital cutting (FGC) and see this as female genital mutilation (FGM). As an anthropologist, I find the term female circumcision or female genital cutting less normative and more fitting to the context in Farabako where FGC is a non-issue that women themselves approve of. *Bolokoli* is the term the women used; they told me that this meant 'to make clean'.

was not a point of (public) discussion in the village and the women did not seem to be aware that women in other countries and even some women in their own country were not circumcised. In Mali, 94% of all women have been circumcised. The Malian government has declared the elimination of FGC as a priority in their strategy for increasing women's empowerment. Nongovernmental organizations in Mali have been active testing strategies to end female genital cutting, but these institutions do not reach Farabako. Almost all the women I spoke to on this subject told me they thought it was a good idea to practice female circumcision. All baby girls were circumcised between one and two months. In Farabako, this is done by the elder women of the blacksmith caste (*numumusokɔrɔbaw*) using a special knife or a razorblade. Excision (FGC type 2),[41] the partial or total removal of the clitoris and the labia minora was the type most common in Farabako. I did see one case of infibulation (FGC type 3, the narrowing of the vaginal opening by cutting and stitching the labia together) during my work in the maternity clinic. Jones et al. (1999) have shown that FGC in Mali leads to an increased risk of childbirth complications. The more severe the FGC, the higher the risk of prolonged labour which increases the risk of new-born deaths. Having said this, most deliveries of women who have been circumcised (in Mali as a whole and Farabako in particular) occur without any complications.

Of the 71 women I spoke to on this subject, nine women (13%) reported that they thought that their being circumcised had made their first delivery more difficult. Bamagan Keita, a young first time mother, told me that her circumcision had made sexual relations painful in the first year of marriage and it had made her delivery difficult, but now 'things were okay for her'. In the same breath she told me that all the girls are circumcised and this is a good thing: 'If the circumcision happens properly the delivery will not be more difficult.' She says she does not know why girls are circumcised; it has been this way since she was born.

It is beyond the scope of this book to delve into the practices and meanings of FGC in Mali. For a discussion on this subject see Diallo (2004). I only want to point out here that FGC can expose the unborn child to a protracted delivery that increases the risk of neonatal death.

In summary, in the womb, unborn babies in Farabako are often exposed to malaria and the poor nutritional status of their mother. This puts babies at risk for preterm labour, low birth weight and neonatal death. A young woman's first

---

[41] The World Health Organization (WHO) has classified female genital cutting into four categories: Type 1, also known as clitoridectomy, is the partial or total removal of the prepuce (clitoral hood) and/ or clitoris. Type 2, also known as excision, refers to the removal of the clitoris and partial or complete removal of the labia minora (inner vaginal lips). Type 3, also known as infibulation or pharaonic circumcision, involves the partial or complete removal of any of the external genitalia, with stitching or narrowing of the vaginal opening. Type 4 is any other procedure involving pricking, piercing, incising, and stretching of the clitoris and/or labia.

child runs an even higher risk of being born too soon, and of succumbing to childbirth complications due to the circumcision and young age of the mother. If a child survives the delivery, he or she is then exposed to unsanitary living conditions and endemic diseases such as malaria and pneumonia. A lack of immunization and food insecurity make children increasingly susceptible to disease and death.

(In)Capacity to cope with health adversity

Until now, the focus of this chapter has been on the physical risk of mortality. The biomedical concept of risk (as probability x harm) and risk aversion are imbedded in our Western institutions. Safe motherhood policies have been critiqued as only concerned with the medical causes of mortality and that this 'official' definition of risk is not women's reality, so we must look at 'unofficial risk'—risks other than the risk of mortality (Allen 2002: 9). This is in line with Douglas (1986), who argues that risk perception is highly socialized cognitive process, a social not an individual process, and that we must try to come to an understanding of the socio-cultural aspects of risk perception. According to Douglas, focusing on coping capabilities is a way of doing this. I now consider the ways in which (future) mothers cope with the risk of childhood death or disease. I explore the women's capacities to generate and mobilize resources to access health care. In this section, I look at how schooling, gender relations, and social capital all influence mothers' capacities to cope with their child's exposure to the risk of death or disease.

Schooling/biomedical knowledge

There is no school in Farabako; only a third of the children walk the four kilometres to the elementary school in a neighbouring village. Twice as many boys as girls go to school. The secondary school is twenty kilometres away and for children to go there, they must stay with a foster family. Of the 53 respondents to the reproductive life history survey, only seven women (13%) had ever attended school. Five of these women had a few years of elementary school or Koranic school, but could not read or write. Two women living in Farabako could read and write a little, but then only with difficulty. At the time of my research, only two girls were attending secondary school. One of these girls, Trayina Traore, was going to school in the capital Bamako when she became pregnant; she was thirteen years old. The baby was born prematurely and died at birth. Despite the shame and scandal in the family, Trayina returned to school. This was possible only because I personally paid for her schooling; otherwise her father would have married her off; 'I am finished with her,' he said. It is rare for girls to reach secondary school and when they do, teenage pregnancy limits the chances of finishing their education. Therefore, few young women have had enough schooling to acquire any biomedical knowledge of disease. Potentially, this knowledge would facilitate their access to prenatal care, improved sanitation and use of malaria prevention.

Indigenous knowledge of female circumcision, pregnancy, birth and children's illnesses are the domain of elder women and often kept secret from young women. However, currently there is a new opportunity for young unschooled girls to acquire medical knowledge—satellite TV. Since 2011, there have been three satellite televisions running on solar energy in Farabako. On the one hand, I have difficulty with the village's priority setting since the money was not spent on the improvement of their children's health or food security, for example. On the other hand, television is a medium that can disseminate knowledge to those who have not been to school and may increase the villagers' capability to cope when a child becomes ill.

Limited reproductive choice

Teenage pregnancies expose (unborn)children to physical risk, yet my female respondents spoke of their inability to prevent being married and becoming pregnant at a young age. Young married women were forbidden to use contraceptives by their husbands.

> People say that you shouldn't become pregnant too young because the uterus is not strong enough and the child could die. In my time there were no medicines [contraceptives]. Now there are, but men will never agree to letting their new young wife use contraceptives because they are afraid that she would then commit adultery. (Kamisa Kante, 40 yrs, January 2012)

One young respondent indicated that there are some women who try to abort the foetus if they become pregnant when they are too young, but that they 'do not have the knowledge' to prevent the death of a first child. Young mothers have little knowledge of birth or children's illnesses.

> If the mother is too young, she will have no knowledge of deliveries and if the midwife or *musokɔrɔbaw* [elder women] do not tell her how to deliver, the baby will become tired and die. (Kòròtun Keita, 20 yrs, January 2009)

In the region, it is the custom for women who are pregnant for the first time to return to their village of birth to deliver in the home of their mother. The survey results indicate that delivering at their parents' home decreased the risk of the first child's death to some extent. Eleven women left Farabako to deliver at their mother's, of the eleven children born, four died (36%). This is significantly lower than the total of 66% of the death of first-borns. Perhaps this can be explained in the following manner. Parents have their daughter's best interest at heart. However, in Farabako, it is the husband's family's best interest that has priority leading to a different priority in health care seeking. It must be said that this sample is too small (and my data was not complete on this indicator), but even so, this is an interesting observation that needs further research. Whereas, many women wanted to go home to deliver their first baby, many women were not permitted to do so by their husbands.

> Some women want to go to their mother's home for their first delivery but the men of Farabako do not want this; they want their children to be born in Farabako and not anywhere else. (Hawa Kante, 35yrs, January 2012)

Men marry women from outside of Farabako. This means that a young married woman has no family of her own in the village other than her younger 'sister' who traditionally accompanies a new bride. If the newly married woman is lucky, she will know several women who were also born in her village and married into Farabako. A young wife is an 'outsider' with a limited social network and has no one other than her husband's family to represent her interests (see also Grosz-Ngaté 1989: 176).

If the pregnant teenage girl is *not* married, she is able to deliver at her parents' home. However, if after her delivery the baby becomes ill, she will have difficulty finding someone to help her pay for the child's medical treatment. A child belongs to the biological father's family. If the child is a boy, the biological father will often 'reclaim' the child once he has been weaned. If the father does not reclaim the child (which is often the case if the child is a girl), the mother will have to take care of the child herself. If she remarries, in some cases the new husband will take care of her child, in other cases, less resources are spent on an illegitimate child (see also chapter 8).

> If the child is not the husband's, the husband will not take care of him. If the woman is not married, she will ask the [biological] father for help, but they often leave and she must take care of the child on her own. (Nakani Kante, 35 yrs, January 2012)

Within the vulnerability context, an individual's social trajectory, interactions with others and the social context in which these interactions take place all influence vulnerability. For example, within the social context of a patriarchal, virilocal society, such as Farabako, a young mother who has just married and moved to the village will not yet have an extensive social network. This can make her and her children more vulnerable to health adversity than say an older married woman.

Social capital

The nature of each parent's social capital influences their capacity to cope with the illness episodes of their children. A mother with an extensive social network (ergo high social capital) may be better able to cope when her child becomes ill than a mother with a limited network. Bourdieu defines social capital as 'the aggregate of the actual or potential resources which are linked to possession of a durable network of more or less institutionalized relationships of mutual acquaintance and recognition' (1986: 248). He makes a distinction between social and symbolic capital. Symbolic capital refers to resources available to an individual on the basis of honour, prestige or recognition, and functions as the embodiment of cultural values. Putnam defines social capital as networks, norms, and trust that all facilitate cooperation for mutual benefit (1995: 67). In this definition there is no clear division between social and symbolic capital, such as Bourdieu makes, rather symbolic capital is part of social capital. I follow Bourdieu in making a distinction between social and symbolic capital, but I also attempt to show how these two forms of capital are interconnected. First, I examine the social capital of the women of Farabako by looking at the social networks by which they can mobilise the necessary resources to access health care. Second, I consider symbolic capital as a factor that influences social capital.

To learn about the social capital of the women of Farabako, I focused on their social networks. I asked 24 mothers to name the people they could ask for help if their children became ill. In the name-generator interviews, respondents were asked to name people they had asked for financial aid, advice or practical support in the past year, when they or their children were ill. The women often found this question difficult to answer, and initially said they had asked no one. Women did not easily admit having asked for help. They found it easier to name the people who they had helped in support transaction interviews. In a support transaction interview, respondents are asked to name the people they have recently helped who were ill.[42] Once the women had made it clear to me that they had helped others, they were more comfortable in telling me who they had asked for help. The women named an average of three people they could turn to for money if one of their children was ill, including their husband. Women often named their husband as the most important person in their network. However, in the dry season their husbands were often absent for weeks or even months on end while 'searching for money' in the goldmines or elsewhere. This posed a real problem, because the women were dependent on their husbands for money; thus, if the husband was absent, there was often no money at all. Formally, the women should ask their brother-in-law for help, but in practice this did not always happen since their brother-in-law was also often away.

In addition to their husbands, the women often named their *jigilamɔgɔ* ('confidant') as someone they could ask for money. A *jigilamɔgɔ* is a person outside of your own household whom you can trust (*jigin* = 'hope') and ask for help; it is someone who will not gossip about you (a co-wife could never be a *jigilamɔgɔ* because she could tell your secrets to your husband or mother-in-law). *Jigilamɔgɔ* are often, but not necessarily, kin. Ties with one's *jigilamɔgɔ*

[42] See Appendix 4 for network analysis.

are built out of mutual trust and trustworthiness is an important element of social capital. If one is seen to be trustworthy, one has a larger network of people to ask for money. Women's networks of people they could ask for advice or practical support if their children were ill, to take over their chores, for example, were larger than the networks of people they could ask for money.

The majority of social network ties were within a woman's own kinship group and of these, most ties were within their own household. A multivariate analysis[43] of the name-generator interviews and support transaction interviews showed no correlation between a woman's socio-economic status[44] and the size of her social network. This is most likely because the women in Farabako have little money of their own and there is minimal socio-economic differentiation in the village. They sustained their ties not through financial means, but by 'taking pity' (*hinɛ*) on each other. Helping their elders if they become ill, taking care of their co-wife's children, cooking or fetching water for a sick neighbour, were all ways of giving support that could be reciprocated in kind. 'Taking pity' was the term used to describe reciprocity between two people who liked each other. Women also had women in their social network that they did not like, for example, a jealous co-wife. Women were reluctant to ask these women for practical support because they would rather not have to reciprocate at a later date.

In conditions of poverty and adversity, rather than extensive unifying social ties of comradeship, one can find few ties fraught with social tensions; Bähre calls this 'reluctant solidarity' (2007: 52). This seems to be the case in Farabako, where women have small networks of material support and there is an atmosphere of mistrust. During the interviews the women often spoke about conflicts with other women (especially co-wives) and they stressed the importance of secrecy to avoid gossip. If a woman was feeling unwell, they sometimes kept it a secret and did not ask for help. This was because if another woman helped her, she would be obliged to work for that woman sometime in the future. There might be gossip; if a woman asked for help often, the other women would say 'she does not work' or 'we always do her work', which is considered a shameful insult in Farabako. Rather than one large close-knit community, there seemed to be only small islands of collaboration in the village.

Social capital appeared to have eroded through individualisation and extreme poverty to such a degree that it could no longer be a source of material support in Farabako (see also Niehof 2008: 221). Women's social capital, although important in terms of practical support ('taking pity') and (reluctant)

---

[43] CATPCA: categorical principle components analysis

[44] Because all of the inhabitants of Farabako live in extreme poverty (less than a dollar a day), income was not a useful indicator of socio-economic status. Therefore, I used indicators such as schooling, type of roof, if the family owned a motorcycle, the number of wives in a polygamous household, the number of chickens, goats and/or cows, if the women had any personal income and how many meals were consumed a day in estimating household socio-economic status.

solidarity, is limited in the sense of not being able to generate the money necessary to access biomedical health care.

In this context of extreme poverty and limited social capital, symbolic capital in the form of a good reputation becomes significant. The symbolic capital of a woman is that which gives her honour and prestige.

One way of being a 'good woman' with a good reputation, in Farabako, is to be a good mother. A good mother takes care of other women's children, specifically the children of her co-wives, as if they were her own. This is part of the harmony norm of *badenya*. Another way of being a 'good woman' is to have 'shame' (*maloya*). Having shame is honourable; it means that you demonstrate the correct deportment such as humility and respect towards your husband and your elders. A woman's *maloya* is the honour of the group of affines she belongs to and thus part of her symbolic capital. A woman who does not have *maloya* is damaging to her husband's family's reputation and by extension her husband's social network. In this way, a child's future can be seen as dependent upon the mother's moral behaviour. A woman who follows the norms of *badenya* and *maloya* is seen to be trustworthy and this raises her social capital and that of her husband. A woman who is seen to be shameless (*malobali*) is publicly ostracized and risks losing her symbolic capital, thereby jeopardizing her social capital and heightening her vulnerability.

Potentiality: The social risk of shame

The potentially serious consequence of the exposure to and inability to cope with health risks may be the death of a child. Shame is another potentially serious consequence of a mother's inability to cope with risk to her child's health. In this section, I argue that the moral discourse of shame (*maloya*) is a significant factor in the vulnerability context. The social risk for the mother of being seen as shameless (*malobali*) mediates the physical risk of death for her child.

Shame influenced the women's health seeking behaviour. Women 'had shame' when they had to ask for the necessary money to pay for a medical treatment or transportation to a clinic. The women often told me that they preferred not asking someone other than their husband for money. Poverty was at the root of this shame; women did not want to 'disturb' others by making them feel uncomfortable if they had to refuse the request due to lack of funds. The next case presents an example of how shame made it difficult for the parents of a sick infant to access adequate health care.

> When I saw Kajatu Kulibali's baby, the baby's breathing was laborious and fast. I suspected the child was in an early stage of pneumonia and gave Kajatu antibiotics and medicine for malaria on credit to give to the baby. The next day, the baby was having more difficulty breathing and had a fever, so I told the mother that now she must take the baby to the doctor in

> Sandama. The next day, I asked around to verify if Kajatu had gone to the doctor—but she had not. By then, it was late in the evening and the baby's condition was worsening, however, it was too late to arrange for transportation. When asked why she had not gone to the doctor, Kajatu said that there was no money. She said that her husband had asked people (she did not know who) for money without success. She said she herself had 'no one she could ask'. In response to further probing, Kajatu said that she had shame in asking me for money because she could not even pay for the medicine I had given her two days earlier. (Fieldnotes March 2007)

Knowing full well that her baby might die, this mother abstained from further health care seeking because she had shame. Asking someone for help to whom you already owe money was perceived as shameless behaviour. Asking someone other than one's husband for money to go to a clinic was also problematic, as it implies that a husband is not a good provider. Women in Farabako are dependent on their husband's family; they have limited access to resources of their own. Protecting their reputation and by extension their husband's family's reputation and his social network is of utmost importance. In this context of extreme poverty, the mother's good reputation (her symbolic capital) is an important factor in increasing child survival.

Identity construction as a 'gelling point'

I now proceed to analyse the intersection of factors in the vulnerability context in terms of identity construction. In so far as illness behaviour is conceived of as coping with social and physical risk, illness behaviour can be conceptualized as an identity building process. Therefore, the study of vulnerability is inseparable from the study of identity processes of coping with risk. Delor and Hubert (2000: 1560) argue that identity construction is the 'gelling point' where various levels of vulnerability within the vulnerability context intersect. Confrontation with risks, such as the risk of a child's death and the risk of shame and social exclusion requires a constant construction and reworking of identity by which each individual endeavours to cope with these risks. In Farabako, the moral discourse of shame is a factor in this identity work.

To come to a deeper understanding of household therapy management of illness, one must look at how people represent themselves to others. Only through exposing the logic behind intersubjective constructs can one understand high child mortality (cf. Biehl et al. 2007). In other words, to understand the simultaneity of parental love and care with not taking action when a child is ill, it is important to look at the subjectivities of parents and the local moral community within which the parent-child relationship is rooted (cf. Gammeltoft 2008). The mothers of Farabako (re)presented themselves as 'good women' who had *maloya*, and this meant that in certain circumstances they refrained from seeking health care or asking for help if they or their children were ill.

Within the vulnerability context, identity construction as a good woman is the gelling point at which the woman's exposure to physical risk, the woman's capability to cope with risk as a mother, and the potential risk of being seen as shameless all come together. Let us take a hypothetical teenage mother as an example.

> A young girl who has just married and moved to her husband's village must show that she has *maloya* towards her in-laws by displaying a humble demeanour and respect. She is exposed to biological risks related to teenage pregnancy due to a lack of reproductive choice. When she becomes pregnant, she hides her pregnancy out of shame and does not seek prenatal care. This young girl, as most other girls in Farabako, has not had enough schooling to acquire the biomedical knowledge necessary to identify (what biomedical discourse considers to be) serious health risks or to be aware of the importance of biomedical health care. For example, she does not know that malaria is caused by mosquitoes and therefore, does not see the necessity of sleeping under a net. She also has not have acquired indigenous medical knowledge, as this is the domain of elder women. As a relative 'stranger' in the village, this young mother has a small social network, and can count on few people to take over her household chores, making it hard to seek medical care for her children. This young mother is economically dependent on and subordinate to her husband and her mother-in-law. She cannot respond autonomously when her child requires medical attention. Her youth and a moral discourse of shame make it difficult for her to ask for financial assistance if her child becomes ill. Thus, she does not ask for help or voice an opinion, but rather waits for others to take action.

This example illustrates that the social trajectory of the mother, social interactions between her and the members of her child's therapy management group, and the moral discourse of *maloya* all play a role in therapy management. *Maloya* is important at the intersection of the social trajectories of the members of a therapy management group. *Maloya* is especially important in hierarchical relations such as between a woman and her husband or a woman and her mother-in-law. The social trajectory, which is the phase of a woman's life, influences the norms of correct behaviour for women in Farabako. The younger the woman, the more *maloya* she should demonstrate. In other words, health adversity is mediated and experienced through a discourse of shame (cf. Johnson-Hanks 2006). The discourse of shame plays a role in the seeming passivity of mothers when their children are ill.

Passivity as agency

Why then was this seemingly passive behaviour of mothers of sick children so difficult for me to accept? I have been socialized in a Western culture that is dominated by denying pain, suffering, and death, and thinking that everything is fixable (by man). My Western (Dutch) predisposition of denying the women's existential vulnerability and limitations made it difficult for me to understand their passivity in the face of mortality. The denial of human limitations includes death itself. Our consumer society is based on a myth of control and the idea that we can solve all our problems with the products (such as medicine) that we can buy. Kleinman calls this 'the big lie…a falsehood at the centre of global culture' (2006: 7). Biomedical discourse does not face suffering and adversity as part of the human condition, but rather as something that needs to be fixed (and I as a medical professional wanted to fix it).

As a midwife, I do not call into question the inevitability and technical superiority of the globalization of biomedical health care. My goal in working in a resource-poor country was to bring about change—to lower maternal and child mortality rates. My idea of agency was to take action to bring about change. But, for the mothers of Farabako, agency can be geared towards non-action, because to take action is not 'correct' behaviour for a woman. By studying this non-action as agency, I have come to a better understanding of women's 'inertia' as a response to health adversity. Yet, I have argued that in the context of the globalization of biomedicine, women's strategy of avoiding shameless behaviour can no longer be considered the most adequate strategy for reducing child mortality. While shame may succeed as a strategy to avoid *social* risk, shame can also lead to problems in accessing the biomedical health care necessary to treat or prevent *physical* risk.[45]

Conclusion

This chapter has shown that poverty, disease, lack of reproductive choice, and difficulty in accessing adequate biomedical health care are factors within the vulnerability context that expose the children of Farabako to physical risk. I have argued that this exposure to physical risk is mediated by the mother's capacity to cope and the potential risk of shame that she faces.

With the arrival of biomedical health care facilities in the area, money is required to ensure adequate biomedical health care. But in Farabako there is no money; social and symbolic capital is generally the only means of accumulation of resources. In Farabako, there is a complicated relationship between social capital and shame. If a woman has shame, she is seen as trustworthy which heightens her social capital. But at the same time, in the context of extreme poverty, shame makes it difficult for women to draw on this social capital, because if a woman has shame she would rather not ask for help from someone who most likely has nothing. Poverty and mistrust limit the capacity of social capital to generate the funds needed. Thus symbolic capital, in the

[45] Similarly, Iliffe (2005: 364) shows how African notions of male and female honour work as obstacles to the behavioural changes necessary to prevent the transmission of HIV/AIDS.

form of the embodied cultural value of shame, becomes an important determining factor in health seeking behaviour. But shame is not only embodied, it is also actively used by women in constructing their identities as 'good women' when faced with health adversity. In the end, when your child is ill and the means run out, it is most important to be a good woman who has shame; morals really matter (see also Kleinman 2006). Having shame is honourable in the vulnerability context of Farabako and accepting suffering is agency.

To understand the simultaneity of parental love and care and not taking action when a child is ill, it is important to look at the risk of a child's death, shame and social exclusion, as well as the means by which mothers strive to cope with these risks. The concept of vulnerability context was constructive in understanding *why* social risk mediates physical risk in the therapy management of children's illnesses, but in order to understand *how* this social risk of shame works, we first need to look more closely at the concept of shame.

5. THE MORALITY AND ETHICS OF SHAME

The previous chapter indicated that a moral discourse of shame is a significant factor in the therapy management of children's illnesses. The social risk of shame mediates the physical risk of disease and death in Farabako. In this chapter, I look more closely at the role that morality and ethics play in the daily lives and therapy management of the women of Farabako. In chapter 6, I will focus more specifically on the role of morality and ethics in the friction between local and biomedical discourse. This chapter starts with a brief overview of the various ways that anthropologists have approached the concept of shame.

I bring several conceptualizations of shame together in a broader context of morality using Zigon's framework of an anthropology of moralities (2007). I use the framework to explore how the discourse of shame (*maloya*) is institutionalized, embodied and publicly articulated in Farabako. Using case studies, I illustrate what people in Farabako actually do when confronted with situations that force them to consciously reflect on the proper ethical response to a health problem. The case studies show that within the moral discourse of shame, women consciously work to be morally correct persons. I use the concept of 'inhabiting a discourse' (Mahmood 2005) to analyse how agency is found not only in acts that resist norms, but also in the various acts of conforming to norms.

Shame and honour

Anthropologists, especially those who study 'honour cultures' in the Mediterranean (e.g. Peristiany 1966; Gilmore 1987; Peristiany and Pitt-Rivers 1992), have considered shame as a defilement of honour, which the family considers a scarce resource and tries to protect. For example, in his work among the Kabylia of Algeria, Bourdieu (2001) found that a woman's reputation and chastity were constituted as a measure of masculine reputation and therefore, symbolic capital of the whole lineage Bourdieu (2001: 45). Love of family honour is the basis of the patrilineal system—the good name and renown of one's ancestors' lineage must remain unsullied. The individual is the group's protagonist and a woman is the guardian of the honour of her group (cf. Bourdieu 1966: 223). Shame is situated with the women, until their misconduct transfers the shame to their menfolk. At this point, the men's honour is compromised and the group's males are made to bear the shame (Pitt-Rivers 1965; see also Goddard 1987). This mediterraneanist approach treats shame as concern for one's reputation. Shame is regarded as a form of defilement of male honour deriving from female misconduct.

Wikan (1984) in her critique of the male bias in previous analyses that attribute honour principally to men, leaving women with, if anything, only shame, argues that honour and shame must not be seen as binary concepts. Honour and shame are both concepts that express a person's value, in his or her own view, or in the eyes of others. Wikan posits that of the two, 'shame' is a better guide to the native's point of view (experience-near), whereas 'honour' is often an anthropologist's construct. In this, I agree with Wikan. During my fieldwork in Farabako, the word for 'having shame' (*ka maloya*) was constantly used by men and women, while I rarely heard words for honour (*danbe*, *bɔnya*). In Farabako, shame is not the opposite or reverse side of honour. In Farabako, I found that it was honourable for a woman to 'have shame', because then she demonstrated 'correct' behaviour. A woman's capacity to be powerful, to be empowered, arose from her relative success in demonstrating correct behaviour. By showing that she had shame, a woman acquired the respect of her affines and the village as a moral community (cf. Ogden 1996).

Shame has also been described as a sense of restraint that discourages anti-social (competitive) behaviour (Kressel 1988; Herzfeld 1980). Shame is demonstrated by the adequate recognition of a social obligation. Shame is also closely related to status differentials. The term is often applied by parents to children, elders to youngsters, or husbands to wives. Jamieson (2000), in his study of the Kakabila in Nicaragua, argues that shame is an embodied sentiment, and that in hierarchical encounters shame is a 'technique of avoidance' by those who deem themselves subordinate. For example, unmarried girls have shame before their suitors, sons-in-law before their mother-in-law, and youth before their elders (2000: 318). Shame 'embodies and polices' cross-sex and cross-generation asymmetries through the creation of ritualized forms of avoidance (Jamieson 2000: 315). Shame ensures that performances of respect keep men and women at arm's length from one another.

Jamieson claims that shame is best treated 'neither as a fixed value nor a virtue, nor an emotion to be theorized, but as a praxis-oriented form of performance' (2000: 312). Demonstrating shame is a discursive practice performed in making particular kinds of subjectivities possible. In other words, shame has to do with the ideal image of the good person that people strive to be (see also Iliffe 2005; Riesman 1977). Jamieson's explanation of the concept of shame is very similar to what I found in Farabako.

In Mali, the Malinke term for shame is *maloya*. *Maloya* is usually translated as 'honte' in French (Bailleul 2000) and 'shame' in English (Grosz-Ngaté 1989; Brand 2000; Schulz 2011). Anthropologists doing research in Mali have described *maloya* as being one of the most fundamental aspects of Mande personhood. According to Grosz-Ngaté (1989) in her study of Bamanan gender construction in the Segu region of Mali, the sense of shame guides action in all domains of social life from proper bodily posture to speech, interpersonal relations, and the division of labour. A person who has a sense of shame is a person who is modest, generous, and honest, does not laugh loudly or speak without thinking and always acts in an honourable manner (1989: 170). Brand (2000), who studied fertility and demographic change in Bamako, defines *maloya* as an important principle within codes for correct behaviour and as a requirement for proper personhood (2000: 133). Schulz (2011), in her study of Islamic renewal in Mali also recognizes the importance of *maloya* for Mande personhood. She defines *maloya* as a 'dispositional and emotional capability' and shows how it is being used in new ways, as part of women's 'self-disciplinary endeavours' to become pious (2011: 99).

In summary, the concept of shame has been approached as defiled honour, a virtue, a technique of avoidance, a code for correct behaviour and a requirement for personhood. How should one research such a complex concept? I do so by conceptualizing shame within the framework of morality as developed by Foucault (1994a, 1994b, 1994c, 1994d), Zigon (2007, 2008, 2009, 2010) and Mahmood (2005).[46] Zigon and Mahmood build on Foucault's work. I first briefly present Foucault's and then Zigon's approach to morality and the related concept of ethics. I then use Zigon's framework for an anthropology of morality as a heuristic tool to present and analyse shame in Farabako. Last, I use Mahmood's concept of inhabiting a discourse to argue that shame can be seen as both an expression and a constituent element of personal identity in a discussion of my findings.

Shame as a technology of the self

For Foucault, morality is comprised of codes, acts and ethics. Codes ('prescriptions') determine the acts that are permitted or forbidden within society. The codes determine the positive or negative value given to various possible behaviours. Acts ('conduits') are people's real behaviour in relation to the moral code. Ethics, then, is defined by Foucault as 'the kind of relationship you ought to have with yourself' ('rapport à soi') (1994b: 263). Ethics determine how the individual constitutes himself or herself as a moral subject of his or her own actions. For Foucault, moralities are institutionalized codes, and ethics is the process of becoming a moral subject.

Foucault distinguishes four aspects of ethics, that is, four aspects of the relationship to oneself. The first aspect is 'ethical substance', that which needs to be worked on (e.g. sexuality). The second aspect is the 'mode of subjectivation' or the way people are impelled to recognize their moral obligation (e.g. glory, immortality, shame). Foucault sees this as a personal choice. The third aspect is a self-forming activity ('practique de soi') or how we change ourselves into a moral subject. The fourth aspect of ethics is '*telos*', the kind of person one wants to be, and the mode of being one seeks to achieve (1994b: 263).

---

[46] To be thorough one cannot overlook the influence of Durkheim, Kant, Nietzsche, and Sartre in studying morality, but this is outside of the scope of this chapter.

Ethics are part of what Foucault calls the 'technologies of the self'. These technologies 'permit individuals to effect by their own means, or with help of others, a certain number of operations on their own bodies and souls, thoughts, conduct, and way of being, so as to transform themselves in order to attain a certain state of happiness, purity, wisdom, perfection or immortality' (1994a: 225). This working on the self happens in moments of, what Foucault calls, problematization (1994c: 117). Problematization occurs when something happens to force one to consciously reflect on the appropriate ethical response. For Foucault, the notion of freedom is central to this project of becoming a moral subject. He speaks not of achieving, but rather of exercising freedom to refer to the extent and ways people can choose. One can have more or less freedom of choice within a moral discourse. The freedom one has takes various forms depending on the historical situation. This is consistent with Foucault's view that human nature is not fixed, and waiting to be discovered and realised, but instead, is continuously reinvented through human choice and action.

Foucault also speaks of freedom as being free of oneself (1994d: 301). For example, for the ancient Greeks it was important not to be a slave to one's desires and passions. Every society puts a value on a person being free of something to become a proper moral subject. To understand the kind of ethics people live by and the kind of moral world they inhabit, we need to explore what society expects their members to be free of (Zigon 2008: 43). I argue that, in Farabako and in many situations, women need to be free of shamelessness (*malobaliya*). And that to understand morality in my research setting, I must examine how the moral 'code' of shame (*maloya*) was used by women to turn themselves into moral subjects. I must also consider the 'technologies of the self' the women used to become the person they wanted to be. I look at the freedom of choice that women in Farabako have to manoeuvre within the moral discourse of shame, and simultaneously address the gender aspects of this freedom. The content of moral codes can only make sense by understanding the ethical project from which they derive (Laidlaw 2002: 326). To study this ethical project of turning oneself into a moral subject, Zigon's (2007) theoretical framework for an anthropology of moralities is useful.

Shame as the performance of ethics

Traditionally, anthropologists have studied unreflective moral dispositions of everyday life (embodied culture, tradition, power). According to Zigon (2007), this is not an anthropology of moralities. What anthropologists should do instead is study the performance of ethics in moments of moral breakdown; that is when a person is forced to step away from unreflective everydayness and think about and respond to ethical dilemmas both at a social and individual level. By studying this (conscious) performance of ethics, one is better able to see the ways that moral dispositions are shaped. Anthropological research must look at what counts as morality in a specific context and the processes by which this morality comes to matter. For Zigon (2010), this should be the goal of an anthropology of moralities.

Like Foucault, Zigon makes a distinction between morality and ethics. However, Zigon defines morality and ethics somewhat differently. Whereas Foucault defines morality as codes, acts and ethics, for Zigon morality includes three aspects: institutional morality, embodied dispositions and public discourse. Ethics is a process aimed at an existential comfort with these moralities (Zigon 2007: 138). Where Foucault sees ethics as an ever-present aspect of moral life, Zigon sees ethics as a state of affairs created when taken-for-granted morality is disrupted.

According to Zigon, the first aspect of morality is institutional morality. Institutional morality is moral discourse supported by power and institutionalized in the law or the church, for example. The second aspect, the public discourse of morality, is comprised of 'all those public articulations of moral beliefs, conceptions, and hopes that are not *directly* articulated by an institution' (Zigon 2008: 163). Some examples of the public discourse of morality are the media, everyday spoken beliefs and opinions, the arts, literature and stories, or parental instructions. The public discourse of morality is also heard in the context of anthropological interviews and conversations. Such moral expressions often differ, sometimes radically, from the dominant institutional moralities of a society. The third aspect of morality is embodied dispositions, not rule-following or conscious reflections on a dilemma, but rather a non-conscious moral habitus, 'one's everyday way of being in the world' (Zigon 2008: 164).

According to Zigon, ethics, then, is the 'conscious and intentional work that cultivates the non-consciously enacted moral habitus' (2010: 8). Ethics is a conscious working on oneself so as to make oneself into a morally correct person. This working on oneself happens in what Zigon calls an 'ethical moment'. An 'ethical moment' is brought about by a 'moral breakdown'. A 'moral breakdown' occurs when some event intrudes into the everyday life of a person and forces that person to consciously reflect on the proper ethical response (Zigon 2008: 165). Zigon's ethical moment is similar to Foucault's notion of problematization. While Zigon agrees with Foucault's view of the ethical process as work on the self, he does not agree with the aim of Foucault's ethics. For Foucault, the aim of ethics is self-mastery and authenticity, for Zigon the aim of the process of ethics is to return to a state of existential comfort.

It is the ability to be non-consciously moral that allows humans to be social beings. To be moral is to inhabit a disposition that is familiar to oneself and most others within one's environment. According to Zigon, it is in this 'familiar sharedness' of moral habitus that one can speak of 'being good' (2007: 135). Moral expectations and dispositions are part of the everyday mode of being in the world; they are normally unquestioned, unreflected upon and simply done. But on rare occasions, something happens that forces one back from the situation to figure out how to handle it. The unconscious becomes conscious and one must 'perform' ethics. What is important in this moment of moral breakdown is not to be 'good' or to be a 'good woman', but to get back to the unconscious moral habitus of everyday life. Ethics is thus a process of returning to an unreflexive state and achieving this return is considered good (Zigon 2007: 140).[47] The process can lead to change. One returns to a new unreflexive state, a state that can be somewhat different from the previous one—a new moral self that can enact a new moral world.

Institutions and public media do not usually have the power to totally implement their moral discourse and one cannot speak of morality as obligatory. Morality is not a totalizing, static discourse. Moral discourse is a 'range of possibilities' of certain ways of speaking, acting and being in the world (Zigon 2008: 134). There are limits to this range of possibilities, but discourse is far from deterministic—there is a freedom of choice within discourse. In various individual and social contexts, the various aspects of moralities and ethics come together as moral and ethical 'assemblages' (Zigon 2010: 13). Morality can thus be thought of as 'a continuous dialogical process within a range of possibilities, during which persons are in constant interaction with their world and the persons in that world, rather than as a set of beliefs from which one picks appropriate responses according to particular situations' (2008; 155). In ethical moments all three spheres of morality come together to influence the ways in which a person works on himself or herself. Following Zigon, I study these moments, these intersections of various spheres in the everyday life of individual persons.

While Zigon focuses on moral breakdowns as an individual experience, Robbins (2007) argues that anthropologists should also study what kinds of intrusions generate this response. According to Robbins, areas of moral difficulty in a society are not random and wholly personal; the shift from morals to ethics occurs when value hierarchies breakdown. People become morally conscious in times of cultural change when new values are introduced.[48] Robbins argues that situations of cultural change are particularly good examples to study how morality shapes culture and experience. Because situations of change often overturn previously stable value hierarchies, they generate the kinds of conflicts that push morality to the foreground. In this, I agree with Robbins. In Farabako, the introduction of biomedicine was a moment of change that instigated a shift from morals to ethics and brought morality to the foreground.

---

[47] It is beyond the scope of this chapter to discuss extreme moral breakdowns such as transition to war or genocide and whether Zigon's concept of ethics, as a return to a state of existential comfort, still applies in these situations (see Richters et al. 2010).

[48] Robbins (2007) gives the example of a community of Urapmin in New Guinea who converted to Christianity. Traditional Urapmin social structural thinking was oriented to the value of relationalism, while their new Christian thought was structured by the value of individualism. These differing values demanded distinct moral choices, and conflicts arose as old values asserted their importance in the face of new ones.

Maloya: Shame in Farabako

I now use Zigon's framework to describe shame (*maloya*) as a morality in Farabako. In this section, I focus on institutional morality, embodied dispositions and the public discourse of shame, illustrating what these concepts mean in practice by giving empirical examples from Farabako.

Institutional shame

Maloya is thought to have originated during an early period, in the time of Sunjata (thirteenth century), when males in the Mande region were constituted as the antithesis of slaves. Slaves (*jɔnw*) were considered to be without shame, as they had no kin group or patrilineal land, and consequently no name to uphold. This history is still visible today as children who misbehave are often called by the slave name *Malobali* ('Shameless One'). Codes for correct behaviour vary according to social category. Members of the social category of freemen/nobles (*hɔrɔnw*) were said to have the strongest sense of shame (*maloya*), whereas those categorised as slaves, were said to have none. My female respondents in the *ɲamakala* category did concede that *maloya* was even more important for nobles, but in conversations and interviews, women of both social categories frequently spoke of *maloya*.

In addition to distinguishing the major social strata, the capacity for shame also serves to differentiate men from women. Men are ranked higher than women. Men claim that their sense of shame is more serious and more fundamental than that of women. Women come from outside of the village and at marriage they are integrated into the patrilineal, virilocal household of their husband. Women are constructed as outsiders who pursue personal interest rather than the interests of the patriliny. They have less shame than men and can achieve personhood (after marriage) only with the help of their affines. It is said by some that women feel no shame because they are able to overcome the negative consequences of any wrongdoing by using their femininity (Grosz-Ngaté 1989). On the other hand, men cannot escape the consequences of shameless conduct. For men, shameless acts can lead to social death. This is illustrated in the following proverb: 'If you find a woman in trouble, help her. But if you find her in a shameful situation, leave her because she will get over it. If you find a man in trouble, leave him because he can get out of it on his own. But if you find him in a shameful situation, get him out of it because otherwise he might die.' (Grosz-Ngaté 1989: 171).

Not only do men have to monitor their own conduct, they are also implicated if their wives engage in a shameless action. Men are shamed, for example, if their wives incur debts without their knowledge and find themselves unable to repay the debt, or if wives are openly disobedient. Both actions imply that a husband has limited authority over his wife and that he is therefore not superior to her. That women are ranked lower than men is articulated, for example, during the creation of a marriage agreement. This is when the intermediary asking for a woman in marriage asks to 'favour … [name of the man] over … [name of the potential bride].' Elders explain this procedure by stating that 'a man has to be a woman's social superior or else he could not marry her' (Grosz-Ngaté 1989: 171). The rules of shame are stricter for women because a woman's reputation is understood to be the responsibility of their husband or father and therefore, her shamelessness also extends to them. As a result, the individual agency of women is often discouraged (Brand 2000: 130). If a woman has *maloya* people assume that all of her family is well brought up. Men show the path that women should take by educating their (young) wives. If a woman does wrong, it is also seen to be the fault of the man.

> Men must always be a role model and must tell women how they must behave. If a woman is *malobali* then a man has *maloya* because this means that he did not bring her up well. (Kali Kamara, 60 yrs, December 2009)

If a man does wrong, it is not the fault of the woman. Since the man is her teacher, the man is responsible. Although the woman may feel humiliated anyway, no one will blame her. If a woman is virtuous, but her husband is not, then people will say that he humiliates her.

In Farabako, shame is institutionalized in social categories and patrilineal marriage relationships. In every society, there are a multitude of institutional moralities that are not always adhered to. Institutional morality can be seen as an influential and pervasive rhetoric; but it is not totalizing.

Embodied shame

According to Zigon, institutional morality is embodied as dispositions (2009). Embodied dispositions influence the non-conscious moral habitus. Structures of social hierarchy are embodied. Social reality that produces hierarchy often confirms the representations that hierarchy invokes to justify itself. This was also the case in Farabako. During interviews, if my female respondents hesitated when answering a question, my interpreter Abdulaye Traore often said 'Elle ne connaît pas, elle est bête' (she does not know, she is stupid). Dispositions are the product of the embodiment of negative prejudice against (young) women that is instituted in the general order, and women constantly confirm this prejudice. For example, my female respondents frequently emphasised that 'women do not have as much knowledge as men', and therefore, it is 'not the work of women' to plan a course of action in case of illness; this is a man's job. This self-fulfilling prophecy leads to inertia (cf. Bourdieu 2001).

The discourse of shame is embodied. Although the discourse of shame also applies to men, the set of prohibitions on what women cannot do is extensive and focuses on their subordinate position in society. In Farabako, in the presence of men, women have a modest demeanour, they do not speak to men until they are spoken to, and they do not voice their opinions. Women take care to position themselves as subordinate to their husbands, male family members, and elders. In Farabako, the potential risk of being seen as shameless can be avoided by not taking too much initiative. Not taking the initiative, delaying taking action, and not asking for help are strategies that Mande men and women use to avoid being seen as shameless (see Jansen 2000: 58). In other words, the embodied moral discourse of shame leads to non-action. Women do not feel able or entitled to actively decide on a course of action, but rather wait for others around them (husbands, in-laws, neighbours) to decide what to do. This can lead to a delay in seeking health care.

Public discourse of shame in Farabako

The verbalization of embodied dispositions is what Zigon calls the public discourse of morality (2009). The term *maloya* was used in two ways. On the one hand, *maloya* was used to mean 'having shame' (*ka maloya*), that is having a deportment that is deemed correct. On the other hand, *ka maloya* was also used to denote an emotion of feeling ashamed. The term *malobali* was used to indicate that a person had no shame, that a person was shameless.

Prohibitions: 'Having shame'

Shame was publicly spoken of as a positive virtue in men and in women, as well as a personal characteristic that one can acquire by following an extensive set of prohibitions. Virtues are not the same as social norms. Virtues are highly valued social and ethical sensibilities. Motherhood, for example, is seen as a virtue, not because it satisfies a social norm, but because it requires certain kinds of sensibilities geared to the child. Thus the mother is not necessarily a 'good woman', but is in fact good at being a woman. And motherhood is not the only way of 'being good at being a woman' (cf. Herzfeld 1985: 16; Zigon 2008: 103). My respondents explained that *maloya* means 'having shame', and 'having shame' is a good thing—it means that one is not shameless (*malobali*). The term *maloya* incorporates many concepts such as respect for one's elders, female chastity, hospitality, trustworthiness, being careful not to upset people, and not speaking without thinking. 'Having shame' was one way for a woman to be good at being a woman.

> *Maloya* is to not do wrong; it is not showing behaviour that you know people would rather not see. (Fatumata Kante, 27 yrs, March 2007)

> *Maloya* means humility, not wanting to disturb someone. *Maloya* is not looking someone in the eye; it is showing respect. *Maloya* is the proper way of doing things. It is refusing to do anything that singles you out. You can excel, but you must be humble, you must not boast, you must be modest. (Kali Kamara, 60 yrs, December 2009)

Maloya is especially important in hierarchical relations. It is an intricate set of prohibitions that come into play in relations between members of another social category, elders and members of the opposite sex. In Farabako, nobles and blacksmiths are said to both have a sense of shame, yet the Keita nobles should refrain from asking something from the Kante blacksmiths. The blacksmiths, on the other hand, have less restraint in asking something of the nobles.

> The Keita will not ask the Kante. The Keita have more *maloya*. This has been so since the time of Sunjata. (…) For example: if his millet is finished, a Kante will ask 'give me some millet'. But Keita have shame to ask something of a Kante. Keita do not have shame to ask other Keita something. (Kanku Kante, 80 yrs, 2009)

Maloya is about not asking for something from a person you respect or an elder (even if only by one year). *Maloya* is also important in relationships with affines. A woman has *maloya* towards her in-laws; for example, she may not express her opinion or joke with her mother-in-law. One respondent told me that she has shame asking her mother-in-law to do something for her. Even if she were ill, she would not ask her mother-in-law to cook for her. A woman should give to her mother-in-law, not take. Speaking openly towards or asking (personal) questions of the elder members of one's husband's family is shameless behaviour as the next example illustrates:

> When during an informal conversation with Baraka Kante, one of the oldest women in the village, I asked the midwife, Jeneba Kante, who spoke a few words of French, to translate a question for me about Baraka's first pregnancy, the midwife said she could not. She could not translate this (personal) question because she had shame. She explained that she had shame because Baraka was her 'older sister'-in-law. (Fieldnotes January 2012)

Shame is important in relationships with one's husband and other members of the opposite sex. A woman who has shame will not argue with her husband. A woman who has *maloya* is confident that her husband will provide for her. She will not 'pester him by asking for money'. For women in Farabako, *maloya* means respecting your male family members. Women should not speak if a man is present. *Maloya* prohibits women from voicing an opinion while a male family member is present as the next example illustrates:

> When I asked Nfali Kante, a man in his late twenties, what *maloya* meant to him, he answered: 'Respect, keeping your promises, and weighing your words. One should not say just anything that comes to mind'. When I asked his aunt Kamisa Kante, who was sitting next to us listening to the conversation, if she agreed with Nfali, she answered 'he is my son', and demons-

> trably said nothing further. Nfali explained 'that [her silence] is *maloya*'. (Fieldnotes March 2007)

During an earlier focus group discussion with only women present, Kamisa had talked freely about what *maloya* meant to her, but with a male family member present she had shame in voicing her opinion. A woman who has shame should not speak when men are present.

Maloya is also important in matters pertaining to the body. Women have shame in showing their naked body. Once married and living with her husband, a woman who has shame will not undress in front of anyone other than her best friend or her husband's younger sister. A woman who has *maloya* will not wear a mini-skirt and her thighs and abdomen should be covered at all times. For example, one male respondent, when explaining to me what *maloya* meant to him, said, that in fourteen years of marriage he had never seen his wife's bare belly, because 'she has shame'. Women have shame both in showing and talking about their bodies. They had shame in speaking about menstruation or disclosing their pregnancy. Pregnant women would often wait until I noticed they were pregnant and ask them to come to the clinic before they would seek prenatal care.

> A woman can have shame in being seen to be pregnant. A woman can have shame in going to the maternity clinic because she is not accustomed to do so. (Nantènè Keita, 25 yrs, January 2012)

If I asked women how they were feeling, in my capacity as a midwife, they always answered that they were feeling better (*a ka fisa*), or that their child was feeling better, even if this was not true. Even Nakani Kante told me she was 'feeling better' after an abortion that went wrong, although she later told me that she had been convinced she was dying at the time. '*A ka fisa*' ('it is better') was a standard reply in Farabako; people did not want to bother, worry, or make me feel uncomfortable so they always said they were feeling better even if they were not. Another reason for always saying they were feeling fine was that to admit being ill could make one more vulnerable to supernatural forces. For the same reasons, women would wait for others to notice that they were ill, and not ask for help outright. They would present their symptoms in an exaggerated way until I would notice something was wrong and *I* would ask them if I could help. In this way the women presented themselves as respectful women who had *maloya*.

Maloya, in the sense of 'having shame', is thus a moral habitus that one acquires by demonstrating proper behaviour by following a set of prohibitions. The strongest prohibition was on committing adultery.

> A woman who has shame (*muso maloya la*) is a woman who does not commit adultery, who does not sleep with men other than her husband. (Narama Keita, 30 yrs, January 2012)

Women in Farabako must possess characteristics, such as humility, trustworthiness and modesty, to be deemed virtuous and as 'having shame'.

One male respondent in Bamako told me that for his wife *maloya* was important; 'she never asks me for anything', he explained this by adding: 'she comes from a village'. The men and women I spoke to in Bamako were adamant that *maloya* was stronger and more important for women in rural areas than in the city. In Bamako, there are fewer prohibitions on both men's and women's public behaviour. There is more communication between the sexes and men and women can sit together, eat together and walk hand in hand. My respondents explained that one reason for this difference was that in Bamako men and women often married for love, while in the rural areas the marriages were generally arranged. In rural areas, marriages are a relationship between two families rather than two individuals. It is therefore important to stress that the term *maloya* may have distinct meanings and importance in various settings. It is not my aim to generalize *maloya* as an integral characteristic of Malinke ethnicity, rather in this specific impoverished rural setting of Farabako, *maloya* is an important part of local moral discourse.[49]

Gossip: Feeling ashamed

The term *maloya* is used to connote a personal characteristic or virtue, as well as an emotion—as feeling ashamed. For example, people feel ashamed when others gossip about them.

> You feel ashamed (*maloya*) when someone frowns upon your conduct. (Fatumata Kante, 30 yrs, March 2007)

One must 'have shame' to avoid gossip and the feeling of shame that accompanies being gossiped about. The two tropes on gossip that I heard frequently were 'people will think you love each other' and 'people will say you don't work'.

> Here [in Bamako] you can sit next to your husband and talk with him. In Bamako you can take a stroll with your husband, 'en brousse' [rural areas] they would say 'you don't work' or 'she loves men'. (Naba Keita, 35 yrs, December 2009)

---

[49] See Breedveld and de Bruijn (1996) for a critique of the concept of *pulaaku* (which has much in common with the concept of *maloya*) as integral to Fulbe ethnicity.

To avoid people saying 'they love each other', men and women do not touch in public, sit next to each other or eat together. Men should not dance with their wives and women would rather not sit behind their husbands on a motorcycle. A husband and wife openly showing love for each could be seen as distracting attention from the collectivity of the family and this threatens household unity. In other words, a woman who has *maloya* shows that she puts the family first.

If a woman asks for help or money, people will gossip and say that she has not worked hard and this is perceived as shameless behaviour.

> *Maloya* is being ashamed to ask something of someone. People will think 'she does not work'. You should be able to manage your own affairs. (Hawa Kamara, 50 yrs, December 2009)

This female respondent told me that she had never asked anyone other than her husband for money. She explained that this is *maloya*. She does not want people to tell others that she has asked for money; she is afraid of gossip. Women also had shame when asking for help from a man who was not their husband because they were afraid this man might think they were making advances. Women were afraid that if their husband heard that they had asked someone for money, it would make the husband feel ashamed because this would imply that the he had not lived up to his responsibility as a provider. Having made her husband feel ashamed would in turn make the wife feel ashamed.

One way my respondents did manage to avoid gossip while asking for financial aid was to send someone else, an intermediary, to ask on their behalf and in secret.[50] A respondent explained that if she could not find the money herself, she would also have difficulty in repaying a loan and she therefore was ashamed to ask for money.

Maloya means not doing things that you suspect will upset people, such as asking for money from someone who has nothing, or asking something of someone you owe money to. One mother told me,

> Poverty is at the root of shame, knowing that someone is poor makes it difficult to ask something of that person, because if this person is not able to help you he will feel ashamed in having to refuse, and then you will feel ashamed for having upset him. (Kamisa Kante, 35 yrs, March 2007)

Poverty also made women feel ashamed due to their inability to take proper care of strangers staying as guests. Women felt ashamed in not being able to give the hospitality a woman usually offers her guests.

---

[50] During the last days of each of my fieldwork periods, people would not ask me directly but would ask my translator to ask me for financial aid.

> When my husband's visitors are not satisfied with the reception, this brings shame to my husband and I also will feel ashamed because I was not a wife who took care of those visitors. (Kadjatu Kante, 20 yrs, January 2012)

Being financially dependent on someone other than one's husband was also a shameful situation, as this example of a mother of six who was abandoned by her husband, demonstrates:

> It is really shameful for a woman to be abandoned by her husband and to end up the responsibility of another man. I am ashamed because I have become the charge of other husbands. Nowadays I meet my family with lowered head. My husband does not assume his responsibility. Everything is left to his younger brother. This brings shame on me (*o bɛ ne maloya*). I am ashamed because [others] have to suffer to help me.

Maloya is thus spoken of as demonstrating virtuous behaviour by adhering to certain prohibitions, and at the same time *maloya* was also spoken of as feeling ashamed because one had not lived up to these conditions of virtuous behaviour.

Shaming: Making someone feel shameless

> *Malobali* ('shamelessness') is not having the dignity of your father. A person without *maloya* is able to do what he wants without thinking of others. (Faramata Kante, 24 yrs, November 2009)

If a woman demonstrates shameless behaviour, if she is deemed *malobali,* she runs the social risk of being insulted or cursed publicly. This next example shows what the consequences can be if a woman does not demonstrate *maloya* towards male family members.

> Today, Hawa Kante and her husband Madi Kante had a fight. It started when Madi's nephew asked for some millet to feed the chickens. Madi told him to take some from the millet Hawa had just pounded. Hawa said that she needed this millet for the evening meal and was afraid that there would not be enough [and she would have to pound more]. His wife's refusal of a request made by a male family member made Madi so angry that he yelled a curse at her in public. He said that all her children would die (five of their eight children had died and she was now pregnant with her ninth child). Hawa cried for hours. She later told me that even children speak ill of her, they also say that all of her children will die. (Fieldnotes 2009)

Hawa's refusal to give her husband's nephew the millet was seen as shameless behaviour; she had not respected her social obligation to her male family members. The sanction for this behaviour was public ostracism, which made her feel shameless. For her, the most painful aspect of this sanction was that her husband even encouraged children to be disrespectful to her. Another woman told me that her husband had cursed her for refusing sex when she was heavily pregnant. He had yelled, 'You will not deliver this baby until you apologize'. Women told me that a public beating by their husband was not as shaming as being cursed.

> I do not see eye to eye with my husband, when he gets into a conflict with me, he insults me in a bad way and he threatens me with divorce. This brings me shame. My husband has no consideration for me at all, now I even feel like going to my father. When there is a conflict between us he also insults my parents and he tells me that I am lazy, that I do not work, these words bring me shame, I am mistreated by my husband, you see how much thinner I have become. (Hawa Kante, 35 yrs, January 2012)

During a focus group discussion sitting under a big tree in a courtyard, I asked three women to tell me about insults. However, before they could answer, my translator, Mahamadou, made it clear that he would not translate questions about insults a man or woman had said to one another during an argument. He had shame in asking the women to repeat the insult; he did not want them to feel uncomfortable. All the women agreed that curses and insults made them feel very ashamed. The women agreed that an insult is a seriously shameful thing that can even lead to a (temporary) divorce. Another female respondent told me that if a woman called her shameless (*'mɔgɔ min tɛ maloya'*), she would consider this a serious insult, and she went on to say that she would fight with this woman.

I have attempted to describe the public discourse of shame, understanding it to be the verbalization of embodied dispositions. But, this is what people say. To try to come to an understanding of how the social risk of shame in health practices really works, we need to look at what people actually do.

Ethical moments: The social risk of being considered shameless

Participatory observation in and around the maternity clinic proved to be a useful tool for studying moments of ethical dilemmas and moments when shame as a moral issue came into focus. Next, are examples of what Zigon calls 'ethical moments'. These are moments when, in the context of health, something happened to force these women to reflect upon the proper ethical response. These stories are about three women and their ethical dilemmas about accessing health care. They are stories about the range of possibilities women in Farabako have within the moral discourse of shame when seeking health care. Women's 'moral agency' becomes visible in these narratives of choosing between alternative normative viewpoints (cf. Schulz 2011). The narratives show how 'having shame' is a 'technique of the self' that women use to become proper wives and good women. The first story is about a widow who was given in levirate to her brother-in-law and her shame before the elder women of the village, the second about a woman who had an unwanted pregnancy and her shame for aborting her husband's child and the third about a woman seeking treatment for epilepsy and her shame in asking someone other than her husband for help.

Binetu's story: A respectful widow

Binetu Bagayogo (37 years) came to the clinic after her husband had explained to my interpreter that she had not become pregnant since she was given to him in levirate four years ago. Her new husband wanted to know if she was ill. Binetu asked if she could speak to me alone. She told me that she had shame in speaking about the change in her menstruation cycle in front of the midwife because the midwife was her former co-wife. When I asked her if she had asked for advice from the *musokɔrɔbaw*, she said yes, just one time. The *musokɔrɔba* said that she was not ill. Binetu did not dare talk about it again, even though she was worried, because she had shame. She was afraid that if she would talk about wanting a pregnancy with her new husband, people would say, 'She does not think of Madu anymore' (Madu was her first husband who had died). This would be seen as disrespectful and shameless.

Binetu chose to abstain from seeking further health care in order to avoid the social risk of being called shameless. Similarly, mothers sometimes chose to abstain from seeking health care for their sick children to avoid the social risk of being called shameless as was illustrated by the case of the baby with pneumonia in the previous chapter.

Nakani's story: An abortion gone wrong

On the third day after arriving in Farabako (in 2009), I did an inventory of the maternity clinic with Jeneba, one of the local midwives. I noticed that a clamp used while cutting the umbilical cord was missing and I asked Jeneba about it. She said 'the clamp is at a woman's home'. I asked why? (I was a bit irritated that the instruments were not clean and complete). Jeneba said that she had done a delivery five days ago and the clamp was still at the woman's home. It took quite some time before I understood that this woman had had a preterm delivery at home. The baby had been born but the placenta had not. The clamp was still attached to the umbilical cord!

Jeneba told me that this woman, Nakani Kante, had induced an abortion by taking traditional medicine and an overdose of chloroquine (an antimalarial). It is possible that this was a spontaneous preterm labour and not an induced abortion. A local physician had assured me that chloroquine does not cause an abortion, but the women in Farabako were convinced that it does, and that this was an abortion.

Five days earlier the baby was stillborn after a pregnancy of approximately five months. The baby had been buried directly after the birth. I had real fear in my heart; a placenta that is retained five days postpartum is a dangerous complication. As anyone who has witnessed a birth knows, the placenta is usually born minutes after the baby, not hours let alone days after.[51] What would I encounter? A woman deathly ill of puerperal fever or bleeding to death? And what could I do (I am not a doctor)? The only means of transportation to a health clinic (twenty kilometres away) was by motorcycle over very rough terrain. I found some medicine in the clinic and went to Nakani's hut.

It was very warm in Nakani's room; a small pot of traditional medicine was simmering on a coal fire next to her bed. On the floor, next to the bed lay the missing clamp still attached to a dried piece of umbilical cord. I examined Nakani; the placenta was indeed still in her uterus. Thankfully, Nakani did not have a fever or other signs of infection and she was not bleeding excessively. I gave Nakani antibiotics and medication to make her uterus contract in the hope that this would expel the placenta. When this was unsuccessful, I gave Nakani's husband money to take her by motorcycle to the doctor at the clinic twenty kilometres away in Sandama. The doctor performed curettage and luckily Nakani recovered.

The only reason anyone had told me of Nakani's abortion-gone-wrong was because I noticed the missing clamp. Why had no one told me when I arrived by hired jeep? Nakani could have been driven to the health clinic by the driver who was returning to Bamako. When I asked Jeneba the midwife about this, she told me that Nakani's husband, Madi Kante was very angry when he heard about the abortion and forbade anyone from buying medicine for her. He did not treat her himself (although he is a *soma*). The midwife had told Nakani's husband that she must be taken to a doctor but instead the husband had asked a nurse-assistant ('infirmière auxiliaire'), who happened to be visiting him at the time, to look at his wife. The nurse had given Nakani an intravenous drip with oxytocine and 'Kinimax' an anti-malarial.[52] She then had tried to express the placenta, but this had not been successful. The intervention had been a few days ago, and since then, the nurse-assistant had taken no further action, nor had the midwife, even though they both recognized the seriousness of the situation.

A few weeks later, when Nakani had recovered from her operation, and I had the use of Mahamadou Faganda Keita as interpreter (from outside of the village), I was able to interview her. Nakani told me that over the five days

---

[51] In the Netherlands if the placenta is not born within an hour after the birth of the baby, it is removed manually under general anaesthetic by an obstetrician/gynaecologist. This is done to prevent infection ascending to the uterus and causing puerperal fever and/or postpartum haemorrhage.

[52] Intravenous Kinimax seems to be a remedy for everything in Farabako; and to a certain extent this is true seeing as everyone has malaria, but a retained placenta will not become looser with this medication. Oxytocine, on the other hand, is an adequate treatment by biomedical standards.

after the abortion that the placenta had not come out, her husband had not visited her once. Nakani said, 'my husband is very good for his guests but very bad for his wives' and that she had been 'waiting for death'.

Nakani went on to tell me that she had first married Brehima Kante with whom she had had seven children. Three of these children died in infancy. When Brehima died in 2003, Nakani was given in levirate to his brother Bala and together they had one son. Shortly thereafter, Bala also died and Nakani was given to yet another brother, Madi. She had little choice in this; she could not marry someone else in Farabako because they are all family (of her affines). She could not marry outside of Farabako because then she would have had to leave her children behind.

She lives in her deceased first husband's house together with her former co-wife who was given in levirate to another 'brother'. Nakani thus lives apart from her new husband's compound where he lives with his other two wives and their children. Nakani feels left out she says because Madi seldom comes to her. She has had serious quarrels with Madi's second wife and there is much jealousy. Nakani feels that her new co-wives are against her.

Nakani had had one child with Madi, but it was stillborn. When she became pregnant again, she told me that she did not want the child because she was alone and this was very difficult for her. Her new husband 'only takes care of her food'. Clothing and other expenditures she takes care of herself. The peanut harvest had not been good that year and she was worried how she would be able to take care of her children.

Nakani Kante was unhappy with her marginal position as a widow in levirate and went against the discourse of *maloya* by inducing an abortion. Afterwards, she was incapable of taking action to save her own life. My respondents told me that the husband must correct his wife if she has behaved shamelessly. Nakani's husband did this by ignoring her and forbidding others to help her. Agency was a scarce resource for Nakani, but also for the local midwife who could not take the initiative to ask me for help. To do so, would have been disrespectful of Nakani's husband and would be seen as shameless behaviour. The shame that Nakani's husband felt at his wife's indiscretion made it difficult for him to ask me for help, but once I offered help he was very happy to take it. My offer gave him a way out of the impasse, about which he seemed to feel quite uncomfortable.

Nakani told me that she felt shame when others talked about her abortion. She felt ashamed that she had 'killed a person', but she added defiantly: 'I'm happy with the result' (of not having to care for yet another child on her own).

Less than a year later, I returned to Farabako. While working in the clinic, Nakani came to me for a prenatal check-up; she was four months pregnant with her eleventh child. Nakani assured me that she was happy with this latest pregnancy. I asked her what had changed. She told me that she was afraid to try an abortion again after looking death in the eye the last time. During this interview, she said nothing but positive things about her husband. She presented herself as a humble and proper wife who had shame. Gone was the shameless woman protesting her marginal position by inducing an abortion.

In both pregnancies, Nakani weighed her ethical options within her range of possibilities. She weighed the risk of being seen to lack *maloya* against her worries of how to take care of her children and the risk of death.

In Farabako, abortion is seen to be shameless (*malobali*). It implies that the woman concerned has no *maloya* and that 'she loves men, but not children'. But nonetheless, attempts to induce an abortion happened quite frequently in Farabako as women had very limited possibilities to space their pregnancies.[53] The fact that Nakani's abortion went wrong (and therefore everyone knew that she had aborted the foetus) made it difficult for all involved. If the abortion had been successful and kept secret, there might have been less shame involved. Bleek (1981), in his work on abortion in Ghana, asserts that activities can only be shameful if they are not secret (cf. also Fessler 2007). If no one has seen the incorrect behaviour, if the abortion is kept secret, there is no shame. But in Farabako there is *maloya* even if the abortion stays secret, as one man explained to me during a focus group discussion:

> Both men and women feel ashamed in the case of an abortion. One marries in order to have children. A woman will feel ashamed even if the abortion is kept secret because abortion is betrayal [of the father's family]. An unmarried girl will also feel ashamed in performing an abortion, even if it is kept secret. She will feel ashamed of having become pregnant too soon, and she will feel ashamed because she should have asked the father [permission for the abortion] because it was his family's child. (Madi Kante, 48 yrs, January 2012)

Whether an abortion is secret or not, the shamelessness is there. *Maloya* is not only relational, but also embodied. The next story is about a woman who first decides on risking shameless behaviour, but later changes course.

Narama's story: Asking for help, or not

Narama Keita developed epilepsy during her sixth pregnancy. I was there when she had her first epileptic fit. Her family and the *somaw* were convinced that she was possessed by a *jinɛ*. They were also convinced that this illness was contagious. The family forbade her from eating with them; thus, she ate alone,

---

[53] Nine per cent of my respondents admitted to have used a substance to induce an abortion. The women spoke very openly about this. The reasons they gave usually had to do with their age; they found they were either too young or too old to have children. These are the cases the women *told* me about. I did not hear of any cases of women in their twenties or thirties trying to induce an abortion; perhaps this is socially less acceptable.

without her children or other women. This made Narama feel like an outcast.[54] Narama was also unhappy because her co-wife was afraid that she would contract the disease through sexual intercourse with their husband and this had disrupted her marriage relations. In her unhappiness, Narama asked me to talk to her husband about this matter and convince him that it was not dangerous to have intimate relations with her.

I did as Narama asked and broached this delicate subject carefully; her husband assured me politely that he understood. He asked me for medicine to cure Narama. I explained to him, and later to Narama, that a treatment for epilepsy requires many visits to a specialist in the capital to determine the proper dosage, a costly and time-consuming endeavour.

A year later, when I returned again to Farabako, Narama assured me that everything was fine and that I mustn't talk to her husband because she did not want him to think that she had asked me to help her again as this would cause problems for her. She told me that she still had to eat alone, she did not like it, but she was used to it now. Narama assured me that her relationship with her husband (and co-wife) was fine. Although earlier in desperation, Narama had shamelessly asked me for help, she now presented herself as a proper wife who had *maloya*'. She did not want to be seen taking initiative; she did not want to disturb her husband. Narama weighed her ethical options and decided not to rock the marriage boat by demonstrating shameless behaviour. A few days later, her husband came to me on his own accord to ask if I could find money for his wife's treatment. After her husband had taken the initiative to ask me for help, Narama did speak of her difficulties to me.

Inhabiting a moral discourse

These examples of ethical dilemmas faced by women in Farabako have shown that agency is found not only in acts that resist norms, but also in the multiple ways in which one inhabits norms. In becoming a subject, the capacity for action is enabled and created by specific relations of subordination. Social norms are not external, but rather the necessary ground by which the woman is realised and comes to enact her agency (cf. Foucault 1990). Mahmood (2005), in her ethnography on the women's mosque movement in Cairo, argues that modesty (and the donning of the veil) expresses both virtue and the means by which virtue is acquired. Wearing a veil is a sign that the woman is virtuous and, at the same time, wearing a veil is a means for a woman to become and actually feel virtuous. Mahmood builds on Foucault's concept of ethics as those practices by which a subject transforms herself to achieve a particular state of being, happiness or truth. Mahmood agrees with Foucault that the aim

[54] In an attempt to convince the villagers that epilepsy is not contagious, I ate together with Narama in front of the head of the village. This did not help, however, as the villagers were convinced that I had a special white man's medicine that protected me.

of ethics is the on-going project of self-improvement. For the Egyptian women in Mahmood's ethnography, a woman's 'failure to enact virtue successfully is perceived to be the marker of an inadequately formed self, one in which the interiority and exteriority of the person are improperly aligned' (2005: 164). Performing virtue was the act of developing the self's potentiality. Mahmood shows that a distinction between a woman's own desires and socially prescribed behaviour cannot be taken for granted, and that submission to certain forms of (external) authority can be 'a condition for achieving the subject's potentiality' (2005: 31). Similarly, Schulz, in her study of Muslim women's groups in Bamako, describes how women remake themselves into a specific kind of moral agent, and that submission to God and their husbands is central in this process of ethical self-remaking (2011: 96). In Farabako, 'having shame' is virtuous behaviour and, at the same time, a means for a woman to feel virtuous. A woman's submission to subordination by males, affines and elders can be a condition for achieving her potentiality and becoming the person she wants to be.

Moral discourse provides the range of possibilities within which women work on themselves to become the kind of person they strive to be. According to Mahmood, agency is not about resistance to the restraints and dominance of structures, rather agency is how women make themselves into the kinds of persons who fit into those structures. That is to say, agency is how they make themselves into socially and morally correct persons. Agency is the active embodiment of structures, so that women can become recognized as virtuous members of the community. Menon (2002) used a similar approach in her study of female power/energy among Hindu women. She shows how Hindu women can gain power and moral authority without resisting unequal societal structures. Proper Hindu women acquire moral authority unattainable by men by embodying the virtues of duty, self-control and service to others, virtues having to do with procreation and nurture. Menon's argument is that 'moral agency' is only possible if there is inequality in gender relations.

Mahmood's agrees with Foucault (1994b) who argues that agency is predicated on the ability to be taught, a condition classically referred to as docility. Docility is often associated with lack of agency, yet the term literally implies the willingness to be taught and yielding to the direction required for someone to be instructed in a particular skill or knowledge, such as being virtuous. In Farabako, a girl must be taught to be moral, first by her own family and then by her husband's family.[55] In this context docility is not a sense of passivity; rather, docility is about hard work, struggle, and achievement (cf. Mahmood 2005: 29).

[55] Similarly, Rydstrøm (2003), in her study on how children embody morality in Northern Vietnam, found that a girl was considered to be a blank slate; she must be trained to be moral first by her own family then her husband's family. This was an embodiment of the patrilineal social structure.

Viewed in this way, female shame in Farabako and the donning of the veil in Mahmood's work may appear to be cases of unacceptable passivity and docility from a feminist point of view; however, they may actually be forms of agency. They could be forms of agency that can be understood only from within the discourses and structures of subordination that create the conditions of its enactment. In this sense, agency is found not only in those acts that resist norms, but also in the many ways in which one inhabits norms (Mahmood 2005: 14). One way to inhabit the discourse of shame is to be docile. Understanding this helps to explain why mothers are sometimes passive in the face of child mortality.

Conclusion

This chapter has shown that the maternity clinic in Farabako was an arena in which women 'performed ethics' in seeking health care for themselves and their children. I have argued that Zigon's concept of ethical moments is useful in understanding how people, when they are forced to step out of their zone of existential comfort (for example, in times of social change), become reflexive about their ethical options. Social change, in the form of increasing individualism and the introduction of biomedicine in Farabako, has illuminated the ethical weighing of the social risk for women of being called shameless.

In Farabako, women are consciously considering how to behave in a morally appropriate manner on a daily basis, and what Zigon calls 'ethical moments' are not rare. Zigon's framework for an anthropology of moralities was a useful methodological tool for studying the discourse of shame (*maloya*) as a morality that is institutionalized, embodied and discursive. The moral discourse of shame is a range of possibilities of speaking, acting and being, within which a 'good woman' can manoeuvre. Mahmood's concept of inhabiting a discourse was useful in examining how shame is the unreflexive embodiment of moral discourse, but at the same time, shame is also a socially performed technique. Shame is *reflexively* embodied in the on-going project of becoming a virtuous woman. This notion of habitus stresses the conscious and intentional work necessary to acquire a particular kind of habitus.[56] Zigon makes a distinction between an unreflexive morality and a reflexive ethics, but here I disagree; in Farabako shame is also a reflexive morality. Shame is a non-conscious as well as a conscious moral habitus. This notion of habitus is similar to Foucault's techniques of the self, which views self-mastery as the aim of ethics.

Zigon posits that the aim of ethics is to return to an existential comfort. Often women will choose an ethical option that shows them to be morally correct (a woman who has shame), and life goes on without having to think too

---

56 Mahmood's notion of habitus is thus different from the mostly unconsciously acquired and socio-economically determined view of habitus given by Bourdieu (1990).

much. But, as the case studies have shown, women sometimes consciously choose an 'uncomfortable' path, and are willing to take the consequences of being seen as shameless. What I am arguing is that in this time of social and medical upheaval and a context of extreme poverty, existential comfort hardly exists as women are constantly faced with ethical dilemmas. In Farabako, shame is a reflexive morality and with the introduction of biomedicine and its accompanying existential *dis*comfort, ethical moments are frequent occurrences in therapy management in and around the maternity clinic.

The next chapter focuses on moralities in health but addresses another question: how are biomedical and local medical (ethical) discourses negotiated in the context of a biomedical health care project?

6. THE MATERNITY CLINIC AS A ZONE OF AWKWARD ENGAGEMENT

Whereas, the previous chapter focused on ethics as an individual technology of the self within a moral discourse of shame, this chapter examines the ethics of good medical practice as perceived by patients, local medical experts and biomedical professionals (including me as a midwife) in the context of the maternity clinic in Farabako. How do these various categories of people form, justify and apply judgements for good medical practice.

My Dutch midwife's perspective on how the maternity clinic functioned in Farabako led me to conceptualize the clinic as a zone of awkward engagement by the imagined universality of biomedicine within the local health and gender arena. Biomedicine was made to fit the local context and attendant specific moralities. The concept of 'friction' as developed by Tsing (2005) is useful for understanding how the so-called 'global' is humanly mediated through the 'local'. Friction is creative; it is a moment of 'productive confusion' when the universal of biomedicine and the particular of Farabako come together and a new medical practice is co-produced. Friction takes place in what Tsing calls 'zones of awkward engagement' (2005: xi). The clinic in Farabako proved to be such a zone. There was an awkward engagement between 'global health' aspirations and the realisation of medical practice in a local context with specific medical and gender discourse and related practices.

Until 2007, it was rare for a woman in Farabako to seek prenatal care (7%) and even more unusual for babies to be born in a clinic or hospital (3%). This is a much lower percentage than in other rural regions in Mali where 26% of pregnant women deliver in biomedical facilities (Gage 2007). In Farabako, only four women had ever given birth in a hospital or clinic and only eight babies of 263 births had been born in a hospital or clinic. Of the 263 deliveries, 85% were home births attended by the *musokɔrɔbaw*. In 10% of births the woman delivered alone; this was either because of preference or because the birth happened too fast to call for the *musokɔrɔbaw*. In most cases, home deliveries went smoothly for the mothers and in only five cases were 'skilled personnel' (doctor, midwife or nurse) called in by the *musokɔrɔbaw* to help because of complications (this was in 2% of all births).[57] While the deliveries generally were without complications for the mothers, the babies did not

[57] These complications included non-progression, breech birth or a retained placenta. Because most women had no prenatal care, they often did not know beforehand that they would deliver twins or have a breech birth. Of the nine breech births, seven were born at home with the help of the *musokɔrɔbaw*, five of these were easy births, two were long and difficult births during which the babies died.

Midwife Jeneba Kante (right) performing a prenatal examination

always fare so well. In Farabako, eighteen of the 263 babies (7%) were reported as stillborn and fifteen babies died in the first week postpartum (6%).[58]

Between the opening of the maternity clinic in 2007 and my return in 2009, the majority of pregnant women in Farabako had come to the new maternity clinic for at least one prenatal check-up and most women had delivered their baby there. This does not imply that the implementation of biomedicine in Farabako went smoothly. The newly trained midwives and I, as a Dutch midwife, introduced a biomedical discourse endorsing a model of pregnancy as a biological event needing medical attention with an emphasis on prevention. This (Dutch) biomedical discourse differed substantially from the local medical discourse on antenatal care with which the midwives and I had to negotiate. The negotiation between the local medical and the biomedical discourse that took place, in and around the maternity clinic, occurred in 'ethical moments' (cf. Zigon 2008). These were moments when patients and midwives reflected on what was good medical practice.

---

[58] Perinatal mortality (babies dying in utero after 28 weeks gestation, during the delivery, or in the first week after birth) in Mali is 50 per 1,000 births (WHO for 2008). If I extrapolate my survey results, perinatal mortality in Farabako is approximately 120 per 1,000 births. My sample is too small and it is impossible to know with any accuracy if the babies reported as stillborn died before or after 28 weeks gestation, but it seems fair to say that in Farabako the perinatal mortality rate is higher than the national average.

A medical discourse gives meaning to illness, determines the role of healers and patients, produces concepts of the normal and abnormal, and generates strategies for prevention, treatment and care. In this chapter, I show that these latter strategies are not only determined by the medical discourse, but also by a society's gender discourse. For example, gender relationships within the household may inhibit women's ability to seek care or to have access to information and resources (see also Mezey 2000; Okojie 1994). In the previous chapter, I analysed how the moral discourse of shame influenced how health care was experienced and used in Farabako. In this chapter, I show how the moral discourse of shame, gender discourse and medical discourse intersect to influence what is considered good medical practice. First, I present the various elements of friction that made the clinic into a zone of awkward engagement. This is followed by a reflection on the ethical dilemmas raised by the new medical practice that developed in the context of the maternity clinic.

Perceptions and practices of obstetric care

While attempting to introduce a Dutch model of midwifery practice in the maternity clinic, in Farabako, it became apparent that reproductive risk assessment and ideas on the use of drugs, pregnancy monitoring and addressing obstetric complications were areas of friction.

Perceptions of reproductive risk

Most women in Farabako had not been exposed to education or media coverage of biomedical views on pregnancy, and thus were unable to recognize what biomedicine considers to be an obstetrical complication or to assess the severity. For example, malaria, which is endemic in the region, was perceived more as a normal part of life than as a serious condition causing obstetrical complications such as premature delivery and stillbirth.

Traditionally, Western biomedicine has studied secondary causes of illness; how the patient became ill. Primary causes, such as the why and wherefore, were best left up to religious experts (cf. Porter 2002: 67). In Farabako, healers concern themselves more with the primary causes of why a particular person becomes ill at a particular time, such as disturbances in the social order or relations with spirits.

Risk assessment and prevention (of secondary causes), pillars of Dutch midwifery, were not a standard of care in Farabako. The *musokɔrɔbaw* did not perform routine prenatal examinations of pregnant women. Preventive measures in Farabako were geared towards primary causes of illness and pregnancy complications. Pregnant women could ask a *musokɔrɔba* to make them a *tafo*—a string over which incantations (*kilisiw*) have been said that is then tied around a pregnant woman's hips to protect her from pain and premature labour. Similar to an amulet, wearing a *tafo* protects a pregnant woman against angry spirits or jealousy.

Baraka Kante, a renowned *musokɔrɔba*, prepared traditional medicine especially for pregnant women. She made this from certain roots mixed with salt and water over which incantations were said. When I asked if there was anything that a pregnant woman could do, or should avoid doing, to have a healthy baby, she said:

> Women should not do hard physical labour, they should not carry anything so heavy that it is difficult for them to put on their head. The [pregnant] woman herself must say when the work is too much; men do not have an eye for this. A woman can ask someone to help her, but then she must pay. Your sister-in-law is the only one who will help for free.

Taboos for pregnant women are closest to biomedical ideas of pregnancy risks and prevention of risks. Baraka told me that there were certain taboos for pregnant women. They must not accept food that is given to them over a wall and they must not knot money in their *fani* (length of cloth worn as a skirt), because if they do this, the child could become a thief. Pregnant women must not eat lemon or baobab as this can cause the baby to be stricken by a skin disease. Pregnant women must not eat hare or mankare (a type of wild goat) for it brings bad luck; their baby could die. These animals are *ɲama*. *Ɲama* has been explained to me in several ways: as sickness, refuse and a kind of (dangerous) energy or (supernatural) force.[59]

Reproductive life history interviews confirmed that before 2007, most pregnant women had not followed a special diet or used traditional or modern medicine. The women had not worked less hard or rested more. They had no system of saving money for medicine or for transport to a clinic in times of emergency. In 274 of 293 pregnancies, the women had not sought prenatal health care in a biomedical health facility. Only when they were very ill with malaria, did the women seek (biomedical) help. If they had had an extremely difficult previous birth, the women sometimes moved to Bamako to deliver in the hospital.

A 'fatalistic' attitude towards pregnancy influenced agency. The pregnant women in Farabako were not always convinced that they could (or should) do anything to improve their pregnancy outcome. If God or fate determines life and death, then interfering in fertility is not always justified or desirable. Brand (2001) calls this fatalism the 'default option'. Pregnancy was perceived to be a special time in a woman's life, but not necessarily a time that needed (what I considered) special care. During a reproductive life history interview in 2007, I asked a mother, who had delivered eight babies at home with the assistance of the *musokɔrɔbaw*, what she had done during her pregnancies to have healthy babies. She responded, 'Nothing'. She persisted when I probed further.

[59] Researchers of the Mande area have produced various theories on what *ɲama* is. See, for example, Brand (2000: 149) and Bird and Kendall (1987: 16).

LH: 'Isn't it necessary to do something different when you are pregnant?'
Mother: 'No, nothing.'
LH: 'Would you have wanted to have prenatal check-ups?'
Mother: 'The idea did not occur to me. That is not the custom here.'

In Farabako, prevention also consists of *not* speaking about pregnancy and birth and not witnessing a birth while pregnant. I explain the reasons for this behaviour below.

Medicine use

The villagers often equated biomedicine with strong effective therapeutic drugs; therefore, the main reason to visit the maternity clinic was not prevention but drugs. If the midwife did not dispense drugs during a prenatal check-up, the care was perceived as ineffective. If drugs were not given in the clinic, then visiting a local medical expert (a *musokɔrɔba* or a *soma*) could be perceived as a more logical choice. If during a delivery, the midwife did not give an injection, she was potentially perceived as 'not having done anything'.[60] This was illustrated in one case when a husband refused to pay the bill for his wife's delivery since no injection had been given. The pregnant or labouring women's demand for drugs made it difficult for the midwives to let nature take its course and not interfere when it was not necessary to interfere.

Biomedical discourse considers drugs as potentially dangerous (especially for pregnant women) and only to be used if necessary (and by prescription). In Farabako, it is possible to buy modern drugs without a prescription at a pharmacy or in the market in a neighbouring town. The drugs are usually not perceived as dangerous and are often not used properly. Most women in Farabako did not realise that modern medicine was potentially dangerous for their unborn children. One exception was chloroquine, an anti-malarial. The women thought that an overdose of chloroquine induced an abortion, and in fact it was used for this purpose.

All the local medical experts I spoke to, said that they thought the availability of Western drugs was a good development: 'Less people die now than ten years ago when pharmacy medicine was not available.' The healers explained that they saw traditional medicine (*furaw*) and biomedicine as complementary. Some illnesses should only be treated by traditional medicine, but in other cases biomedical treatment is seen as superior. For example, if a patient has *sayi* (jaundice), biomedical treatment is thought to be dangerous, or even fatal. On the other hand, for haemorrhage biomedical treatment is the preferred treatment.

Traditional medicine (*furaw*) can be taken even if the patient is not ill. It is often taken to give strength, much as we in the West take vitamin pills. The

[60] This strong preference for 'Western' medicines is widespread in the region (cf. Van der Geest and Whyte 2003).

only reason local medical experts gave for patients not taking traditional medicine, was that certain medicine was dangerous for pregnant women and too strong for small children. The main reason given not to take Western drugs (if one was ill or not) was that they were too expensive, not that they were dangerous. The local medical experts and villagers both agreed that taking drugs was beneficial, even if a person was not ill.

> A mother whose child I had treated for an infection with antibiotics came to me to tell me how happy she was that her child had recovered so quickly. She said 'that was good medicine' (*fura a ka nyi*) and asked if she could buy some more to give to her child to keep him strong. She wanted to continue the treatment even though her son was no longer ill. (Fieldnotes 2011)

The biomedical idea that bacteria can become resistant to antibiotics, and therefore one should only use antibiotics if necessary to treat an infection, is unfamiliar to the healers and villagers of Farabako. Biomedical doctors in health clinics in the region prescribe antibiotics abundantly.

> An older man complaining of stomach-aches came to me at the maternity clinic. Only after I had asked specifically, did he mention that he had already been to a doctor in Bamako. The doctor had prescribed medicine without telling the man what his diagnosis was. I asked him to show me the prescription. The doctor had prescribed ten kinds of medicine including four antibiotics, all to be taken at the same time. (Fieldnotes 2009)

The reaction of this man and his companion was that the doctor did not know what he was doing and had prescribed all the medicine available at the pharmacy. According to my respondents, this was not the sign of a good healer. However, no one voiced concerns about the medicalization, resistance or side-effects that immediately came to my mind.

Monitoring the foetus

One important aspect of biomedical prenatal care is to monitor of the growth of the foetus. In the Netherlands, midwives do this by comparing the growth of the uterus (in centimetres) to the number of weeks that the woman is pregnant. In Farabako, the women did not use a calendar in their daily life. They did not know the precise date of their last menstruation, and thus could not say with any accuracy how many weeks pregnant they were. While the midwives used calendar months to follow a pregnancy, in Farabako, pregnant women spoke of a normal gestation as lasting 9-11 lunar months.

Because it was impossible to calculate the gestation by date, I taught the midwives to estimate the duration of pregnancy by measuring the uterus using a measuring tape. The midwives found this difficult, as they had never used a measuring tape before. I tried to make it easier for them by using a visual aid. I drew a pregnant abdomen in each month of pregnancy including the corresponding number of centimetres on the wall of the clinic. However, this only confused the midwives as the link between the drawing on the wall and the pregnant belly they were examining was not obvious to them. Finally, I was successful by repeating over and over the number of centimetres that corresponded to the number of (lunar) months of a pregnancy.

In this way, a biomedical prenatal care technique was re-interpreted to fit the situation in Farabako. The midwives were socialized in an oral culture, barely literate and unaccustomed to visual aids. Instead of comparing centimetres of growth to a date on a calendar, the midwives used centimetres of growth to estimate the date (duration) of the pregnancy. In this way the midwives could estimate when a woman was due and when she should be referred to a hospital in the capital for cases of a breech presentation, twins or a previously difficult birth.

Managing obstetric complications

For the Farabako biomedical project to work as intended, midwives should have been able to refer pregnant women with (anticipated) complications to the government health care system. In the indigenous medical discourse of Farabako, however, severe illnesses were often regarded as disturbances of the social order. They concerned relations with spirits or relations with other people within the community (see also Imperato 1977; Slobin 1991). For example, if the illness was thought to be caused by *jinɛw* or betrayal by an enemy, the preferred cure could be a sacrifice and not drugs. If obstructed labour was thought to be caused by a woman's infidelity, then confession rather than transport to a health clinic could be seen as the proper treatment.

In Farabako, referral to a clinic during the second or third stage of labour was not an option. It is practically impossible to transport a woman in an advanced stage of labour on the back of a motorcycle over rough terrain. The only option was for the midwife to ask a man from the village to go by motorcycle to fetch a doctor or midwife from the neighbouring town. To do this, the midwives needed to take initiative and they needed to take action. However, action can be problematic. In the Mande region, change is seen as 'hot and dangerous' and delay in taking action and waiting for someone else to take the initiative are deliberate strategies for 'cooling down' society (Jansen 2000: 5-9). Deliberately postponing or delaying action slows down the process of change (in this case the change from normal to problematical delivery). In this way, waiting and doing nothing can be understood as a health care strategy for the midwives and villagers of Farabako.

Although the midwives in Farabako were 'skilled personnel' as a result of their biomedical training, their ability to handle obstetric complications was limited. This is illustrated by a story one of the two midwives told, in 2009, about a delivery she had assisted the year before.

> Hawa Keita had come to the maternity clinic to deliver her first baby. After an uncomplicated first stage of labour, the second stage stagnated due to the fact that Hawa had been circumcised. The midwife did not dare to perform an episiotomy because she had never done this before. After Hawa had been pushing for one hour, the midwife sent a family member to fetch another midwife who worked in the health centre in Nioumamakana, which took two hours. By the time this midwife arrived and delivered the baby (after performing an episiotomy), the baby had died. (Fieldnotes January 2009)

When the maternity clinic was set up, the stakeholders agreed that the *musokɔrɔbaw*, with all their experience, should be present at deliveries in order to assist the newly trained (and relatively inexperienced) midwives. But as it turned out, young women coming to the clinic often did not want the *musokɔrɔbaw* to attend their delivery. They were afraid that the *musokɔrɔbaw* would gossip about their comportment during birth. The young women perceived the maternity clinic as a modern space[61] where they could avoid involvement of a *musokɔrɔbaw* (and their family) in their delivery. The disadvantage of this development was that the midwives could not benefit from the expertise of the *musokɔrɔbaw* in handling obstetric complications.

Prenatal care in a landscape of shame

For a woman, it was especially difficult to reach state health care facilities, as she needed her husband's permission to seek prenatal care and his money for transport. As noted in the previous chapters, *maloya* plays a role in therapy management. Young women do not always perceive themselves as able or entitled to make health care decisions and women often 'have shame' asking for money to pay for a consultation. Furthermore, in Farabako it was unseemly for a woman to sit behind her husband on a motorcycle, as people might think that the man and woman 'love each other' and this made the women feel shameless. Unfortunately, a motorcycle was the only means of transportation for a woman to reach the health care facilities that were twenty kilometres away. Shame not only made it difficult for women to access biomedical care, but also effected the quality of care once they reach a health facility.

Women 'had' shame if they spoke about their pregnancy, which was considered boasting and therefore shameless behaviour. I asked a young woman, who was heavily pregnant, if she wanted to go to the clinic for a prenatal check-up,

---

[61] Similarly, Hunt (1999) found that in Congo, delivering in the modern space of a clinic was a metaphor for development.

and to my surprise her response was, 'I am not pregnant'. Women were afraid of gossip, as a young mother explained during a focus group discussion:

> Women only tell their best friends when they are pregnant, not everyone. They are afraid others will gossip 'look, she is pregnant' which is the same as saying 'look she has sex with her husband'. When a doctor says 'you are pregnant' the woman also has shame. (Nantènè Kante, 23 yrs, December 2009)

Nantènè explained further that she waited until others saw that she was pregnant before talking about it. She was afraid that if someone knew she was pregnant they would 'faire gris-gris' because of jealousy (*kɛlɛya*) and egoism (*ɲɛgoya*) and doing evil (*juguya*). For example, a woman who had fewer children than she had might be motivated to use 'gris-gris' against her. 'Gris-gris', a French word, is a magical substance, which can be used, in amulets, to protect the wearer, but 'gris-gris' can also be used to bring bad luck.

Fanta Kante, a *musokɔrɔba* who had delivered many children, told me that it is not the custom to speak about birth with women who have not yet had

Musokɔrɔba *Fanta Kante collecting medicinal plants*

children themselves. Fanta only gives information on the birth process during the delivery, not before. She explains that this is because of *maloya*; women have shame in talking about pregnancy and birth. She only talks to her own daughters about pregnancy and birth, and then only in the privacy of her own house. Women will not tell others that they are pregnant because they have shame. Even women in Fanta's own compound will not tell her that they are pregnant, but will keep it secret as long as possible. For this reason, pregnant women often came for their first prenatal check-up when they were six months along and could no longer hide their pregnancy. Or pregnant women waited for local midwives to notice their swollen belly before going to the maternity clinic.

Once inside the clinic, women 'had shame' when uncovering their abdomen during an examination, which made them uncomfortable. In public (and sometimes even in private) a woman's thighs and belly should be covered at all times. In Farabako it is shameless for a woman to be seen naked by a woman who is younger than she is. Sometimes this was problematic in the maternity clinic since the midwife Kamisajè Kulibali was only thirty years old. If a woman older than Kamisajè was in labour, the other midwife, Jeneba Kante, who was approximately fifty years old, had to be called in.

Perceptions of good medical practice

The previous section pointed out that the fear of being considered as shameless made accessing biomedical health care facilities difficult for women. Due to shame in disclosing their pregnancy, women often did not seek health care until relatively late in their pregnancy. Shame for being seen naked by a younger woman meant that the young midwife was often not able to perform her duties. Not speaking out about a pregnancy and not disclosing a pregnancy can be seen as strategies pregnant women use to avoid shame. This section sheds light on reasons, other than shame, that made talking about pregnancy and health problems problematic in Farabako, and thus influenced the quality of care provided in the local clinic. These factors include perceptions of the nature of medical knowledge and what it means to be a good healer, as well as the undesirability of privacy.

The secrecy and danger of knowledge

Indigenous medical knowledge is not standardised or accessible to everyone in Farabako. Whereas, postmenopausal women had knowledge of matters pertaining to pregnancy and birth, young women and men did not (see also Brand 2000: 150; Castle 1993; Slobin 1991). Each *musokɔrɔba* or *soma* had personal secret knowledge (*dalilu*) of the required incantations (*kilisiw*) for preparing specific traditional medicines (*furaw*). *Musokɔrɔbaw* did not talk with each other about their knowledge and did not know exactly what the others knew. Their personal knowledge was not shared with their patients. This is in contrast to the Netherlands, where midwives share standardised knowledge about pregnancy and childbirth and it is generally clear to their patients what that knowledge is.

'Knowledge is the domain of secrets', the *musokɔrɔba* Kinyèba Fofana told me. She explained that 'every knowledge has its conditions'; certain medical knowledge is only effective if kept secret. Medical knowledge is kept secret to enhance the power of the medicine and the healer and also to protect the patient.

Certain traditional medicine made from roots, leaves and bark, only becomes effective once incantations (*kilisiw*) are said over them. Some incantations are family incantations and may only be used to treat family members. If a healer were to use family incantations to treat non-family, this could be dangerous as it breaks the rules of the knowledge; it is like breaking an oath. Incantations are secret. The well respected *musokɔrɔba* Fanta Kante does not divulge her secret knowledge to her patients because to do so would mean that she would lose her patients' trust and thereby her power to treat them.

Another reason that local medical experts do not share their knowledge is because it is said to lead to jealousy. By keeping their knowledge secret, every healer has their own specialty and there is little competition. If a healer refers a patient to another healer, the first healer will not always explain the treatment that has already been given. Healers will share their knowledge and incantations only with a select group of other healers whom they trust completely. They claim that they will never share all their knowledge but keep some behind to protect themselves in case the other healers want to do them harm.

The patient must also be protected from others wanting to do evil. The *musokɔrɔba* Baraka Kante told me that when she collects plants for traditional medicine, she never lets anyone see the plants because if someone wants to do evil they can do so by looking at the plants. Thus secret knowledge protects the patient and the healer.

In Farabako, knowledge is not only secret but it is also perceived as dangerous. Knowledge of pregnancy and childbirth is thought to be dangerous; it can cause a miscarriage or premature labour. Therefore, young (potentially pregnant) women were not given this knowledge. A pregnant woman may not see another woman deliver a baby. It is said that the potential fear generated by seeing another woman in labour might cause a miscarriage. Seeing a delivery is not only dangerous for pregnant women but also for young women in general.

> Masitan Keita is one of two women in Farabako who can read and write. It is for this reason that I encouraged her to help in the maternity clinic. Masitan enjoyed assisting the midwives during the deliveries but at a certain moment she developed a pain in her eyes. The *musokɔrɔbaw* told her that she was too young to see a birth and that this caused her pain. On the advice of the older women, Masitan stopped working in the clinic despite her ambitions to follow a course in nursing. (Fieldnotes February 2011)

Although I, as an outsider, was allowed to provide information on pregnancy and birth to the pregnant women of Farabako, the newly trained midwives, unaccustomed to speaking openly about pregnancy and birth, were reticent to give anything more than the most basic information.

Characteristics of a good healer

Biomedical health care for pregnant women is based on providing patients with (standardised) information on recognition and prevention of complications and asking women a fairly standardised set of questions. Biomedical encounters feature an 'incitement to speak', constructing the patient as a communicating subject and using language as a tool for 'truthful reference to inner states' (Wilce 2009: 206). While in biomedical care, the patient does a great deal of talking in response to a doctor's questions, in indigenous healing practices, in Farabako, the situation is often reversed. In this village, the patient offered the healer only a limited amount of information and the healer did most of the talking. A sign of a good healer is one who quickly knows the diagnosis, sometimes with the aid of divination (see Jansen 2011). A healer's diagnosis is made without having to ask numerous questions about the patient's physical state. To the people of Farabako, therefore, the sign of a good healer is someone who asks very few questions, since a healer should sense or know the diagnosis by other means. Therefore, it cannot be taken for granted that the midwives at the clinic can ask the questions they need to ask in order to give good prenatal advice from a biomedical viewpoint, and still acquire the status of a 'good healer'. In 2009, the midwives in the clinic asked pregnant women a few questions and provided little information. The pregnant women, who were not used to being asked questions, were shy and reticent when answering them. I experienced that asking questions during a consultation could be problematic when Sekuba Keita, a young man of twenty, came to me for help because he was feeling very ill:

> Sekuba told me that he had *sayi* (jaundice). I started by asking about his symptoms and then went on to ask what kind of treatment he had already had. When it was not clear to me if and when he had seen a doctor, I posed yet another question. At this point, fed up with all my questions, Sekuba got up and left the clinic. He no longer had any confidence that I could help him. (Fieldnotes February 2011).

In Farabako, patients do not expect to be given information with which they must decide whether or not they consent to a treatment. They put their trust in a healer who decides for them. Healers assure their patients that they will recover and give them confidence that the healer will be able to cure them. Even if a healer thinks a patient will die, he does not give this information, but rather tries to take away the patient's fear by reassuring them. It is believed that it is psychologically too difficult for the patient to have all the information on his or her illness and that this could even aggravate their condition. This is much like Hippocratic medicine in Europe before antibiotics or analgesics when the 'bedside manner' of a physician whose ability to inspire confidence and comfort the patient was seen as the most important characteristic of a 'good doctor' (cf. Porter 2002: 39).

In March 2007, when I asked Musa Kante, a *soma*, how his patient was he said: 'He will be cured'. The next day, when the patient was visibly worse, Musa said (to me): 'Un peu, un peu'. When the patient went into a coma Musa told me: 'He is very tired'. When the patient died Musa said, 'It is God'. Musa was well aware of the severity of the patient's illness, but a healer does not admit publicly that a patient is dying. Musa knew beforehand that this was a difficult, perhaps even hopeless, case of *boni korote* (magical poison throwing). The patient had been cursed and sand divination had told Musa that he could *not* be cured. However, since the patient was too ill to be moved to his home village, Musa treated him anyway.

It is rare for a healer to be blamed if a patient dies in Farabako. If a patient dies, it is said that 'the day has arrived that he would die'. It is not the fault of the healer; it is God's will.

> In a hospital people pay a lot and think that therefore everything can be cured. There, people have a different mentality, but here [in Farabako] there is no blame; it is God. (Namagan Kante, 47, yrs, February 2011)

Only if a healer acts in an untrustworthy manner can they be accused of doing evil, for example, by not informing a husband when prescribing medicine that could cause his wife to abort. But, healers will not be blamed if they have a good reputation and are seen as trustworthy.

When I asked healers in Farabako what kind of information they gave to their patients, they always started by telling me that they assured the patient that he or she would not die and would be cured. The dosage and method of preparation of traditional medicine was explained to the patient. The names of the plants used in the traditional medicine were divulged only if the plants were effective without incantations. If incantations were necessary, then the names of the plants had to remain secret. In most cases, the healer told the patient the name of the illness. If the healer did not know for sure which illness the patient was suffering from, they would not say that they did not know. The healer would make a hypothesis and see if the treatment worked. If the treatment did not work then it must be another illness requiring another treatment. The healers did not ask consent of their patients to start a specific treatment. They gave the medicine and said, 'this will cure you'. The healer only asked the patient's permission for the treatment if side-effects were expected. Little or no information was given on the cause of the illness unless the cause was supernatural. No explanation was given about symptoms or what the patient could expect.

> A woman came into Namagan Kante's compound. Namagan was sitting in a chair and the woman stood a few feet away, a bit behind him and told him she wanted medicine for a pain in her belly. Namagan did not look at the woman and did not ask her any questions, he told a child to get the medicine (a bundle of leaves) from his room. The child gave this to the woman. The only advice Namagan told her was not to use everything at once, and the woman left. (Fieldnotes February 2011)

Both healers, in Farabako, and biomedically trained health professionals are not accustomed to giving their patients extensive information. Next, is an example of how little information is given to mothers by members of a vaccination team.

> The midwife and the pharmacist from Nioumamakana came to Farabako to vaccinate the children. The pharmacist wrote down the names of all the children in his ledger and wrote down which vaccinations were necessary in a booklet. He gave this booklet to the midwife who then gave the child the vaccinations. The mother was not told for which diseases the child was being vaccinated. It was not explained why vaccinations were important. The mothers could not read what had been written in their booklets. Pregnant women were given mosquito nets. The midwife opened the plastic bag the net came in to prevent the woman from selling it. All that the midwife said to the woman was, 'sleep under this'. She gave no explanation that the net protects against mosquitoes or that mosquitoes cause malaria. (Fieldnotes February 2011)

That so little information is given, explains why almost all of the women in Farabako told me that they did not know the cause of malaria. Most women do not make the link between malaria and mosquitoes, which in turn explains why so few women in Farabako sleep under mosquito nets (and those who do sleep under nets do not name malaria as the reason).

Healing in Farabako is all about trust, not about giving information. A healer must be trustworthy and the patient must put his trust in the healer. It is my contention that it cannot be taken for granted that the midwives in the clinic can give the information they should give (from a biomedical perspective) and still gain the trust of the pregnant women that they are good healers.

> The midwife Jeneba Kante was worried that Nantènè Keita would have a difficult delivery and she advised her family to send her to Bamako for the birth (as I had done in her previous pregnancy). The villagers understood

> this to mean that Jeneba could not do the delivery. They sent for a nurse who happened to be in a neighbouring village. This imposing lady came and assured everyone that of course she could do the delivery. Luckily for the mother and child the delivery went well, but sadly for the midwife her reputation was damaged. (Fieldnotes January 2012)

The villagers interpreted Jeneba's risk assessment and preventive measures, which were all justified from a biomedical perspective, as a lack of expertise. This led them to no longer trust her. Next, is another example of what the consequences can be of giving too much information.

> A mother from another village came to the clinic with her sick child. The baby was a week old and having convulsions. I gave the baby antibiotics and an anti-malarial. I did not know for sure what kind of infection this child had and I wanted the mother to take the baby to the doctor in Sandama. Because I knew how reluctant parents were to take their children to the doctor, I told the mother that the child had *kɔnɔ* (an illness term denoting a severe infection with convulsions) thinking that this would make the mother understand how serious her child's condition was. I told her that I was not sure if my medicine would work and that she must take the child to the doctor. I added that if she did not do this, the child could die. This surprised the mother and she was shocked. I was perplexed as everyone speaks of *kɔnɔ* as a serious disease killing many children. Why was this mother so surprised when I told her the baby could die? A few days later I heard that she had not followed my advice and had not gone to the doctor, but that luckily the child had recovered. (Fieldnotes March 2007)

Why did this mother not follow my advice and why was she so surprised to hear that her baby could die when everyone knows that kɔnɔ is often fatal? The answer, I now realise lies in the fact that I broke the first rule of being a good healer. I did not reassure her that I could treat the child and I made it psychologically difficult for her by telling her that the baby could die. I was clearly not a good healer, so it should not come as a surprise that she did not follow my advice. I had given too much information.

Lack of privacy and autonomy

In Farabako, women are not autonomous patients and privacy during a consultation with a healer is next to impossible and could even be considered undesirable. This can inhibit women from speaking about health matters. In Farabako, there is certain patient-healer confidentiality; healers do not talk about their patients with others. After a sand divination, for example, a *soma* will not speak with others about the outcome. But there is an exception to this rule; sometimes it is necessary to involve the husband in the treatment of his wife.

The *soma* Musa Kante, gave the following example:

> If a woman comes to me for a treatment of infertility, I will have to inform the husband because the husband must perform a sacrifice for the treatment to be effective. (February 2011)

Musa Kante gave another example of when it was justified to violate patient-healer confidentiality:

> *Jinɛbafe* ['the *jinɛ* wants her'] is an illness whereby a pregnant woman is possessed by a *jinɛ*. In her dreams the woman has sex with the *jinɛ* this is a form of masturbation. *Jinɛbafe* can cause a miscarriage. A woman that suffers from *jinɛbafe* does not want sex with her husband. The husband must understand the cause; otherwise, he might think that she is a bad woman for refusing sex. In this case, it is important that the healer inform the husband. (February 2011)

When I asked if a woman can ask for a treatment without her husband or mother-in-law knowing about it, Fanta Kante, a *musokɔrɔba,* told me the following. If a woman comes to her for a treatment for irregular menstruation, Fanta will ask the woman if her husband knows that she is seeking treatment, because the traditional medicine Fanta uses for this treatment can also cause an abortion. Fanta does treat female family members in secret, but she is very careful when treating women from other villages.

> Here it is dangerous to give medicine to women just like that. The husband will think you are doing evil. This will lead to conflict; the husband will say 'why did you do this without telling me?' (February 2011)

Namagan Kante will treat a woman without telling her husband, especially if the husband is away at the time. But if a woman comes to him and specifically asks him not to tell her husband, he would rather not treat her because then 'something is not right' and if the husband finds out he could 'attack' Namagan. Similarly Fawulen Keita, an herbalist, tells me that it is always the husband or the mother-in-law who comes to him to ask for a treatment for a woman. He has never treated a woman without her husband knowing about it. If a woman asked him to keep a treatment secret he would refuse to treat her because this would create problems. If the woman died, he could be accused of killing her. People will say, 'Why did you give medicine without witnesses?'

Pregnant women are not individual autonomous patients. They need their husband's and mother-in-law's approval to go to the maternity clinic. Women often do not have personal income and are thus dependent on their husbands to pay for a consultation or delivery in the clinic. Women have little privacy in health seeking. If a woman has a health complaint, frequently her husband or mother-in-law asks the healer for help, not the woman herself. The idea of a private consultation was strange to the women of Farabako. During a consultation in the maternity clinic, female friends and neighbours were often present as well as older women who happened to pass by. Privacy is practically impossible in such a small village, but also undesirable. A midwife working on her own is open to gossip. Being open and transparent and having witnesses to her mode of work builds trust; having witnesses protects the midwife against gossip. I would go as far as to say that in Farabako, in the context of health, witnessing can be more important than privacy. This makes it difficult for women to access health care when illnesses are perceived as shameful, or when the woman wants to go against the wishes of her husband, for example in using contraceptives.

Social and economic conditions under which midwives work

The social conditions under which the midwives in Farabako had to work were not always conducive to continuity of care. The midwives had to wait for the male village elders to 'ask them to work' before they could do their job in the clinic. One of the midwives was unable to work in the maternity clinic for a year because of a conflict between specific men in the village and her husband's brother regarding the misappropriation of money destined for a village development project. Therefore, she had not been asked to work in the clinic. Also the *musokɔrɔbaw* proved to have some authority over the midwives. When Kamisajè Kulibali, the youngest midwife, became pregnant, the *musokɔrɔbaw* forbade her to work in the clinic because seeing women in labour would be dangerous for her and her unborn baby.

Another reason that midwives were absent from the clinic was their economic situation. The midwives' pay was so meagre that they were obliged to cultivate millet and peanuts in their fields in order to feed their families. During a village meeting, the men had agreed to help the midwives by working in their fields, but despite these good intentions, this help had not materialized. This meant that the midwives were often not in attendance at the clinic. In December 2009, the doors of the clinic were often closed: one midwife was away working in her fields, 10 kilometres from Farabako and the second midwife went to the goldmines most days to 'look for money'.

An extra burden for the local midwives was that they lodged and fed women from other villages who came to Farabako to deliver at the clinic, just as many women in the village did. The Farabako women seemed to see this as hospitality that was taken for granted and for which they were not paid.

The ethical dilemmas of a new biomedical practice

The findings presented above, demonstrate how the result of the friction between biomedicine and local medical discourse was a new biomedical practice borne out of negotiation that did not function according to standard (Dutch) biomedical procedures. My role as midwife enabled me to identify areas of friction and my anthropological research helped to provide an understanding of how that friction was generated and operated. I now reflect on the outcome of the health care project—the Farabako maternity clinic—as it developed during the first five years using a primarily Dutch midwifery perspective. Ideally, more ethnographic research would be needed to evaluate the project from the perspective of the Farabako community. I suggest that such research should be done by an anthropologist with no medical role in the clinic, since such a role significantly influences what people say and do not say in response to questions. On the other hand, the advantage of my double role was direct access for observing the friction in which biomedicine operated in the clinic.

From a biomedical midwifery perspective, biomedicine's awkward engagement in Farabako did lead to the improvement of the quality of care for pregnant women in certain areas. The pregnant women had access to malaria prophylaxis, iron tablets to treat their (often severe) anaemia, and medication to prevent postpartum haemorrhage. Antibiotics and oral rehydration salts were available for the children. However, perhaps the most important outcome of the health care project for the pregnant women was the realisation that prenatal care was now available and this had the potential to empower them. On the other hand, the implementation of the local maternity clinic led to a new medical practice that from a biomedical perspective raised some ethical dilemmas.

There is a now a risk that the expertise of the *musokɔrɔbaw* will be lost in Farabako. Before the clinic was established, the maternal mortality rate was relatively low. One reason may have been that the *musokɔrɔbaw* did not interfere in the natural process of childbirth. Their assistance consisted of saying incantations and giving moral support. The newly trained midwives can perform pelvic examinations, artificially break membranes and give injections. Their relative inexperience and the pressure to give drugs make it difficult to take no action when appropriate and let nature take its course. Thus, in all likelihood, this clinic (like so many biomedical prenatal care facilities) will increase the medicalization of pregnancy and birth. Medicalization can be seen as an agent of social control (especially over women) as it makes people unnecessarily dependent on medical experts and pharmaceuticals. The biomedical discourse of reproductive risk targets certain populations for intervention. In this way, globalization in the form of biomedicine could even be seen as the re-colonization of a woman's body (Mohanty 2003). On the other hand, responses to new medical technologies are often pragmatic; individuals are not just victims of biomedical hegemony, but rather act on what is perceived by them to be in their best interests (Lock 2001). Women, in Farbako, often embrace new medical possibilities as enabling, particularly in connection with fertility.

Civil society projects, such as the Farabako maternity clinic, can have the undesired effect of masking the state's institutional shortcomings and this can lead to the demobilization of villagers working to improve their health care situation (Brown et al. 2008: 26). The maternity clinic has not solved the health care problems in Farabako. Thinking that the clinic would suffice while it is ill-equipped and poorly staffed to handle obstetric emergencies, can be dangerous; it can lead to a delay in getting to a facility that can perform the necessary intervention. Pregnant women who are at risk for obstetrical complications must still be referred to the capital in order to have access to adequate treatment (and this referral is difficult for the midwives to do).

The implementation of the project has unintentionally led to an increased burden for the women of the village, who house and feed pregnant women coming to deliver in the clinic. In a context of extreme poverty and lack of autonomy for women, the midwives were not always able to work in the clinic, which jeopardized the continuity of care. From a Western feminist perspective, the ideal would be a clinic that works as a space of empowerment, where knowledge about pregnancy is shared (even if only to a limited degree) and where pregnant women would perceive themselves as able and entitled to make health care decisions (Parpart et al. 2002: 240). In this sense, empowerment is about individual conscientization, whereas, a focus on the individual may be problematic in Farabako.

Autonomy, one of the principles of (Western) bioethics,[62] asserts that the individual patient must have a freedom of choice in treatment, thereby inferring individual responsibility (Finkler 2008). In order to make a choice, the patient must have adequate disclosure of pertinent information from their health professional. Patient autonomy depends on the information an individual patient possesses and this information can vary according to social status and gender. In Farabako, 'informed consent' is problematic. First, the individual and the family are one in Farabako; for pregnant women, choices are seldom made autonomously. Second, the *musokɔrɔbaw*, who initially had a monopoly on the (secret) knowledge of pregnancy and birth, may fear a loss of status/power if this kind of knowledge becomes 'common' knowledge. Third, midwives may be reticent to provide information on pregnancy and birth because this information is thought to be dangerous for pregnant women. Furthermore, a 'good healer' in Farabako is expected to assure the patient that everything will be fine, not give extensive information. Midwives are not accustomed to giving their patients information and their patients are not accustomed to

[62] Bioethics is often regarded as universally applicable to biomedical practice. Individual, principle-based bioethics stands on four pillars: beneficence, non-malfeasance, autonomy, and distributive justice, and generally addresses problems relating to the individual and the doctor–patient relationship. It is grounded in individual rights. These 'global' bioethics often work out quite differently in various local settings (e.g. Finkler 2008). The principles of bioethics are not always entirely compatible with local moral discourses in some parts of the world.

receiving it. It is difficult to determine what adequate disclosure is in Farabako; too much information could cause harm (cf. Cox Macpherson and Connolly 2002: 7).

I argue that small-scale private health initiatives can do more harm than good, or at the least provoke ethical dilemmas in circumstances of extreme poverty, gender inequality and poor infrastructure, and should therefore be implemented with caution. The project in Farabako has shown that before implementing a biomedical health care project, ethnographic investigation of reproductive health, as it is locally understood, is needed. It is crucial to pay special attention to a gender-sensitive appraisal of the social relations of health care delivery. Furthermore, there should be accountability for what transpires when health messages are introduced into a community. Patient-provider interactions should be approached as having dynamic on-going effects; this means that community responses must be monitored over time (see also Boonmongkon et al. 2002).

Conclusion

In this chapter I have argued that the maternity clinic in Farabako was a zone of awkward engagement where the so-called universal of biomedicine and the particular of a small Malian village came together. In areas of friction, negotiation of competing discourses and practices took place, which over time resulted in a new biomedical practice. Biomedically trained midwives working in the clinic perceived the dissemination of information on pregnancy and birth as potentially dangerous and equated 'modern' health care with dispensing drugs. The midwives were not autonomous and experienced logistical and existential challenges when referring patients with obstetric complications to a higher level of care. Gender relations and a moral discourse of shame inhibited pregnant women's access to health care facilities and local perceptions of the power of words impacted the quality of care. Biomedicine was made to fit the local context with attendant specific moralities. However, this new practice is in danger of masking institutional shortcomings, increasing women's burdens and leading to the medicalization of birth and pregnancy. An appraisal of the five-year process of engagement thus raises the question of whether this new practice will be effective and justifiable according to Western and local medical-ethical standards.

In this chapter I have explored how claims that biomedicine is universally applicable, work out in the particular context of a private health care project in a non-Western setting. I have shown that local medical ethical discourse can differ in a fundamental way from Western biomedical-ethical discourse. For example, in Farabako, patient autonomy and informed consent were often perceived as undesirable. I found that moral issues, such as what it meant to be a 'good healer' and a 'good woman', were at the core of the friction out of which a new biomedical practice was born. With the descriptive ethnography in this chapter, I have attempted to contribute to a more inclusive engagement between the biomedical discourse and local medical discourse by looking at how patients and healers justify and apply judgements on good medical practice (cf. Fassin and Stoczkowski 2008: 332).

This chapter has confirmed that understanding local medical discourse with its specific moralities is a prerequisite for understanding how mothers use, or do not use, (bio)medical health care facilities in therapy management. The next chapter will focus on the management of children's illness episodes and the multiple social realities of illness in Farabako.

7. ILLNESS NARRATIVES OF THERAPY MANAGEMENT: THE MULTIPLE SOCIAL REALITIES OF ILLNESS

The focus of this chapter is on the particularities of therapy management of children's illnesses in Farabako. What do therapy group members do (and not do) when a child becomes ill and what are the illnesses children suffer from? In international public health research, surveys are used in certain countries to try to explain the high rates of child mortality. The underlying assumption of this research is that a proper understanding of health-seeking behaviour has the potential to reduce delay in diagnosis, increase treatment compliance and implement effective health promotion strategies. My goal was to contribute to this research with a qualitative exploration of how people reach therapy management decisions in the context of their daily, socially and culturally embedded lives and in a context of medical pluralism. In short, I explore the micro-politics of decision-making about health care strategies at a household level (cf. Kamat 2008).

To be more precise, in this chapter, I look beyond cultural knowledge and etiological beliefs to the variations in the therapeutic pathways that household members follow. It is not my goal to reify cultural perceptions and representations of health as independent variables, but to evaluate them in relation to local contingencies, economics and politics of responsibility (cf. Nichter 2008). I first present the various research methods I applied, successively. In my empirical research how various household members represented a child's illnesses was an issue. Therefore, I give a short literature review of how illness narratives can be viewed as performative representations. I then give a case study of the household therapy management of a child's illness episode. The analysis of this case study and additional case studies shed light on the multiple social realities of illness in Farabako, and the various ways illness narratives are produced in the dialogue between respondent and interviewer. The previous chapter highlighted medical ethics and the role of moral discourse in the use of, and access to, (bio)medical health care. This chapter highlights the influence of the local moral and gender discourse on illness representations in Farabako. The chapter shows that in order to understand the therapy management of children's illnesses, one needs to understand that the medical system in Farabako operates as a social system and the details of how that system works are essential to understand child mortality.

Methodology

To first obtain information on what kinds of illness children in Farabako suffer from, I started with a series of free-listing interviews with healers (*musokɔrɔbaw*, *somaw* and herbalists) and parents. I asked all of them to name all the children's illnesses that they knew (see Appendix 2). The illness categories that were named most often, as serious children's illnesses in Farabako, were: *sumaya*, *kɔnɔ* and *kolobɔbana*. The illness term *sumaya* corresponds to the biomedical category of uncomplicated malaria. *Kɔnɔ* was a serious illness with convulsions that was caused by a bird-witch that 'eats' children in the night, according to some. Others spoke of *kɔnɔ* as the aggravated form of *sumaya*; '*sumaya* becomes *kɔnɔ*'. This leads me to believe that *kɔnɔ* corresponds with the biomedical category of cerebral malaria, yet I suspect that the term is also used for all (near) fatal infections. *Kolobɔbana*, 'a fever of the teeth', or literally teething illness, is an illness term used commonly to describe a large range of ailments afflicting very young children. It is considered dangerous and can be fatal. The symptoms often, but not always, include fever, vomiting and diarrhoea. *Kolobɔbana* does not correspond with a single biomedical category. After these free-listing interviews, I had a beginner's vocabulary of childhood diseases in Farabako, and I could talk with parents about their children's illness episodes.

I proceeded by conducting in-depth interviews with mothers, fathers, mother-in-laws and healers about the same illness episode of a child that had taken place in the past year. In total, I collected seventy illness narratives. After asking my respondents to recount the illness episode of a child, I subsequently conducted a survey based on the WHO verbal autopsy list (Soleman et al. 2006) A verbal autopsy includes lists of symptoms used in health surveys to determine the cause of morbidity and mortality in settings where there are no medical records. In this chapter, I focus mainly on the eleven cases in which I had interviews with two or more therapy group members concerning the same illness episode.

Illness narratives as performative representations

Patients' illness narratives have been viewed as a significant source of information in the overall process of arriving at a more complete picture of the clinical problem and are helpful in sorting through and resolving problems of diagnosis and treatment (Kleinman 1988). Although patients' stories are clearly a significant source of data, they are usually treated from the standpoint of the biomedical model of illness, with an emphasis on their utility for physicians to achieve their clinical tasks more effectively.

Simply defined, narrative refers to the stories people tell about various phenomena (including their experiences of illness), while discourse refers to the more general process of verbal communication or conversation. Narrative cannot be examined as a self-contained and independent text; it is a constructed reality. In other words, the significance of a narrative does not depend on the text, but rather on how people construct and use the text to generate particular meanings in specific contexts, and how others interpret and react to the messages they receive (Migliore 2001).

As Good suggests, stories (in this case parents' narratives of their children's illness episode) 'are a means of organizing and interpreting experience, of projecting idealized and anticipated experiences, a distinctive way of formulating reality and idealized ways of interacting with it'. An illness narrative is not simply a way of depicting reality, but a way of constructing it (1994: 80). An illness narrative can be seen as contextual co-production. Together, my respondents and I constructed multiple representations of therapy management in Farabako. Ultimately, I used an interpretive approach in which I attempted to gain insight into the meaning produced by the inter-subjective experience of health and illness (cf. Good 1994). I address the question of how parents' 'storying' their children's illnesses functioned for them, and how this helped them understand and adapt to their problems within the socio-cultural contexts of their lives (cf. Hyden and Mishler 1999).

Narratives can be described as inter-subjective and emerging from negotiations between the narrator and interviewer. These negotiations occur in the context of community and culture. Radley and Billig state, 'People use health beliefs to make themselves accountable *to others* and to articulate *for others* their own position in the world' (1996: 222). In the particular context of my research, 'others' refer to me, the anthropologist-midwife conducting the interviews. The conditions wherein the interviews took place—the research project (and the fact that it was part of a medical development project), the objectives, the interviews, etc.—must be considered while analysing parents' accounts. In other words, illness narratives are not only reflexive accounts of the past; they also create future possibilities. Illness narratives are action oriented and performative. 'Illness narratives may thus respond to the disruption of identity, creating a new place in the social world that resolves conflicts and difficulties rooted in the broad context of the teller's life' (Hunt 2000: 90). Individuals can use a narrative as a strategic device to achieve certain effects in social interactions, for example, to assert their own moral value as parents or to justify their own actions (see also Riessman 1990; Gammeltoft 2006).

In one of the few studies of parents' narratives of their children's illness, Lauritzen (2004) found that parents (notably mothers) seem to base their understandings of their children's health on detailed observations of the child's body, bodily changes and behaviour. At the same time, their accounts of child health were intertwined with presentations of themselves as parents and often as devoted and competent parents. In this process, the values of health and what they understand as important indicators of child health or illness surfaced in interesting ways in their stories. In Farabako, similarly, the accounts of child health by therapy management group members were intertwined with presentations of themselves as competent parents, successful healers, and obedient daughters-in-laws, etc. as is illustrated in the next case study.

Varying accounts of Baba's illness episode: A case study of household therapy management

This case study is based on the illness narratives of one therapy management group. These narratives tell of the illness episode of Baba, a one-year-old boy. The household that forms Baba's therapy management group is headed by: the child's grandfather, Mamaduba Kante; his second wife, Dusuba Sinayogo; the father of the child, Kanda Kante; Kanda's first wife and mother of the child, Fatumata Kante; Kanda's second wife, Sise Kante and ten children (see figure 1). A month before the interview, Baba had been ill for several days, but recovered quickly after having received traditional and biomedical treatment. Each family member had his or her own representation of little Baba's illness episode.

Father Kanda's account

According to Kanda, the first day that Baba was ill he had had a fever in the night. In the morning, his wife Fatumata told Kanda that she had not slept that night. Kanda saw that it was serious because the fever was high and the child had not slept. He decided that he would go to the doctor in Nioumamakana, but first he gave Baba traditional medicine because he was fearful and woke up frightened. Kanda called this illness '*siran*' ('fear'); the child saw something that scared him, 'like a bad dream'. Kanda gave the medicine to protect Baba against sorcery. Sorcerers are considered to be beings that are selfish; they can transform themselves and do evil. Kanda is a *soma.* He told me that someone had wanted to harm him, but could not hurt him because he is strong and protected by his amulets. So that person tried to hurt the child instead.

Kanda based his explanation of what had happened on what he discovered during a sand divination. As a *soma*, he consults the sand when a child has a headache or a stomach-ache that does not go away. He sees in the sand if the child will live or not, and which medicine will help. In the case of his own child, Baba, the sand told him that the child would live. However, he said that even if the sand had said the child would die, he would have taken Baba to the doctor anyway, although it probably would not have helped.

Kanda took Fatumata and the child on the motorcycle to the doctor in Nioumamakana. The doctor diagnosed *sumaya* (uncomplicated malaria) and gave him a bottle of syrup and tablets that cost 2,250 FCFA (3.5 euros). The father found the treatment to be effective as on the second day, the child was much better.

The symptoms that Kanda mentioned spontaneously were fever, not sleeping, and fear. Only after I asked him directly, did he mention that Baba was also coughing and vomiting, and that his fontanel was sunken.

Mother Fatumata's account

According to Fatumata, the first day that Baba was ill, he vomited and had a

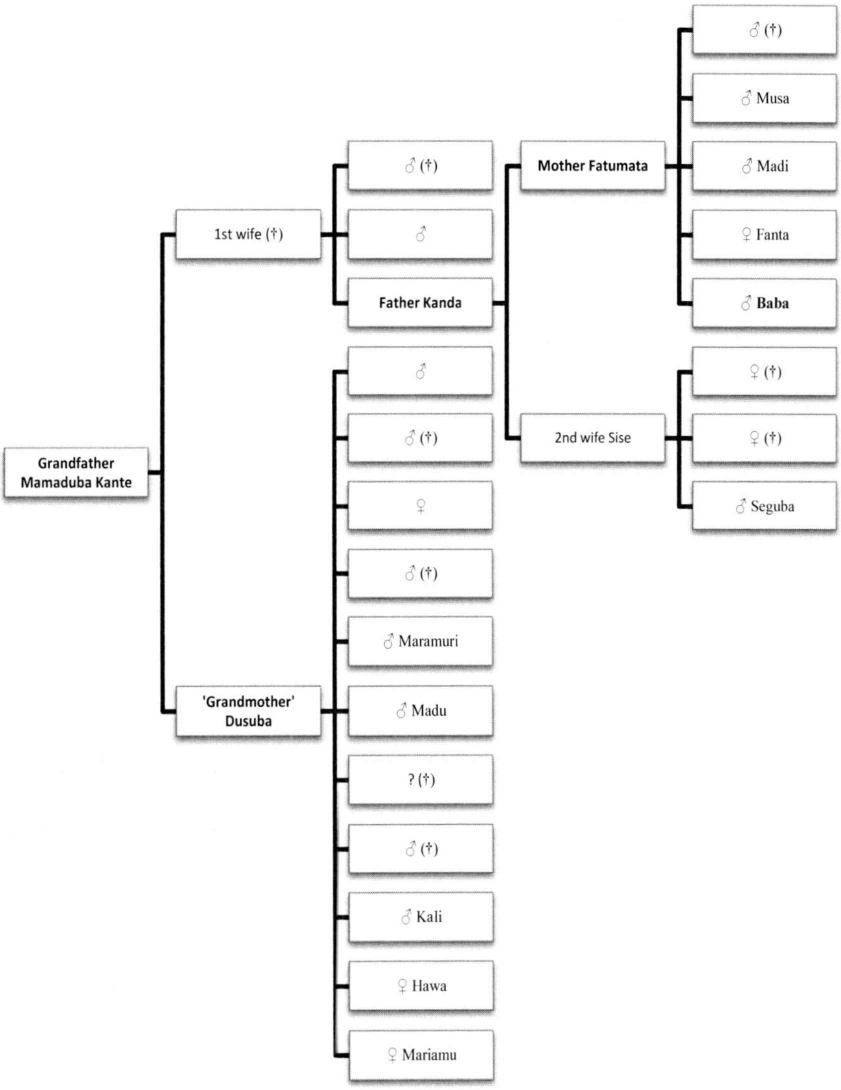

Figure 1. Household members of infant Baba's therapy management group (where no name is mentioned this person is deceased or no longer living in Farabako)

fever. Fatumata showed Baba to her husband, Kanda. They saw that it was serious because the infant did not drink. Fatumata also showed Baba to her mother-in-law Dusuba. It was so serious that they decided not to give him traditional medicine first. Although Kanda and Dusuba knew right away that Baba had *sumaya* (uncomplicated malaria), Fatumata did not know what it was. Kanda took the child on the motorcycle to the doctor in Nioumamakana. The doctor diagnosed *sumaya* and gave syrup and tablets. Fatumata does not know how much the medicine cost. She found the treatment to be effective.

After four days the infant was better, he drank and ate again. He no longer vomited and was playing. Fatumata did not give Baba traditional medicine. Dusuba had traditional medicine for *kolobɔbana* (fever of the teeth), but Fatumata saw that this was another illness.

Fatumata spontaneously mentioned the symptoms of fever, vomiting, not drinking, and not playing. After I asked her directly, she also said the child had lost weight.

'Grandmother' Dusuba's account

On the first day of Baba's illness, Fatumata (his mother) showed her the infant, it was as if the child was injured in his chest—she saw that it was *mugu*. She saw this because when she picked the child up, he started to cry. *Mugu* is caused by children falling while playing. She gave the child a traditional medicine called *kolokolo*,[63] but this did not work so she tried another medicine, *kɔrɔngɛyin*,[64] which was also not effective.

On the third day, Baba had a fever and was always sleeping. Dusuba now thought his illness was becoming *sandafɛ*[65] (a serious illness with convulsions). Kanda decided to take the child to the doctor. Kanda said that it was not *mugu*, but he did not say what he thought it was. The same day the infant was better. Dusuba does not know what the doctor said or did because Kanda did not tell her. She knows that Kanda performed a sand divination, but he told her nothing about it.

The symptoms that Dusuba mentioned spontaneously were pain in the chest, crying when picked up, fever, and sleepiness. After I asked her directly, she also named coughing, difficulty breathing, diarrhoea, vomiting, a swollen belly, a stiff neck, spasms, loss of weight and paleness of the skin.

Baba's case is interesting for it shows the multiple representations of one illness episode by members of the same therapy management group (see Figure 2). Each member of the therapy management group agreed that little Baba had had a fever and was taken to the doctor. But each member gave a very distinct account of events. Each person emphasised specific aspects of what

---

[63] Pericopsis laxiflora, Bailleul (2000).

[64] Opilia amentacea, ibid.

[65] *Sandafɛ* is different from '*kɔnɔ*'. Both denote a serious illness with convulsions. With *sandafɛ*, the child has open fists, while with *kɔnɔ* the fists are clenched.

had happened. To understand how and why these accounts differed, one needs information on the context in which these narratives were told.

Therapy group member	Symptoms	Diagnosis	Therapy	Duration of illness
Father	Fever Fear	*Siran*	Sand divination Traditional medicine Doctor	2 days
Mother	Fever Vomiting	*Sumaya*	Doctor	4 days
'Grandmother'	Chest pain Fever Sleepiness	*Mugu* *Sandafɛ*	Traditional medicine Doctor	3 days

Figure 2. Multiple representations of one illness episode

Context in which the narrative was told

It is not clear if Mamaduba Kante, the grandfather, was consulted during Baba's illness episode (no one mentioned it), but it is highly likely that he was, as he was the head of the extended family (*dutigi*) and lived in the same compound with Kanda and his wives. Mamaduba was in his seventies. He was the oldest inhabitant of Farabako and bedridden at this time. Sadly he died a few months after the interview I had with him. Mamaduba was known for his knowledge of children's illnesses. He was a *soma*, as is his son Kanda.

Of Mamaduba's sons, Kanda is the eldest son who is currently living in Farabako. Kanda is a good-looking man approximately 35 years old. He has two wives and six (living) children. Kanda, as almost all men of his age group and older, had not had formal schooling and cannot read and write. He speaks only a few words of French. Kanda makes money doing sand divinations in Bamako and the nearby goldmines. In 2009, he spent two months doing divinations in Kayes. A sand divination for a client wanting to get a job can bring in up to 50,000 FCFA (80 euros) and can take years. A sand divination to treat an illness is only paid for if the treatment is effective. Kanda seemed a bit more cosmopolitan than most men in Farabako. He sometimes wore colourful tracksuits with gold chains rather than a boubou (a wide sleeved robe worn by men in much of West Africa). His wives were among the best-dressed women in the village. Kanda seemed a bit more prosperous than the other men in Farabako.

In 2007, Kanda told me that he had a 'photograph' of the snake *jinɛ* that roams around Farabako. The 'photograph' turned out to be a photocopy of a drawing of a snake that Kanda had drawn himself after having seen the snake *jinɛ* in his dream. He sold this drawing to me for 10,000 FCFA (15 euros) while letting me know that this was a special price for me.[66] In Bamako, he sold them for much more. Kanda told me that this 'photo' of the snake *jinɛ* of Farabako would protect me.

Of all the *somaw* in Farabako, Kanda was the only *soma* who did not collaborate with me medically. The other *somaw* consulted me when they thought one of their patients needed modern medicine. I consulted with them when I was ill or when a patient came to me with symptoms that I did not recognize. The *somaw* had no problem with me treating their patients. They told me that they found Western medicine and traditional medicine to be complementary. Only Kanda seemed to have another opinion, and did not want me to treat his patients.[67]

Kanda did not object to his second wife Sise delivering her baby at the maternity clinic, but he did object to paying the bill afterwards. The midwife, Jeneba Kante, on her own initiative had hiked up the price for the delivery as a penalty because Sise had not come for prenatal check-ups. Kanda refused to pay the bill for the delivery because the midwife 'had not done anything'. When I asked what he meant, my translator explained that the midwife had not given an injection thus she had not done anything special. Kanda is the only villager who (in this oblique way) voiced his doubts on the usefulness of the clinic.[68] Kanda's account of his son's illness was a story of sorcery and sand divination that positioned him firmly as a *soma*.

Fatumata Kante, Baba's mother, is Kanda's first wife. She is approximately 28 years old and has delivered five children. Her first child died at one due to a 'fever of the teeth' (*koloboɔbana*) for which she had not sought biomedical help. In 2007, when I asked Fatumata her reproductive life history, one of the

---

[66] I paid for chickens, a goat and a sheep that were needed as sacrifices during divinations done for me by another Kante family member. I also gave money for a ceremony to honour the fetishes of the Kante family. But, Kanda was the only one to ask directly for money for his services.

[67] While I was walking through the village one morning I saw a woman who I had not seen before. She had a bandage on her foot. She was clearly in pain and leaning heavily on a crutch. I asked her if she wanted me to look at her foot. She said no. When I asked why not, she told me that she had been to a doctor and that he had 'cut her with scissors' and that she was afraid of the pain. When I told her that I promised I would only look, that I would not hurt her, she still refused. She told me that she was a patient of Kanda. She was from another village, but was staying in Farabako for her treatment. She also told me that Kanda did not want me to treat her. A month later she was still limping badly. The week before I was to leave Farabako and return to the Netherlands she hung around in the compound where I was staying. She had seen that I had treated another young woman with an infection on her leg, and that this girl was now walking again without pain. She did not ask outright for my help and I did not dare treat her for fear of ruining the relationship I had with Kanda.

[68] This is not to say that Kanda and I didn't get along, we did. He was always friendly and came to greet me every morning (his compound was next to the one I was staying in). When I was ill, he brought me tea bags. It is a running joke that he wants to marry my daughter.

questions I asked was if she had ever been to a hospital. She told me she had been to a hospital five years ago when her husband had beaten her so badly that she had to seek medical help in Bamako. She also told me that the difficult relationship between her and her husband was the reason she wanted to use contraceptives, but she was pretty sure he would not approve. She said:

> Men want many children. A woman with few children is looked down upon, but mostly by men. Men want children quickly one after the other, women don't.

Fatumata was unable to use contraceptives and had a baby boy, Baba, in 2008.

Fatumata's household is not always a harmonious one; she openly dislikes her co-wife Sise, and they quarrel a lot. Fatumata insinuated during our interviews that Sise did not take good care of her own children and did not help out with the household chores. During my visit in November 2009, Fatumata and Kanda had been fighting and Fatumata was visibly unhappy. No one wanted to tell me what the fight had been about, but the tension in their household was palpable.

In 2008, Fatumata had a personal income of 25,000 FCFA (40 euros) from cultivating her field. In 2009, she had made another 25,000 FCFA by working in the gold mine. In that year she had not asked anyone for financial help. She told me that even when one of her children is very ill she does not ask others for money (except for her husband and her husband's brother). She said that she has shame; she is afraid they would say no. If one of her children is ill, she gives them traditional medicine for a few days. If this does not work, she would take the child to a doctor, but transport is a problem: 'It is difficult to ask someone when your husband is away'. Fatumata was happy that medicine was now available in the pharmacy in Farabako.

> Now, with your arrival at Farabako, you have helped motherhood a lot. Our children are taken care of easily these days and this puts us at ease and saves us from shame. We would like it a lot if you would carry on bringing us help, especially medical help. The care brought to the motherhood of Farabako assists enormously in the realm of the children's health and that of the mother's. We are taken care of at home without the worry of having to go elsewhere, which costs a lot. And all this is thanks to you, Dusuba [=LH]; this is why we are always ready to talk to you.

My translator, Abdulaye Traore, asked me several times to let Fatumata work in the clinic. He told me that he found that Fatumata was very intelligent. One day he brought Fatumata to me and asked her to read to me to persuade me to let Fatumata work in the maternity clinic. She immediately took on a humble demeanour and sat on a small stool, much lower than the one I was sitting on, and with great difficulty read aloud a few sentences out of a book. This was the book Abdulaye had been teaching her to read from. She knew these few sentences by heart. I found this kind of initiative and ambition unusual for women in Farabako. Fatumata wanted to work in the maternity clinic with me. In her account of her son's illness, she stressed her faith in doctors and biomedicine, which was the opposite position of her husband.

Dusuba Sinayogo is the second and youngest wife of Mamaduba Kante and was the co-wife of Kanda's mother (who is deceased). She is now the only *musokɔrɔba* in the household. She is in her late forties and has had eleven children of whom four have died.

Dusuba is a potter, as many blacksmith women are. She sells her clay pots and the peanuts she has harvested at the market in the nearby village of Sakorodaba. Last year this brought in 50,000 FCFA (80 euros). If she needs money, Dusuba has no one to ask because everyone knows that 'she has nothing' (which means she will have difficulty repaying). She can't ask Kanda for money because there is a conflict between them (that she does not want to talk about).[69] She has asked men of the Keita family for money when one of her children was seriously ill, but did not get any. She could ask her friend (a *musokɔrɔba* of the Kante family) for money but she usually doesn't have any either. She complained that Kanda's wives do nothing for her. Her husband cannot help her because he is ill (and old). For practical support she must turn to her sons, but they are still relatively young. Her oldest son often drinks alcohol and she worries about him. Dusuba presented herself to me as a woman with a very small support network and as a victim of uncaring family members.

Dusuba said that many people come to her when their children are ill. She is good at treating *sandafɛ* (a kind of *kɔnɔ*), *dino* (cold) and difficulty breathing. She acquired this knowledge of traditional medicine from the mother of the village chief (a woman of the Keita family). Dusuba had given her clothes as payment for this knowledge. She told me that in the past year she has treated five children (not all in her own household). Although Dusuba extolled her knowledge of traditional medicine for children's illnesses, Fatumata, her daughter-in-law, said that she only had medicine for one illness—*kolobɔbana*. Dusuba gave an account of the child's illness that stressed her importance in the household as a *musokɔrɔba* with indispensable knowledge of traditional medicine.

[69] Structurally, in the Mande world, there is competition between the sons of co-wives for family resources. This is possibly the reason Dusuba does not get along well with Kanda, the son of her former co-wife.

Conflicting stories

Symptoms and diagnoses

As was the case with Baba's illness, in other cases, it was rare that two people within a therapy group named the same symptoms of an illness episode (see Appendix 5). For example, in the case of one-year-old Baba's symptoms, his mother named vomiting and fever, his father only fear and fever and the grandmother named pain in the chest and fever. Very few symptoms were named spontaneously. Similarly, the grandmother of Bobo Kante (household 8), in an interview the day after her grandson had died, named only skin lesions when I asked what was wrong with the child. His mother named only diarrhoea as a symptom. I had seen the child the day he died; he had had a fever, diarrhoea, and was extremely emaciated with oedema of the face and feet. In the case of the five-year-old Mambi Kante (household 9), the only symptom of his illness episode that his mother mentioned was fear; the child was afraid of something 'he saw'. Only after I asked her specifically, did she also name diarrhoea, a swollen belly, difficulty breathing and erythema over all of the child's body.

The few times that all members of a therapy group named the same symptoms, they gave differing diagnoses. For example, in the illness episode of Faseme Kante (household 4) all the members of the therapy group named diarrhoea as symptom, but each gave one of the following diagnoses: *kolobɔbana* (fever of the teeth), *sɔgɔsɔgɔ* (coughing) and *sumaya* (uncomplicated malaria). The one therapy group whose members all gave the same diagnosis (of *sumaya*) for an illness episode, each named different symptoms (household 2). In the majority of cases, members of a therapy group named symptoms and diagnoses that differed.

Mothers, especially young mothers, seldom named a diagnosis; they spoke in terms of symptoms. The same was true for young fathers (unless they were *somaw*). Both often told me that they did not know what illness their child had, and left it to their elders to name the illness.

Diagnoses sometimes changed over time. For example, in the case of Mambi Kante (household 9), the child's father, a *soma*, first gave the diagnosis of *jinɛbana*, an illness caused by *jinɛw*. He sought treatment for his son from a *soma* living close to the Guinean border, a specialist in curing diseases caused by jinn. When this therapy did not prove to be effective, the father concluded that it must be another illness—*sumaya*—and he took his son to a doctor.

Treatment

As for Baba's illness episode, the accounts by various therapy group members of the treatment given to a sick child often differed. For example, one mother told me how she had bought Nivaquine tablets (an anti-malarial) from a travelling drug seller and paracetamol syrup at the maternity clinic in Farabako for her son who was ill. Her husband said nothing to me about the treatment his wife had already given the child, but told me that he took the child to the herbalist and bought Amoxycycline (an anti-biotic) at the maternity clinic. The mother-in-law did not mention the herbalist or the antibiotics, she stressed the role of her other son whose incantations had cured the child (household 7). How and if fathers and mothers and mothers-in-law communicated about therapy choices was not always clear. The mother did not always know what action the father had undertaken and vice versa. Men often did not mention that their wives had consulted the *musokɔrɔbaw*. For example, one father knew that his wife had taken their child to the *musokɔrɔbaw*, but he did not know which *musokɔrɔba* his wife had consulted or what she had said or done.

There were often also conflicting accounts of who had paid for the treatment. Usually fathers told me that they had paid for the treatment, while several mothers-in-law assured me that they had paid for the treatment themselves (e.g. household 6).

Duration of illness

Within one therapy management group, there were often conflicting accounts of how long the illness episode had lasted. This was also the case in the accounts of Baba's illness episode, although the difference of two to four days was not as great as in narratives from other households. In the interviews, I asked the respondents to describe the first day their child was ill. Mothers often started counting on the day they took action; they seldom counted the days leading up to the full-blown illness. Fathers, who had been absent, often started counting from the day they saw their child, and often did not know how long the child had been ill before they came back. The discrepancies were sometimes quite significant. One mother said her son had been ill for thirty days, while her mother-in-law told me the child had been ill for ninety days (household 3).

Not all therapy management groups gave conflicting stories of an illness episode. Of the eleven households for which I was able to interview two or more members of the therapy management group, three household members told similar narratives. These cases concerned families that were a bit more prosperous and who had extensive ties with Bamako or had migrated to the outskirts of Bamako. For example, one of these households (household 2) was headed by Fasuru Keita. Fasuru is a merchant who owns the only (small) shop in Farabako where he sells rice, sugar, coffee and candy. He is also the local gold buyer. He buys the gold that inhabitants of Farabako have found in the mines nearby. He owns a motorcycle and frequently goes to Bamako. His wife, Masitan, sometimes helps out in the maternity clinic. She has had some schooling and is one of the two women in the village who can read and write. Fasuru, his wife and his 'aunt' all named similar symptoms and mentioned the diagnosis *sumaya* when describing one of their children's illness episodes. All members also stressed the importance of biomedicine.

Health surveys: The child gets lost in the telling

Why do members of the same therapy management group often tell such differing stories about their sick child? And, what can one conclude from such conflicting accounts of one and the same illness episode? I will attempt to answer these questions in this section.

The illness narratives presented above say little about the biological facts of children's illnesses in Farabako. They do not fulfil a Western health professional's need for (biological) explanation and scientific closure. I still do not know from which (biomedical categories of) illnesses little Baba and the other children in Farabako suffer. There is no such thing as an 'actual illness episode', or if there is, an illness narrative cannot 'uncover' it. Language (and health surveys) do not have a direct link to the 'objective reality' of a disease, but rather they are a link to multiple social realities of illness. The narratives did give insight into how ideal gender roles are affirmed and contested and how medical knowledge is gendered within the medical pluralism of Farabako.

Positioning within medical pluralism and status within the household

So why all these differing stories about the same sick child? One reason, I argue, is that various therapy management group members had different stakes in telling me the story of their child's illness episode. My stake in listening to their stories was to gain information that might improve the health situation for children. It is possible that the respondents' stakes in talking to me were not so much about the health of their children. Perhaps they did not see me as someone who could improve their health situation. I believed that I was bringing 'the truth' of biomedicine to Farabako, while they perceived 'my medicine' as one of many alternatives. Biomedicine was perceived as complementary, not a replacement for traditional medicine. If many illnesses are seen to be caused by sorcery, and living and dying are determined by God, what can one midwife from *Peyiba* do? They did see me as bringing money and opportunity to their village and were keen on nurturing the relationship between the Netherlands and Farabako. My respondents' stakes included being connected to the maternity clinic (and money from the Netherlands) and receiving free medical consultations during my stay. Their stakes also included asserting their own status/power/importance in therapeutic decision-making and treatment within local medical pluralism.

Positioning oneself within medical pluralism cannot be seen separately from relational power dynamics in a household. In the case study above, the father, Kanda Kante, was the only *soma* in Farabako who did not want me to treat his patients. His account of his son's illness is a story of sorcery and sand divination, thus firmly positioning him as a *soma*. His wife Fatumata wanted to work in the maternity clinic with me. In her account of her son's illness, she stressed her faith in doctors and biomedicine. Dusuba is the second wife of Kanda's father. She and Kanda, the son of her former co-wife, had a structural authority conflict. Her position (although she was the only *musokɔrɔba* in the household) was difficult as her husband was dying. Her account of the child's illness stressed her importance as a *musokɔrɔba* with indispensable knowledge of traditional medicine.

Contesting/affirming ideal gender roles

In most narratives, men presented themselves as good providers, women presented themselves as obedient wives and daughters-in-law, and mothers-in-law presented themselves as knowledgeable and indispensable for protecting the family. Thereby, all affirmed their ideal gender role and status within the household. As we have seen in Baba's illness episode, his father presented himself as a devoted parent and good provider. The mother deferred to her husband and mother-in-law. And the mother-in-law was important in protecting the family. But, illness narratives were also a medium by which ideal gender roles could be contested without openly criticising the gender order. In her narrative, the mother Fatumata positioned herself firmly on the side of biomedicine which was a position opposing her husband's position of a *soma* who did not want to collaborate with biomedicine. Ten months earlier, in an illness narrative about another of Fatumata's children, she had stressed her husband's knowledge and that it was not necessary at the time to give the child anything other than his traditional medicine. In the context of her unhappy marriage and recent fights she was having with her husband, it is possible that her most recent narrative was an act of defiance. Illness narratives gave respondents an opportunity to complain about other members of the therapy management group

In many illness narratives, mothers-in-law presented themselves as powerful, competent and indispensable. They sometimes spoke of their daughters-in-law as being incompetent, especially if their relationship was not a harmonious one. Mothers-in-law protect the family. They promote their sons and keep a watchful, critical eye on their daughters-in-law. The younger the mother is and the fewer daughters-in-law in the household, the lower the mother's status. This makes it difficult for a young mother to make therapy decisions herself. In households where the father's birth mother is deceased and a co-wife is the eldest woman in the household, young women have more freedom to undertake action on their own.

Gendered knowledge: 'Women know nothing'

Fatumata, a young mother, told me that she did not know what illness Baba had. When she saw that her child was ill, she immediately consulted her husband and mother-in-law. In talks with me, young mothers gave the impression that they did not feel capable or entitled to take action when their children were ill and that they did not have the knowledge necessary to do so.

When speaking about health matters, my male respondents often stressed that (young) 'women know nothing'. Fathers give their knowledge to their sons, not their daughters. Women give their knowledge to their daughters not their sons. Women's knowledge is separate from men's. The *musokɔrɔbaw* have their own personal secret knowledge of children's illnesses and their treatments. This knowledge is not standardised and is not freely shared with young mothers. Mothers will wait until their daughters are in menopause before sharing their knowledge of incantations. Most of my respondents had had no formal schooling and thus no source of knowledge other than the older women and what they saw and heard in the village.

When I asked young mothers to name the childhood illnesses they knew, in almost all cases, the mothers could name only a few illnesses (two or three). These were often illnesses they had seen recently in their own children or in neighbours' children. For example, when I asked a mother with six children which children's illnesses she could name, she answered:

> *Sandafɛ* [a serious illness with convulsions], *sɔgɔsɔgɔ* [coughing] and *kolobɔbana* [fever of the teeth]. That's all I know, these are the illnesses that my children have had. (Narama Keita, 27 yrs, January 2009)

When asked, Soro Keita, a first time young mother, could name only two children's illnesses she knew: *sinkɔrɔntalen* (pneumonia) which could be treated by the *musokɔrɔbaw* and *kunkolodimi* (headache) which could be treated with paracetamol.

It is not the task of young women to make therapeutic choices. If a young mother sees that her child is ill she should consult her mother-in-law and her husband and leave it up to them to decide on the course of action. Young mothers were instructed by their mother-in-law in how to use traditional medicine, for example, if it needed to be boiled or should be used to wash with or to drink. For the use of medicine against sorcery, the husband must instruct the mother, as one *soma* told me:

> There are medicines that protect against sorcery. The father must tell the mother how to use this medicine because women know nothing of this. (Namagan Kante, 45 yrs, January 2009)

If a mother consulted a *musokɔrɔba,* she would not always tell her husband what the older woman had said or which treatment she had recommended. These consultations were women's business as Namagan went on to tell me:

> Women know which *musokɔrɔbaw* can treat which illness; I do not know this because I do not consult the *musokɔrɔbaw*.

In many cases when a child fell ill, the mother would consult the eldest woman in the household who would advise her which traditional medicine to use or which other *musokɔrɔbaw* to consult. Often only after traditional medicine was given and found not to be effective would the husband take action and look for alternatives such as buying medicine from a drug seller or taking the child to a doctor.

If a father took his sick child to a doctor he would not always tell his wife what the doctor had said, and women did not always ask. If women went along to the doctor, and the doctor did not volunteer information on the nature of the child's illness, the women were not accustomed to asking the doctor questions. Communication between household members about health matters did not always occur. Consensus within the therapy management group did not seem to be a priority in Farabako; ultimately, it was the father of the child who decided on the action to be taken.

Young women are given little information and are told they know nothing. They have embodied the notion that they do not have the knowledge necessary to treat their sick child. I believe that this is one of the reasons why young women in Farabako wait for others to take action when their child is ill. This passivity is further reinforced by the women's lack of resources, as this next case illustrates:

> Salimata Kante saw that her son Mambi was ill; he had 'fear' (*siran*), he 'saw something'. She took him to an old man to ask for traditional medicine and shea oil to rub onto the child's skin. The old man gave this free of charge. After this, she undertook no further action and waited three months for her husband to return and take over the care, and take the child to a doctor (household 9). (November 2009)

I wonder if this embodiment of inferiority does not also make it difficult for young mothers to use the knowledge they *do* have in the therapy management of their children's illnesses, as the next case demonstrates.

> Rokia Keita came to talk to me about the fatal illness episode of one of her twin girls. The first twin had died of '*sumaya* in the belly'. While Rokia was telling this story, the surviving twin, Nasira, was sleeping in her lap. After the interview had been going on for about a half an hour, Nasira woke up and I realised that she was seriously ill. She was coughing, had a fever and difficulty breathing. I examined her and suspected pneumonia. All during the interview Rokia had said nothing to me about this twin. It seemed as if she did not realise how ill the child was. I asked her why she did not bring the child to my attention. Was it that she was waiting for me to notice her myself? Rokia told me no, it was because she did not think the child was that ill, just that she had had a cough for the past three days. When I asked specifically, she told me that the first twin had had these symptoms too, before she died. Yet she said nothing. (Fieldnotes January 2009)

Even if young mothers, from first-hand experience, have knowledge of symptoms of serious illnesses, it is not clear whether they feel they can or should use this knowledge in therapy management, or that they are able and entitled to make health care decisions.

Gendered diagnoses: diagnose and treat that which you know

Because the production of knowledge is gendered, it is not surprising that diagnoses are gendered as well. In the case study above, the father Kanda is a *soma*. He diagnosed *siran* ('fear'), an illness caused by sorcery. He was able to diagnose this with the help of a sand divination. He treated this illness with traditional medicine. His mother-in-law diagnosed *mugu*, an illness caused by falling during play, and later she diagnosed *sandafɛ*. She was able to diagnose this because of her extensive knowledge of children's illnesses. Her treatment consisted of traditional medicine. The mother, Fatumata, stressed that she did not know what illness her child had.

The link between clinical symptoms and diagnosis seems to be a biomedical fixation that is not accorded the same importance in Farabako (cf. Feierman and Janzen 1992). The diagnosis given by villagers seems to be more dependent on the age, gender and expertise of the person giving the diagnosis than on the symptoms. *Kolobɔbana* (fever of the teeth) and *kɔnɔ* (caused by a bird witch) are diagnoses usually only given and treated by (female) *musokɔrɔbaw*. Sorcery, *siran*, *jinɛbana*, *dabali* (illnesses caused by witches or *jinɛw*) are diagnoses only given and treated by (male) *somaw* and male herbalists. Mothers, especially young mothers, seldom name a diagnosis themselves. They speak in terms of symptoms. The same is true for young fathers (who are not *somaw*).

The illness narratives gave insight into the multiple social realities of illness. They demonstrated how therapy group members positioned themselves within medical pluralism and status in the household. They also illustrated the ideal gender roles and how medical knowledge is gendered in Farabako.

Fitting narratives into biomedical discourse

I set out to study the household therapy management of children's illnesses, and became aware of my deeply ingrained biomedical assumptions about medical language. It was my biomedical assumption that symptoms in a disease category simply reflect their association with an objective reality. I attempted to elicit illness narratives as a means of placing local knowledge in relation to the 'truth' of biomedicine. I used narratives to connect individual patients with *my* medical knowledge and experience. I tried to fit information from my respondents into my own biomedical categories of symptoms, diagnosis and treatment of children's illnesses, and this proved rather futile. In Farabako, diagnoses were sometimes the result of power-related aspects of the consultative procedure, rather than being linked to clinical symptoms (see also Castle 1994). It turned out to be more fruitful to explore the view that diseases are not constituted as natural entities, but rather as social realities (cf. Good 1977: 25). In this view, medical language has more than just a naming function—it constructs the disease.

Interpretation of illness is produced in the dialogue between respondent and interviewer. Illness narratives do not unlock 'local knowledge'. Knowledge is relational and interaction produces and manipulates knowledge (cf. Pool 1994). The 'local knowledge' derived from the participation and interviews with the villagers, as represented in this chapter, reflect and endorse *my* external analysis of problems and solutions. I take responsibility for shaping the research and interpreting the events. While I describe the stories of the villagers of Farabako, it is *my* involvement, my bias, and my values and interpretations that impose the framework that forms this narrative (cf. Mosse 2005: 14). I chose the topics and I recorded the information according to what I found relevant. I was researching the local model of health and illness while at the same time endorsing the biomedical model of health in the maternity clinic. Of course, this influenced the kind of information my informants gave me.

Focusing on the narratives and trying to fit them into my biomedical discourse was not productive. Looking at the conditions underlying the research and their impact on the type of account furnished by the respondents turned out to be a more successful way of gaining information on how individuals address relational power dynamics and gender constructions of ideal roles within the household production of health. These stories were not only talking about a medical practice, but also about a social system (cf. Nichter 2008; Janzen 1978).

Conclusion

In this chapter, I argued that health surveys and illness narratives of parents say little about the 'actual illness episode' of the child, and that the child gets lost in the telling. The way parents narrate their child's illness episode can say more about how the parents wish to position themselves within medical pluralism and how they want to present themselves towards the interviewer (and her development project of the maternity clinic) than how therapy management actually took place. The 'actual illness episode' of the child was often hidden in the illness narratives of the parents. As a consequence, I did not obtain the information I set out to acquire, namely information that I thought would help to improve (biomedical) health care provision for children. I cannot say what diseases these children had and after how many days what treatment was given to them with accuracy.

What has been presented here is a representation that I co-produced with my respondents during the course of my stay with them (see also Pool 1994). This does not mean that what are presented here as local beliefs and understandings bear no relation to how people in Farabako think about, and in particular talk about the therapy management of children's illnesses. By articulating the relationship between my assumptions, my methodology, my findings and my conclusions (comparing narratives and participant observation to understand the context in which narratives are told), I believe (cf. Thorne 2009) that this representation of therapy management in Farabako has gone beyond just being a good story told somewhere to someone at some time.

These illness narratives, together with months of participant observation, did turn out to be a useful tool to learn about the social system that is the 'medical system' in Farabako. This chapter has shed light on the (gender)relational power dynamics in the household production of health in Farabako. The next chapter will continue to focus on therapy management, and the lack of fit between biomedical and local medical discourses. First, however, I focus on the particular case of the therapy management of malnutrition in Farabako.

8. THERAPY MANAGEMENT OF MALNUTRITION: A SHAMEFUL ILLNESS OR A PROBLEM OF FOOD?

In the previous chapter, I illustrated why an understanding of local medical and moral discourse is a prerequisite for understanding therapy management of children's illnesses in general, in Farabako. In this chapter, I focus on the specific case of malnutrition. My argument is that a biomedical discourse and local medical discourse must be negotiated to find a common ground—an overlap—an aspect that fits both discourses. Only when this overlap is found can an (medical) intervention be acceptable.

> Anger wells up in me. I had to suppress my anger; it sometimes wells up in me like a blast of adrenaline. Like today when a woman with an extremely malnourished and sick child came to me asking for medicine. Her little boy was two years old, he used to be able to walk, but he had stopped; his legs were just too thin. The mother asked me for medicine so that he could walk again. I asked her how long he was sick; she answered 'a year'. I asked her if she had gone to the doctor; she said no. I asked her what she had done for her child. She said she gave him tea with sugar. How to understand this passiveness? How can you see your child wasting away for a year and do nothing but give him tea? (Fieldnotes January 2007)

As a midwife, in Mali for the first time, I found the seeming passiveness of mothers incomprehensible and extremely frustrating in cases of what I diagnosed as malnourishment in their child. As an anthropologist, I wanted to understand how it could be that mothers and I were looking at the same symptoms of extreme emaciation, yet coming to such disparate conclusions regarding an appropriate response. I conducted interviews and focus group discussions with mothers, elderly women (*musokɔrɔbaw*) and traditional healers (*somaw*) on their perceptions, treatment and therapy management of (what I call) malnutrition. My goal was to come to an understanding of the lack of fit between the dominant Western biomedical discourse on malnutrition and local conceptions in Farabako. I was in the ideal position to observe this lack of fit because I was giving biomedical treatment to children who were severely malnourished in the maternity clinic. I used my frustration as a tool to gain insight into the problem of (what I call) malnutrition.

In this chapter, I first describe what could be considered as causes of malnutrition according to biomedical discourse. That the biomedical discourse on malnutrition did not fit well in Farabako will become clear in a case study of the local therapy management of (what I call) malnutrition. I then describe the local medical discourse on malnutrition (*sede*). Subsequently, I present a second case study of my biomedical treatment of a child suffering from severe malnutrition. In the discussion, I return to the lack of fit between local and biomedical discourses and argue that malnutrition in Farabako is not primarily about food.

Biomedical and public health discourse on malnutrition

Despite abundant research in Mali on the economic, agricultural, educational and cultural factors influencing malnutrition (Sidibé et al. 2007; Teft et al. 2003; Simon et al. 2002; Dettwyler 1994, 1989, 1986), and despite nutritional programs, malnutrition is still endemic in Mali as it is in much of sub-Sahara Africa.

While the relationship between poverty, household food (in)security and child malnutrition is well established, measures of socioeconomic status have shed little light on the mechanisms by which malnutrition is created and/or prevented (Simon et al. 2002; Millard 1994). There is no single causal factor of severe malnutrition. Even when children share the same diet, some can develop severe malnutrition while others do not.

Young and Jaspers (2006: 7), building on Millard's (1994) causal model of child mortality, present a three-tiered conceptual framework of child malnutrition. Proximate causes of child malnutrition, such as protein deficiency aggravated by infection, are influenced by three main categories of intermediate factors: access to food and adequate health services, and child-care (feeding) practices. These, in turn, are influenced at the macro-level by resource availability and distribution and by political ideology. Malnutrition is a complex web of biological, ecological, economic, social and cultural factors. Below, I present factors that are situated on various levels of causality, which contribute to malnutrition.

Proximate causes and prevalence of malnutrition

In rural Mali, the context is poverty, high exposure to disease and poor quality diets.[70] Therefore, a large proportion of children are nutritionally vulnerable. An episode of diarrhoea, fever or abrupt weaning can trigger the downward spiral of malnutrition. In Mali, 38.5% of the children under five years old are stunted (low height for age). This reflects the cumulative effects of malnutrition and infections beginning in utero. Stunted growth can therefore be interpreted as an indication of poor environmental conditions or long-term restriction of a child's growth potential. In Mali, 27.9% of the children are underweight (low weight for age) and 15.3% suffer from wasting (i.e. low weight for height), indicating acute weight loss (WHO for 2006). Decreasing child mortality depends heavily on reducing malnutrition, which is responsible, directly or indirectly, for 35% of deaths among children under five.

[70] See chapter 3 for a detailed description of the vulnerability context of Farabako.

Mother and child clinic: weighing the under-fives

Severe acute malnutrition is defined as a very low weight for height (below 3z scores of the median WHO growth standards), visible severe wasting or the presence of oedema (swelling of the face, hands and feet). The under-five case-fatality rate for severe acute malnutrition typically ranges from 30% to 50% (WHO for 2006).

In Farabako, in 2011, I weighed and measured all the children under five years old (seventy-seven children in total). Ten children (13%) suffered from wasting (low weight for height) and six of these children suffered from severe acute malnutrition (very low weight for height). These results were similar to earlier years when 10-13% of the children suffered from wasting. In many cases, it was difficult to determine the age of the children so I also measured their mid upper arm circumference.

Kwashiorkor and marasmus are two biomedical illness categories for severe malnutrition. Kwashiorkor is characterized by a swelling of the face, hands and feet (oedema), irritability, loss of appetite, ulcerating skin lesions and discolouration of the hair. According to a biomedical explanation, kwashiorkor is caused by insufficient protein consumption even with sufficient caloric intake, which distinguishes it from marasmus. More recently, micronutrient and antioxidant deficiencies have come to be recognized as contributory for kwashiorkor. Marasmus is caused by insufficient caloric intake and is characterized by extreme emaciation. In clinical practice, many children manifest symptoms of both kwashiorkor and marasmus and these are referred to as marasmic kwashiorkor, or more recently as protein-energy malnutrition (PEM). I treated three children with marasmic kwashiorkor in Farabako; two survived. The term kwashiorkor comes from the Krobo-Ga-Adangbe language of Ghana and means 'the disease of the deposed baby when the next one is born' (Williams 1933). It refers to the condition of the older child who has been weaned from the breast when a younger sibling is born. In Farabako, the term '*sede*'[71] is used to denote this condition. The biomedical explanation is that breast milk contains proteins vital to a child's growth. Kwashiorkor can develop when a mother weans her child replacing breast milk with a diet high in carbohydrates, but deficient in protein. I will come back to this point later.

Intermediate factors contributing to malnutrition

Access to food and health care as well as feeding practices at the household level are examples of intermediate factors contributing to malnutrition. In Farabako, in the dry season after the harvest, there is enough food, but the diet is not varied. The inhabitants live from subsistence farming; they eat only what they are able to produce. What they cannot grow, such as sugar, salt, bouillon cubes, tea and coffee, is bought at the market in neighbouring towns.

Villagers start their day with a meal of millet, rice or corn porridge. In the afternoon and evening, they eat rice or millet with okra sauce, onion and tomato sauce, green leaf sauce or a sauce using a peanut paste. Meat is only eaten if someone has performed a sacrifice, and even then, one chicken is divided among many mouths. There are fruit trees in Farabako and in the months that they bear fruit, children eat mangoes, oranges and papayas. Fish and potatoes are thought to be good food for babies, but they are not available in Farabako and money is rarely spent buying them at the market. Babies are given thin rice porridge (*sɛri*). Most extended families own a cow, when a cow has a calf there is milk for a few months. However, I seldom saw people in Farabako drink milk.

In the months preceding the next harvest, when the reserves of millet and corn have been depleted, villagers buy sacks of millet elsewhere to feed their families. But there is often not enough money and people go hungry. From 2009 through 2011, many villagers went to work in the goldmines and neglected their fields. Most villagers did not find gold and as a result, these were very lean years for most villagers of Farabako.

Illnesses such as measles and diarrhoea often trigger or aggravate a negative spiral leading to severe malnutrition. Therefore, treatment of infections is important for the prevention and treatment of malnutrition. Doctors in health clinics twenty kilometres away, in Sandama and Nioumamakana, are able to

---

[71] The official spelling (Bailleul 2000) is *sere*, but as my respondents all pronounced the term with a 'd', as did I in the many interviews on malnutrition, I choose to use the (for me) phonetic spelling of *sede*.

treat children's infections. They also distribute free packets of milk-feed powder to malnourished children. But, as became clear in the previous chapters, health care is not easily accessible for the mothers of Farabako. And even if they do manage to reach the doctor and receive the milk-feed, this does not necessarily mean that they will use it (in the way intended).

I interviewed Sise Kante, a young mother who had delivered her fourth and fifth child within fifteen months of each other. The older of the two was malnourished and ill. Her husband had taken the child to the doctor. The doctor gave him two packets of milk-feed powder. After several days, the father found that this treatment was not effective; therefore, he consulted a healer in another village. The traditional medicine that the healer gave was seen to be effective, so the mother stopped giving the milk-feed. Several months later, although the mother conceded that her child was still extremely thin and weak, the packet of milk-feed lay unopened. She had not been convinced of the necessity of giving it to her child.[72]

I base this section on months of participant observation and on a small observational study of feeding practices. The observational study was conducted in one compound in Farabako by my daughter Claudia Klumper (MA in Child and Education studies) and Merel Joosten, who accompanied me for ten days during my fieldwork in 2012.

In Farabako, the best food went to adults. For example, if a chicken had been sacrificed, children would be lucky to get any meat at all. However, on the rare occasions that there was extra food available (often in the form of my left-overs) it was given to the smallest children in the household.

In Farabako, most babies are breast fed for approximately two years. As a supplement to breast milk, babies start eating solid foods between eight and twelve months by joining the family meal. Mothers do not spoon feed their children, but rather give them a small bowl of food from which they can eat with their hands. I did not see mothers putting food directly into a child's mouth.

Children three years and older, eat together from one large dish set in front of them on the ground. There is little supervision. Therefore, it is difficult to know how much a child eats, especially when older siblings take care of young children when mothers are at work. The child who eats the fastest eats the most. The child without an appetite will eat the least. Mealtimes in Farabako are structured; children are offered food three times a day, and the women of the household decide how often the children eat. However, only the child decides how much to eat.

---

[72] Jackson (2005: 33) gives an example of young mothers not taking the paper prescriptions written for their sick babies to the dispensary. Instead, they would chew them, and then dissolve them. Finally, they would drink the concoction, much as one would wash Koranic suras from a tablet and drink the writing to effect a cure. This procedure was familiar to the mothers and made them confident in the cure in a way that foreign treatment with pills did not.

In Farabako, mothers say that all children receive the same amount and type of food. Children who were seen to be vulnerable (e.g. too thin) were not given special treatment, 'otherwise it is thought that the child is favoured'. In practice, the smallest children, younger than three years old, ate with their mother and were often given extras.

Hawa Kante (35 yrs) explained that if a child refuses to eat, she first encourages them to eat. If this is not successful, her conclusion is that the child is ill and needs medicine. Hawa named Nivaquine as the medicine she would try to buy. Nivaquine is an anti-malarial that is no longer recommended since mosquitos have become resistant to it. It is often sold as individual tablets by travelling drug sellers for only a few FCFA per tablet. Hawa would not give the child a new or more varied diet. A lack of appetite is considered a normal part of many childhood illnesses, in Farabako. There are no special foods for sick children and mothers do not prepare favourite foods to tempt a child to eat. There is a strong belief that children will eat if they are hungry and that children should not be given food against their will.

Macro level management of malnutrition

In 2001, UNICEF and the Mali Ministry of Health initiated a program known as the 'Strategy for Accelerated Child Survival and Growth' (ASCD) to reduce child mortality due to disease and malnutrition. Part of this programme involved training health staff to treat malnutrition according to Integrated Management of Childhood Illness (ICMI) guidelines (Sidibé et al. 2007). The programme also included an immunization campaign and the promotion of antenatal care and skilled delivery. But as we saw in chapter 2, Farabako is geographically remote; government health centres are difficult to reach due to a lack of infrastructure. The immunization campaign reached Farabako only sporadically and very few children were fully vaccinated. Distribution of mosquito nets and vitamin A supplementation is also infrequent. Thus, all these issues contributed to the susceptibility of the children in Farabako for diseases such as malaria and measles that can cause a negative spiral into malnutrition.

In sum, according to the public health and biomedical discourses on malnutrition, children in Farabako are nutritionally vulnerable because of their lack of access to a varied diet and frequent food scarcity. Biomedical health care is not always utilized due to the lack of money necessary for transport. Not all parents are convinced that biomedical treatment is best for their child. Children are quite autonomous in how much they eat. A sick child will not be forced to eat and this can lead to weakness that makes recovery from illness lengthier; this in turn, can be the start of a negative spiral of malnutrition. To illustrate how people in Farabako approach malnutrition I present a case study of the illness episode that led up to the death of Bobo Kante (see also household 8 in Appendix 5).

Case study Bobo: A local approach to malnutrition

> 'It is nothing, don't cry, it is Allah,' says Kanku to me after I leave the hut where Bobo just died. Kanku takes me back to my compound, sits me down in my chair and sternly forbids me to cry. Even the mother may not cry. (Fieldnotes December 2009)

One day, my neighbour came to tell me that there was a very sick child in the compound adjoining ours. I immediately went to see the two-year-old boy, Bobo. He was extremely emaciated; he had sunken eyes and oedema of his feet. He was vomiting and had diarrhoea. My diagnosis was that this was a serious case of marasmic kwashiorkhor, dehydration and any number of infections. I immediately gave him antibiotics and an anti-malarial. I spoon-fed him a little milk fortified with sugar, vegetable oil and vitamins. While I was doing this, I realised that the situation was much more serious than I had thought. The child developed convulsions and difficulty breathing. He also had difficulty swallowing and I was worried that he would aspirate the medicine. I gave a quinine injection, knowing that I was too late. The child needed to be rehydrated; he needed a doctor. I asked my host Namagan to take him by motorcycle to the doctor, but before he could do so, Bobo died. I had never seen a death like this one before. The first thing the grandmother, with an angry tone of voice, said to me afterwards is 'how will I pay for the medicine?'.

My first reaction was: Why had they let this child die? Why didn't they do anything? I didn't understand. Why had no one asked me to help? I had been in the village for five days before Bobo died and no one told me he was ill. My translator Abdulaye said it was because Faramata Kante, the mother-in-law, did not want to spend any money on a child that was not of her family; her son was not Bobo's biological father. I decided to interview as many people as possible who had been involved in this illness episode to try and understand what had just happened. This case study is based on interviews with Naba Bagayogo, the mother of the child, Faramata Kante, her mother-in-law, Fanta Kante and Baraka Kante, two *musokɔrɔbaw*, Jeneba Kante, the midwife and Sala Kante, a *soma*, who were all involved in Bobo's therapy management.

Bobo's mother, Naba Bagayogo, is twentyyears old. She is married to Madu Kante and lives with him in another village. Naba has two children. The father of these children is not her husband. The man had promised to marry her, but then did not. Her first son lives with Naba's grandmother. Naba married Madu while pregnant by the other man with her second son, Bobo. She says that Madu did not see this as a problem because he loved her. Madu has always taken care of Bobo and loves him. Naba is now pregnant with Madu's child, her third.

Madu's father is another story; 'he does not want to see Bobo because he is not his blood'. Naba is thinking about going to stay with her parents because

Madu's father is not nice to her. 'He refuses water if I offer it.' According to Naba, Madu's father hates Bobo.

The first day that Bobo was ill, Naba noticed that he had diarrhoea. Naba showed him to a *musokɔrɔba* in her village who gave him traditional medicine. She also told her husband, who then gave Bobo traditional medicine for diarrhoea (*kɔnɔboli*) and *sede* 'because Naba was pregnant'. A few days later, when Bobo had not improved, Naba bought four tablets from a traveling drug seller. She does not know the name of the tablets. She only paid 25 FCFA (4 euro cents), because the drug seller had 'taken pity on her'. After two weeks, Bobo was still not better and her husband, Madu, told Naba to go to Farabako where his mother, Faramata Kante, was staying and to ask her for money for a medical treatment. Naba took Bobo to Farabako and told her mother-in-law that the child had *kɔnɔrɔjoli* ('wounds in the belly', blood in the stools). At this time, Bobo also had a fever, cough, spasms, weight loss, swollen feet, pale skin, worms, and skin lesions. Faramata did not give her any money. Next, Naba's husband, Madu, came to Farabako and also asked his mother for money, but Faramata again refused. Naba is sure her mother in law had the money, and that if Bobo had been Madu's child, she would have given it. She had overheard her sister-in-law telling Faramata 'you must not treat this child because he is not of our family'.

But Faramata assured me that it made no difference to her that Bobo was a bastard grandson. She would take care of him as if he was her own blood. It was her husband who hated the child; she herself loved him. It was difficult to find money in Farabako, she explained. Last year, when she was sick, she had asked for money from three male family members, but they all had said no. Therefore, she did not ask now that Bobo was ill. Her daughter worked in the gold mines and she had found some gold, but she had spent it on clothes and jewelry. When Faramata asked her daughter for money, she said no.

When Faramata first saw Bobo, she saw that he had skin lesions in his groin. Naba had told her that he had 'wounds in the belly'. Faramata showed the child to Sala Kante, an apprentice of the divination expert, Namagan Kante. Sala Kante had been studying sand divination for one and a half years. He is originally from Siguiri in Guinea. He does not often do sand divinations for children; however, in the past year, he did approximately seven. He often gives traditional medicine and does incantations.

Faramata asked him to do a divination. When Sala saw Bobo, the child was vomiting; he had diarrhoea and skin lesions. Sala gave traditional medicine and oil with incantations for the skin lesions. This medicine was effective without a sacrifice. According to Sala, the cause of Bobo's illness was Naba's old boyfriend (who was also a *soma*) doing evil (*dabali*) with the sand. Maybe the evil was meant for Naba, but hit the child instead. People can do evil by asking their fetish to hurt someone, or for example, by burying a live chicken and putting kola nuts in a hollow tree. Sala saw in the sand that the child would die. He did not want to tell the grandmother this, so he said that she must sacrifice two chickens to *sinsin* (the twin fetish) and walk up the mountain and back with a stone (also a kind of sacrifice). Sala knew that this would take so long that the child would probably be dead after Faramata's return. But, if she did this, then maybe the child would not die from this disease (but rather from another disease in the future). According to Sala, Faramata did not perform the sacrifice, because she did not have the time since she was working in the goldmine. Faramata told me that she had found only one chicken because there were no other chickens for sale in Farabako. Chicken pest is endemic in the region and a scarcity of chickens is frequent. The sand also called for five specific plants, but these would only be effective with the sacrifice of the two chickens. Faramata did not give the chickens, so Sala did not go to get the plants (he had to do this himself). If the plants were laid on the sand and the chickens were sacrificed, then the chickens would die rather than the child. Sala did not ask Faramata for money because he knew she had none. If the child recovered, Faramata would have gone to Sala to thank him and pay her respect by giving him something.

The day before Bobo died, Faramata took him to Fanta Kante, a *musokɔrɔba* renowned for her healing abilities. Fanta Kante saw that the child had swollen feet. She asked if the mother of the child was pregnant. The child was very thin and she thought he had *sede*. Fanta told Faramata to find the fruit of the seretoro[73] tree and the fruit of the *dakɛsɛbu*. Faramata should pound these fruits with some salt in a mortar and then give it to the child to eat. Faramata said that she could not find these trees and she asked the child's mother Naba to go in the bush to search for them, but Naba did not do this.

Fanta Kante did not tell Faramata to go to me because she thought that Faramata had already consulted me since we are neighbours. According to Fanta, they did not consult me because they did not care about the child. She does not understand; 'everyone calls the help of a doctor when the doctor is in the village'. Fanta added that Naba should have paid her respects to Fanta after the child died, but she had not done this; 'Naba is shameless' (*malobali*).

Faramata then showed the child to Jeneba, the midwife. Jeneba said that she did not have the knowledge of what medicine was needed and that Faramata must take the child to a doctor. Faramata did not do this because she had no money. Later, Faramata showed the child to old Bala Kante, who gave her traditional medicine for the wounds. Next, she showed the child to a visitor from Guinea, who subsequently gave traditional medicine to wash the child with. Knowledge coming from elsewhere might be successful when the knowledge in Farabako had not been. Knowledge coming from outside the village was seen as more prestigious.

On the day of Bobo's death, Faramata warmed the child in front of the fire.

---

[73] Ficus capensis (Bailleul 2000).

She then gave the child to his mother who took him on her back when she went to pound millet. Faramata did not realise that the child was gravely ill, and she left for the goldmine. Naba went to Baraka Kante, another *musokɔrɔba* renowned for her healing skills, and told her that Bobo had wounds. Baraka did not see the child herself, and had not known that the child was ill. Baraka told Naba to look for leaves of the *mɔgɔjiri*[74] tree, and Naba said she would do this. In the meantime, my neighbour, in whose compound Faramata lived, called me to come look at Bobo. Despite my best (but unfortunately inadequate) efforts, Bobo died two hours later. According to his family, Bobo had been ill for approximately three weeks, I suspected that his malnutrition had been going on for several months.

When I asked Faramata why she had not asked me to look at the child earlier, she told me that she thought that I would not be able to treat this illness (even though she does know of the story of Samba, another child with the same symptoms whom I had treated successfully). Then she said that she forgot to ask my help because she was always in the gold mines and came home late and she thought that the traditional medicine would help. Later she said that the real reason was that she had no money, but she had been ashamed to say so. This case raises questions of entitlement. Within this context of extreme poverty, was Bobo, as a bastard child, entitled to medical care that cost money? Seemingly not, but perhaps there really was no money.

This case illustrates two other points. First, whereas I thought they 'had done nothing', the family of the child had actually consulted seven healers. Three *musokɔrɔbaw*, one traveling drug seller, a local midwife, two sand divination experts, a visitor from Guinea and I had been consulted. Whereas, it was my assumption that as long as the family had not taken the child to a doctor, they had not reacted adequately (I might have even gone so far as to think that this family was being negligent), the family saw my Western medicine as an expensive, but not necessarily superior alternative.

My second point is that nowhere in the accounts of Bobo's illness did anyone speak about food. The term *sede* was used by various members of his therapy group and the term *sede* corresponds to the biomedical term, kwashiorkor, and kwashiorkor is caused by malnutrition, and malnutrition is about food. So why had no one mentioned Bobo's diet? To understand this, let us now look more closely at the illness term *sede*.

---

[74] Stereospermum Kuntianum (ibid.)

Sede

Becoming pregnant too soon

Because I assumed that *sede* corresponded with my biomedical category of malnutrition due to early weaning, I asked many questions about *sede* while expecting to hear answers about malnutrition. In fact, I got answers about pregnancy instead. When I asked 'what is the cause of *sede*?', my respondents would answer, 'when a woman becomes pregnant too soon'.

> The first months after the delivery are called 'den turu tɛ kalow' if a woman has her menstruation during this time, her child could have *sede*. (Fadima Kulibali, 30 yrs, Focus group discussion February 2011)

The phrase 'den turu tɛ kalow' was explained to me as meaning the months that a woman should not become pregnant again because her child has not matured enough. Like a rooster needs time to grow a crest, so the child needs time to grow. The women mentioned pregnancy as the cause of *sede* and not early weaning. When I asked about the treatment for *sede*, my respondents answered—contraceptives. But contraceptives were not always available in or around Farabako, and if they were, not all husbands approved of their wives using them.

> Nantakadi Kamara was pregnant for the fourth time in four years. She took *surumugu*, a traditional medicine, used as an abortificant and prepared by the *musokɔrɔbaw*, because the pregnancies were too close together and she was afraid of her third child getting '*sede*'. The *surumugu* did not help and the baby was born. Of the nine children Nantakadi went on to bear, five died. (Fieldnotes 2007)

Two respondents had heard of women using a *tafo* to prevent becoming pregnant. A *tafo* is a string with knots over which incantations have been said that is worn around the waist. However, most respondents named abortion using traditional medicine (leaves of the *dɔdɔturu* or *surumugu*) as the only (unreliable) treatment for *sede*. So the talk turned to the women's limitations for spacing their children.

Lack of reproductive choice

In the reproductive life history survey I conducted, 46 of the 263 (17.5%) children were born within less than two years of each other. Thus, they had possibly been at risk for malnutrition due to early weaning. The women told me that after a forty-day postpartum abstinence period, they resumed sexual relations with their husbands.

> Sali Keita has had three children in three years. I have never seen her smile. She is tired because the second child cannot walk yet: 'I cannot carry two children on my back'. She is afraid of *sede* and her second child. She says that her husband does not share her fear. If a woman refuses sex, her husband may hit her. (Fieldnotes 2007)

The women were unable to refuse sex. As one female respondent told me, 'a good wife may have a discussion with her husband, but she may never say no'. The sanctions for refusing sex included being hit and publicly chastised or cursed. These measures were experienced as extremely shameful by the women.

> If you refuse your husband sex and the next morning he hits you in front of the whole family, then you feel shame. It is shameful when your husband pronounces a curse over you. For example: 'I will not pardon you, I will leave it up to God'. Or when you refuse sex during pregnancy, he may say: 'You will not deliver this baby until you apologize'. Only in the last month of pregnancy can a woman refuse sex, but some men do not respect this. (Nakani Kante, 33 yrs, January 2009)

Both men and women said three years was the optimal time between deliveries to avoid *sede*. Although their wives were breastfeeding, their husbands did not abstain or lower the frequency of sexual relations. One young mother, living in a polygamous household, had had three caesarean sections and had been advised by the doctor not to have any more children. She told me:

> The [contraceptive] pill is the only way to treat *sede*. Refusing my husband sex is impossible, that would lead to war. I cannot refuse him even though he is also afraid of another pregnancy and delivery. (Fadima Kulibali, 30 yrs, Focus group discussion February 2011)

The women assured me that having a co-wife did not mean that their husband would abstain from sex and go to the other wife if she was breastfeeding. It was important that their husbands gave equal attention to all wives at all times to avoid jealousy among the co-wives.

My male respondents told me that after the forty-day period of abstention, men resumed sex with the same frequency as before the delivery, even if they also worried about their wife becoming pregnant too soon. As one man explained: 'If we need, we need.' Two of this man's children had died of *sede*. Another man said that his wife could lock her door if she did not want sex. However, this was not something the women admitted to, which is understandable, seeing as that action could be seen as shameful behaviour. If women did become pregnant, their husbands often thought it was the woman's fault, because men suspected that women knew when they were fertile. The women denied knowing this, but even if they had known it, this did not mean they could refuse their husbands.

A shameful diagnosis

If a woman is unable to prevent becoming pregnant while breastfeeding, she will have shame (*maloya*). People will say that 'she could not control herself' or 'they have sex often'. Both men and women feel ashamed about the pregnancy. However, according to a male respondent, for *sede*, 'women have more shame than men'. Female respondents agreed; in cases of *sede* women have shame because they are often blamed for becoming pregnant too soon. It is for this reason that women will keep their pregnancy a secret as long as possible. Women sometimes deny being pregnant when asked. A woman is reticent to say that her child has *sede*, because to say so is to admit to being pregnant. A woman may not seek treatment as long as she is still able to hide her new pregnancy. *Sede* is a shameful diagnosis, especially in the beginning of a pregnancy. As one young mother explained:

> Yes, women whose child has *sede* have shame, it is not as it should be; they put their child in danger. (Fadima Kulibali, 30 yrs, Focus group discussion February 2011)

No one named *sede* as a cause of illness in the illness episode interviews, nor was *sede* mentioned as a children's disease during the free-listing interviews. When describing the illness episode of their children, mothers almost never spontaneously named symptoms of malnutrition or the illness term *sede*. In one typical example, a mother recounting the illness of her one-year-old daughter (who had died) mentioned only fever and *dino* ('feet as cold as ice') as symptoms. Only after I asked directly (in a verbal autopsy), did she tell me that her child had also been coughing and vomiting, was emaciated and had swollen feet and pale skin, all signs of (what I call) malnutrition aggravated by infection.

In 2009, seventy mothers, fathers and mothers-in-law told me about the illness episodes of their forty-two children. Eleven children had showed symptoms of severe malnutrition (emaciation and oedema). In only five cases had the parents mentioned these symptoms spontaneously. For the eleven cases of emaciation and oedema, ten children were between 1 and 2 years old and four of the eleven had died. In only two cases, was the diagnosis *sede* mentioned. Both concerned children I had treated, which meant that I had already broached the subject of *sede* with the parents. It is impossible for me to say to what extent shame plays a role in not mentioning these symptoms. In two other cases, in which the children had died and I suspect that malnutrition played a role, the mothers had used the neutral illness term '*fasara*' which means 'has become thinner', rather than the morally laden *sede*, which means becoming pregnant too soon. With so many underweight children, maybe emaciation does not strike the parents as a serious symptom, especially because, in almost all of these cases, the children also had infections, the symptoms of which were more noticeable.

Dangerously hot belly

If a woman overcomes her shame and seeks advice from the *musokɔrɔbaw* on how to treat *sede*, the *musokɔrɔba* will tell her that she must stop breastfeeding as soon as possible. She should preferably stop as soon as she finds out that she is pregnant again. A pregnant woman is said to have a 'hot belly' (*kɔnɔ funteni*). The heat that a pregnant woman gives off can be dangerous for the child she is breastfeeding. The heat can cause the child to have a fever and diarrhoea. It is for this reason that the *musokɔrɔbaw* advise women to keep their distance from the child and stop breastfeeding. This heat can also be dangerous for older children, as the next case illustrates.

> Kajatu Kante (age 4) was sick; she had a fever. Her mother said that the fever had been caused by the child sleeping with her while she was pregnant. She explained that a pregnant woman gives off a great deal of heat and this can be dangerous. She washed the child with water in which medicinal plants had boiled and the fever went down. (Fatumata Kante, 28 yrs, January 2009)

One male respondent told me that having sex with a pregnant woman could cause a man to become ill. In Farabako, it is not the (early) weaning of the child that is seen to be dangerous, but rather the physical contact between child and pregnant mother. It is not the perception that weaning leads to malnutrition due to lack of protein, but rather the heat of pregnancy that leads to the illness *sede*.

Treatment of sede

During a demonstration of how to prepare oral rehydration salts as a treatment for diarrhoea at the maternity clinic one morning, I took the opportunity to ask the young women present what they gave their children if they had *sede*. The women answered that they gave tea and thin millet porridge and 'for the rest, it is up to God'. When I asked why tea? I was told that the tea, prepared with sugar, was light to digest and easy to drink. It is used as a remedy because it makes it possible for a sick child, who has no appetite, to eat at least a little bit. Tea is also said to give 'liveliness to the blood' and this is thought to be necessary to ward off illness.

Several respondents named the *musokɔrɔba* Kinyèba Fofana as the expert in treating *sede* in Farabako. During an interview, Kinyèba confirmed that indeed she was an expert and that *sede* was a serious illness that kills many children. When mothers come to her some say that their child is ill, and some say that their child has *sede*. Many women are ashamed to say that their child has *sede*. 'A woman who has a child who suffers from *sede* is not appreciated in the village, this is because of *maloya*.' Shame will not keep her from seeking a treatment, but it will keep her from saying that her child has *sede*. The shame is greatest when the new pregnancy is not visible. Once everyone can see that the woman is pregnant, she can ask for a treatment for her child's *sede* without problems. Women have confidence in her treatment and know that Kinyèba does not gossip; therefore, some women come to her also early in their pregnancy.

Kinyèba's treatment consists of an infusion of seretoro and *dakɛsɛbu* leaves over which she has spoken incantations (*kilisiw*). The child is washed with this infusion (four times if a girl and three times if a boy).[75] When I asked why four times if a girl and three times if a boy, Kinyèba Fofana said that she does not know; 'it has always been this way' (this is the answer I got from all my respondents). The child is also given this infusion to drink. Kinyèba has three distinct incantations to choose from. She chooses one and if it does not work she will try another. She does not have a fixed method. She learned the incantations from *musokɔrɔbaw* in her natal village. The incantations are secret since it would be violating the rules to give them to others.

Kinyèba Fofana explained that a child who suffers from *sede* often has other illnesses such as *tɛgɛjɛ* (anaemia, literally 'white hands'), *sandafɛ* and *kɔnɔ* (illness categories that correspond with serious infection with convulsions). Kinyèba can also treat these illnesses. When I asked Kinyèba if it takes a long time to treat *sede* she answered: 'It depends, some recover quickly, others slowly. Some children recover at the moment of the delivery of their mother. This happens often if it is only *sede*, not complicated by other illnesses, because after the delivery the heat goes down.' She explains again that a pregnant woman's belly gives off heat and that it is not good for the child to be too close to the mother because this can cause diarrhoea. She advises women to stop breastfeeding and keep their distance. The woman should give her child cow's milk. If this is not possible she can (out of necessity) give the breast. If the child is old enough to eat, Kinyèba advises that the mother should give her child soup with meat, a paste made from peanuts and a sauce made from the leaves of the seretoro. She tells me that she does not know if women follow her advice.

Kinyèba Fofana is not the only *musokɔrɔba* in Farabako who treats *sede*. For example, Fanta Kante treated Bobo in the case above using the same treatment that Kinyèba described, *seretɔrɔ* and *dakɛsɛbu*. Baraka Kante's treatment of *sede* is similar and consists of saying incantations over *tɔrɔjugudenw* (fruit

[75] The gender number four for a girl and three for a boy is universal in the Mande region.

of the evil [!] *seretɔrɔ*) and then pounding the fruit into a powder. This powder is given a little at a time to improve the child's appetite. The focus of treatment given by *musokɔrɔbaw* is on enhancing the child's appetite not the child's diet.

Kinyèba Fofana was the only one in the village who I talked to who named cow's milk as a substitute for breast milk. It is possible that she did so, because the year before I had given demonstrations in the maternity clinic about how to prepare powdered cow's milk and fortify it with sugar, oil and vitamins. I had repeatedly talked about milk as a treatment for *sede*, and Kinyèba probably knew that I had bought a cow with the purpose of giving the milk to the malnourished children in Farabako.

Case study Samba: A biomedical approach to malnutrition

Let me now present a case study as an example of my biomedical approach to the treatment of malnutrition in Farabako. This case illustrates that despite the fact that the child recovered after receiving biomedical treatment, the link between malnutrition and quality of food was not thereby apparent to his caretakers.

In November 2009, I treated the little boy Samba Kante (1½ yrs) for a severe case of what I call marasmic kwashiorkor. When I first saw Samba, he was dying. It was evening and he was lying alone on a bed in his grandmother's room. He was hypothermic. His family had lost hope that he would recover and he was left to die. Samba was extremely emaciated; you could see every bone in his body. Where his bottom used to be there were folds of skin. His face, hands and feet were swollen (oedema) and he was having great difficulty breathing. This was a case of marasmic kwashiorkor aggravated by an infection and/or malaria. I immediately gave antibiotics and an antimalarial. While I asked Samba's grandmother to explain what had happened, I tried to warm the child and spoon-fed him some milk. His grandmother Mariamu Kante told me his story.

Samba's mother had become pregnant four months after his birth. She delivered a new baby when Samba was a little over a year old. His mother could not 'carry two children on her back' so Samba was given in fosterage to his grandmother. The grandmother, Mariamu Kante, who has delivered eight children, finds this 'tiring but obligatory'. It is the custom that a foster child stays until he can go to the fields (which is usually around 4 years old). When I saw Samba for the first time he had been in Farabako for five months. His mother lives in her husband's village, which is twenty kilometres from Farabako, and had not been able to visit him since he was given in fosterage.

According to his grandmother Mariamu, all this time he had been very skinny. In the past month Samba's hands and feet had become swollen, he had white palms and a fever. Her mother-in-law (the child's great-grandmother and a *musokɔrɔba*) thought the child had '*dino*' (cold), and gave him traditional medicine. Mariamu did not think this treatment was effective so she sent someone to Niamu, where Samba's parents live, to tell the father that the child was ill. The father told the messenger to tell Mariamu to try traditional medicine. The father did not come to see the child.

After a week, Mariamu took Samba to another *musokɔrɔba* who diagnosed *tɛgɛjɛ* (anaemia, literally 'white hands') and gave traditional medicine. Mariamu did not have to pay for this treatment (if the child recovered, she might pay a few FCFA or kola nuts). This treatment helped a bit.

When after two weeks there was no improvement, Mariamu decided to take the child to the doctor in Nioumamakana after consulting her mother-in-law, who now thought it was *sede*. A male family member took her on a motorcycle (he did not ask money for the gasoline). The doctor diagnosed *jolitala* (anaemia, 'no blood') and gave her iron syrup, an antibiotic and anti-malarial medicine. This cost 5,000 FCFA (7.5 euros). Mariamu paid this with money she had earned by selling peanut seed. Back in Farabako, Jeneba Kante (the midwife) also examined the child, she also thought that it was *tɛgɛjɛ* and she gave traditional medicine.[76]

Samba had been ill for a month by the time I saw him. My diagnosis was severe malnutrition complicated by a respiratory infection and/or malaria. I gave Samba powdered milk that I had brought from Bamako for my own use since there was none for sale in Farabako and the cows were not giving milk at the time. I fortified the milk with sugar, vitamins and vegetable oil. I showed his grandmother Mariamu how to prepare this. I explained that she needed to feed him eight times a day, small amounts at a time, and that she must keep him close to her and warm. I gave Samba medication for malaria, and respiratory infection and worms. I was doing my best, but I had never seen or treated a severe case of malnutrition before and felt that this child must go to a doctor. I also knew that a hospital treatment for malnutrition takes weeks or even months and would be a costly undertaking. I asked Mariamu 'who is responsible for this child?'. She answered, the father, but because he was in another village, the grandfather was responsible. However, the grandfather was away in Gabon earning money doing sand divinations. This meant that the brothers of the grandfather were responsible for the child, but they were also traveling. The only brother left in the household was Madu, who was eighteen years old and had no money. He was responsible for more than thirty people living in his compound. I asked if someone could send for the father of the child so that we could talk about the best course of treatment.

Samba's father came to Farabako the next day. He lives in Niamou with his two wives and seven children. His first wife was ill and he was worried about her. He has no brothers to help him in his household. He looked as if he was at

[76] This surprised me. I would have expected that the midwife, with her biomedical training, would have given the advice to go to a doctor rather than giving traditional medicine. But this is the grandmother's account of events, not the midwife's. I was not able to interview the midwife about this illness episode.

his wit's end. I explained that this child should go to the hospital in Bamako for treatment and I stressed that his condition was very serious. But the father did not want his son to go to Bamako, even after I offered to pay the initial costs, because he had no money for such a long treatment. I asked how much a consultation in the hospital would cost, but no one would tell me, I had the strong feeling the father did not want me to give him money. After talking for a very long time, we decided that I would continue treating Samba as best I could in Farabako (I explained that this was beyond my expertise) and if he worsened in the coming days we would reconsider going to the hospital in Bamako. I found this a difficult ethical dilemma; how much should I interfere when a child's life is at stake?

As luck would have it, the next day the new doctor from Sandama happened to come by. On his way back to his village, his motorcycle had problems and he made a stop in Farabako. He was offered food in the compound where Samba lives, but no one asked him to look at the child. Why? Had they not realised that he was a doctor (he was new in the area)? Or were they worried he would ask for money? No one gave me a straight answer when I asked. Luckily, he stopped by my compound to greet me, so I was able to ask him to examine Samba. He looked at the child and said 'It is kwashiorkor, the child will get better'. He agreed with my treatment but advised me to give even stronger antibiotics and quinine injections. He had bags of special milk-feed powder especially for malnourished children that I could pick up for free in Sandama the next day.

So, I continued treating Samba. Giving him quinine injections against malaria was heart-wrenching because he had no buttocks left and I had to inject the medicine into his skinny little legs with little muscle and this was painful for him. Every morning and every evening for two months, I went to his grandmother's house and together we prepared the milk. Some days, he would vomit and we would worry. Other days, he seemed more alert and we were hopeful. After about one month, we began to see improvement. We carefully started giving Samba solid foods high in protein such as beans. The villagers always joked about my penchant for beans.[77] After two months, the swelling in Samba's face and feet had gone down and he began to gain weight, was able to sit up and he even smiled. Amazingly, Samba survived a measles epidemic that swept over the region a month later. Samba's family told me that they had been convinced that Samba would die, but because of me he was alive.

I had hoped that this case would be educational for all the mothers of Farabako and that this case would prove that milk and a varied diet could cure *sede*. A year before, I had bought a cow. The cow had a calf and was giving milk just

[77] My name in Farabako was Dusuba Kante. Kante because I was living with a Kante family. It is a running joke, for the Keita as joking partners (*senankunw*) of the Kante, that members of the Kante family are bean-eaters, and as a Kante I was not spared from these jokes.

before I left Farabako. So I left in a hopeful mood—now there was milk for the children with *sede*.

When I returned in 2011, a little more than a year later, Samba was still seriously underweight, however, he was in reasonably good health and walking and playing and smiling. To me Samba was my success story. That is until his grandmother Mariamu Kante (the same woman I had prepared milk and special food with twice a day, every day for two months) came to me and said, 'Samba still sometimes gets a swollen face and feet, what should I do?' In reply, I asked what Samba ate. She answered, '*kini* (rice with sauce) with the rest of the family'. I asked if she ever gave him special food. She said no. I asked if she ever gave him milk, beans or fruit. She said no, and looked at me as if this was the first time she had ever heard of this. How could this be? Mariamu recognized the signs of malnutrition and she had learned how to treat malnutrition, yet she did not practice what she had learned. Why had she not done anything? I believe that the reason Mariamu had not paid special attention to Samba's diet after I left was because I had not convinced her that *sede* was about food.[78]

For Mariamu, Samba's *sede* was an illness caused by the 'hot belly' of his mother. Mariamu probably thought that my medicine was responsible for curing this illness, and that the milk and beans were a custom from my country, *Peyiba*. Samba now had the same symptoms as he had had the year before, but this did not mean that Mariamu saw them as the same illness. This time, it may not have been seen as *sede*, because now there was no clear link with a pregnant mother. What was clear was that seeing the symptoms of malnutrition did not make Mariamu think of paying special attention to Samba's diet.

I realise that I have achieved little besides saving one life. The case of Bobo's death that I described in this chapter is a case in point. My assumption that education on the importance of nutrition would make a difference had proved false. Actually none of my biomedical assumptions were very useful in bringing about change. This is perhaps the base of my frustration—with my feminist-action-research approach, I had wanted to improve the health of the women and children in Farabako, but was not successful.

The complex of factors leading to 'passivity'

I started this chapter with a description of my frustration about mothers 'not doing anything' when their children suffered from malnutrition. On closer consideration, I realised that this frustration had to do with my biomedical assumptions about appropriate behaviour in cases of severe malnutrition—going to a doctor. The awkward engagement of my biomedical discourse with the local moral and medical discourses in Farabako brought into focus the

[78] Similarly, Dettwyler (1994) describes a woman asking for medicine for her malnourished child despite her having told her that food was the cure.

factors that hinder mothers in seeking biomedical health care for their malnourished children. Let me sum up and discuss the various factors leading to what I perceived as passivity.

Women have little social power

Once a mother becomes pregnant (too soon), she will give her child thin millet porridge and tea and wash the child with traditional medicine to treat fevers or diarrhoea, but in the end it is 'up to God'. Western biomedical treatment of malnutrition, consisting of milk-feed and medicine for the infections malnourished children often suffer was available in Farabako. Yet this treatment was seen as one (expensive) health care option, and not necessarily a superior one. Adequate biomedical health care is not easily accessible for women in Farabako. Extreme poverty, limited social capital and a discourse of shame make it difficult for women to seek health care for their children.

Parents' perceived lack of control over the fate of their children has been described as a factor contributing to the problem of malnutrition. It is God, not food who will make a sick child better (cf. Hampshire et al. 2009: 761). Simon et al. (2002), in their study on child malnutrition in Mali, found that a woman's social power, her felt potential to influence outcomes and not 'leave everything up to God', mediated the impact of poverty on childhood nutrition. Women with more social power had fewer malnourished children (see also Castle 1993). Simon et al. (2002) defined social power as favourable social characteristics such as having a large social network, and favourable 'psychological characteristics' such as feeling entitled to take action. These characteristics have a positive effect on child nutrition, whereas passivity and a feeling of helplessness have a negative effect. As we have seen in the preceding chapters, women have little social power in Farabako. They have limited social capital and often do not feel entitled or capable of taking action. I agree that passivity and feelings of helplessness have a negative effect on child mortality in Farabako. However, I disagree heartily that passivity is an individual psychological characteristic. In Farabako, passivity has to do with the embodiment of the moral discourse of shame within a context of vulnerability.

Children's entitlement to food

At the household level, child-feeding practices have been seen as contributing to malnutrition (Hampshire et al. 2009; Engle et al. 2000; Dettwyler 1986, 1989, 1994). For example, a laissez-faire approach to feeding may result in malnutrition. Mothers are described as having a laissez faire approach when children decide when and if they want to eat. In Mali, in general, infants are not fed, they are 'allowed to eat' (Dettwyler 1986: 657). This was also the case in Farabako, albeit that mothers did offer food to their children at fixed times.

Another factor said to contribute to malnutrition in Mali, is that good food is thought to be wasted on children, who do not appreciate it. It is said that the best food should go to the people who work the hardest or the elderly who will die soon (Dettwyler 1994). A sense of equalitarianism (all children receive the same amount and type of food) rather than discrimination (more food for a malnourished child) has been described as a factor contributing to malnutrition (cf. Messer 1997). That sense of equalitarianism can explain why in certain households mothers fail to differentiate in favour of the most vulnerable child. This has also been described as a form of selective neglect (Hampshire et al. 2009; cf. Scheper-Hughes 1992). Mothers must balance the needs of the sick and of other household members and spread the risk of malnutrition over the collective rather than focusing on the individual risk of one sick child. In a context of poverty and food insecurity, long-term livelihood security can be more important than short-term investments in children's health and nutrition (Baro and Deubel 2006).

On the one hand, in Farabako, a sick child is not necessarily entitled to better food than children who are not ill; all children are said to be entitled to the same amount and kind of food. Money is not spent on milk for vulnerable children. On the other hand, the case studies presented here raise questions of entitlement: are illegitimate and foster children as entitled to resources (food and money for treatment) as biological children? In her study in Sierre Leone, Bledsoe (1995) found that both men and women feel pressure to allocate household resources disproportionally to children of unions they value the most. Children from existing unions fare better than (illegitimate) children coming from previous ones. The same can be said of foster children; young foster children had poorer diets, less access to medical care and higher rates of malnutrition than children living with their mother (Bledsoe et al. 1988). Further research is necessary to see if this is also the case in Farabako.

I argue that rather than being a case of selective neglect or spreading the risk of malnutrition over the collective, in Farabako, vulnerable children do not get more food because food is not thought to make a sick child better. This is in line with Dettwyler's findings that while many mothers noticed that their children had become very thin during an illness, the mothers seldom recognized an explicit connection between diet and health (Dettwyler 1986).

Local theories on illness; sede *is not about food*

What much of the research on malnutrition and the programs for the prevention and treatment of malnutrition have in common, is their underlying assumption that malnutrition is about food: household food security, food consumption, cultural beliefs about food and feeding practices. However, anthropological studies have shown that people do not always relate malnutrition to food, and that to understand malnutrition one must understand cultural beliefs about illness. For example, for the Luo of Kenya, the illness category *ayieny* (which corresponds to the biomedical term kwashiorkor) is not related to diet entirely, but rather it can be caused by witchcraft. *Chira* (which corresponds to the biomedical term marasmus) is seen to be caused by breaking taboos, for example if a man has sex with another woman within four days of the birth of his son (Olenja 1991). For the Tabenken of Cameroon, the illness term *ngang* (which corresponds roughly with kwashiorkor) had several causes other than diet, such as female impropriety, witchcraft or being born as a 'single twin' (Pool 1994).

In Farabako, *sede* is the illness term that comes closest to my term kwashiorkor, but *sede* is not a nutritional problem caused by lack of protein. *Sede* is an *illness* caused by the heat that a pregnant mother gives off. *Sede* is caused by heat and the mother's 'hot belly' can give the child fever and diarrhoea. The treatment of *sede* is thus the separation of mother and child. From a biomedical perspective, one would advise mothers to continue breastfeeding as long as possible, right up to the delivery. A child is most at risk for malnutrition *after* the birth of the new baby when there is no more breast milk for the older sibling. However, it is a widespread belief in Mali that pregnant women should not nurse (Dettwyler 1986). In Farabako, the most dangerous time for *sede* is the time *before* the birth of the new sibling. The heat that causes *sede* subsides once the mother delivers the new baby. Early weaning is thus not always thought of as a problem as it protects the child against the mother's hot belly. In Mali, early weaning is sometimes even used as a method to increase food intake and to force children to eat solid foods. Dettwyler (1987) found that in Bamako early weaning even led to increased weight gain. This has not been studied in Farabako, but it is reasonable to believe that this is not the case in Farabako due to the times of food scarcity, the limited variation in diet (mostly millet and rice) and the unavailability of foodstuffs high in protein

Nutritional health education does not work

In 2001, UNICEF and the Mali ministry of health initiated a program known as the 'Strategy for Accelerated Child Survival and Growth' (ACSD) to reduce child mortality due to disease and malnutrition by at least 25% by the end of 2006. Bryce et al. (2010) undertook a retrospective evaluation of the programme, but could find no significant improvements in nutritional status attributable to the ACSD. In another assessment of the programme, Sidibé et al. (2007) also found disappointing results. The nutritional status assessment of children by health staff was neglected because of a lack of training and ' ignorance about the importance of malnutrition'. The authors recommended training the health staff and the 'intensification of behavioural change communication for mothers'. This is a typical approach to the problem of malnutrition—parental agency must change through education by trained health staff. A shift in parental agency is seen to be necessary for a nutritional program to work. Malnutrition is portrayed as an invisible problem; there is a lack of awareness that must be remedied by education (Tefft et al. 2003). Yet despite nutritional health education programs, malnutrition is still endemic in Mali.

My assumption that health education would convince the women of Farabako that *sede* is about nutrition proved false, as the case of Samba illustrated. Despite months of giving demonstrations on how to make fortified milk to supplement the diets of children with *sede*, and despite the fact that Samba recovered, once I left Farabako, Samba's grandmother no longer paid special attention to his diet. I had not convinced her that *sede* was about food and it was presumptuous of me to think that she would see me as an authority on the subject.

Contraceptives are the only method of prevention

Prevention of malnutrition from my biomedical standpoint was geared towards insuring that the child has a diet with sufficient protein and energy. To this end, I started several small projects that, sadly, had little effect on children's diets. I had a vegetable garden planted with vegetables high in iron and vitamin A, especially for the children. Everyone—men, women and children—ate the vegetables. The idea that children need a different diet from adults because they are growing is a Western concept. In Farabako, the people who work the hardest are the ones in need of the best food. To further supplement the children's diet, I bought ten chickens and a cow to produce eggs and milk. But in Farabako, people normally do not eat eggs, since chickens are valued for sacrifices. Unfortunately, all but one of my chickens died from the chicken pest that is endemic in the region. My cow gave milk for a few months, but it was not easy for women to ask for milk because having a child with *sede* is considered shameful. Saying 'my child has *sede* may I have milk?' is like saying 'look at me, I could not control myself, I like sex'.

The women of Farabako assured me that prevention of *sede* is only possible by adequate child spacing, that is, by not becoming pregnant too soon. Therefore, I introduced contraceptives in Farabako and the women eagerly (although often secretly) made use of them. The introduction of contraceptives was perhaps the only effective intervention I did. That child spacing is a factor contributing to malnutrition was the only part of the biomedical discourse that fit with the local medical discourse regarding *sede* in Farabako.

Conclusion

I have argued that understanding local medical and moral discourse is one of the prerequisites for understanding the therapy management of malnutrition. This chapter has highlighted the (almost) complete lack of fit between the dominant Western public health and biomedical discourses on malnutrition and local conceptions in Farabako (cf. Pool 1994). From a biomedical standpoint, the cases of severe malnutrition that I have described here were caused by a protein-energy deficiency, in other words malnutrition is caused by not eating enough food or eating the wrong kind of food. Malnutrition was presumably caused by early weaning and by not substituting breast milk with cow's milk or other foodstuffs high in protein. However, from a local standpoint, malnutrition in Farabako is not primarily about food. It is a shameful illness caused by lack of reproductive choice within a context of vulnerability.

This lack of fit is one explanation of why biomedical treatment and prevention programs, such as UNICEF, have had little effect. For a program to be effective, biomedical and local medical discourse must be negotiated to find a common ground, an overlap, or an aspect that fits both discourses. In Farabako, the necessity of child spacing fits both discourses and therefore, making contraceptives available in the village pharmacy was accepted by the mothers of Farabako as a useful intervention.

The next chapter also focuses on local health discourse, but now with a new question in mind: What words do women in Farabako use to speak about their health and how does their own health impact the therapy management of their children's illnesses?

9. MOTHERS ACCEPTING SUFFERING TO MAINTAIN THE MARRIAGE ALLIANCE: THE DARK SIDE OF SOCIAL CAPITAL

In previous chapters, a fragmented picture emerged of what it means to be a mother in Farabako and how women's position and experiences as wives and mothers are related to their role in the therapy management of their children. In this chapter, I complete this picture by asking the women to speak freely about their lives without predetermined questions. I did, however, ask them to specifically focus on their health. What surfaces from women's narratives is that they have to compromise their well-being to ensure that their children receive at least minimal care.

My interest in listening to and analysing women's stories lies in the types of stories women tell, how they tell them and the emerging themes. Before I let women speak about their lives and health, in this chapter, I present my theoretical perspective on the narrative construction of identity. I also address the methods I used to collect and analyse the women's narratives. Subsequently, I present a case study that illustrates many of the themes present in the women's narratives. The two main themes I identified in the women's stories were that women felt they were not well taken care of and that the acceptance of the (physical and psychological) 'everyday violence' that they experienced was needed to keep their social ties intact. This chapter provides more in-depth insight into women's role in therapy management.

My methodological approach

In 2011, when I went back to Farabako, I wanted to do open interviews to analyse the women's exact words after having done so many semi-structured interviews and surveys. I chose ten women I knew well. I thought these women might feel reasonably comfortable responding to my request to tell me their life history. The women were from six distinct households (of the total fifteen in Farabako), four Kante and two Keita families. All the women were in polygamous marriages. Four women were part of the large polygamous household I was staying in. I chose these women in the hope that listening to their stories would give me some insight into the dynamics of a polygamous family. The ages of the respondents ranged from 25 to 70 years old; all were married or widowed and all had children. The life history interviews took place in the maternity clinic or in the women's homes when only one of my two assistants (Mahamadou Faganda Keita or Abdulaye Traore) and I were present. All the quotations in this chapter are from these life history interviews conducted in February 2011, unless specifically stated otherwise.

The interviews were taped, and later transcribed and translated by Mahamadou Faganda Keita. The transcripts were analysed using both a narrative analysis (Riessman 1993) and a grounded theory method (Charmaz 2006). In a narrative, events are selected, organized, connected and evaluated as meaningful for a particular audience. A narrative analysis explores the extended account, while interpreting similarities and differences in participants' stories. A grounded theory approach, on the other hand, fragments the transcripts into meaning-laden moments and thematic categories. Both approaches pay attention to how and why events are storied, and which discourses the stories draw on rather than simply the content to which language refers (cf. Riessman and Speedy 2007).

Narrative construction of the self

I chose life history interviews because the narratives they produce are not only expressions of personal states, but also a manifestation of social and cultural patterns. They are not just subjective and private, but also public and shared because interpretations of a life are always produced using the available discourses and cultural repertoire. There is a close relationship between the stories we tell and hear and who we are. One could even go so far as to say that selves are narratively constructed (Bruner 1990: 99). Our stories are the building blocks of our identities. Yet, stories are never wholly personal; how we construct, interpret and recount our own experiences for others bears a strong resemblance to the storylines that are already 'out there' (Andrews et al. 2004: 112). Narration can thus be seen as embodied discourse, illuminating individual lives *and* broader social processes. Thus, women's stories are not only subjective and personal, but also an autobiographical expression of women's subject positions (Squire et al. 2008).

Narratives are co-constructed. The speakers intent is always met with the researcher's interpretation which in turn is situated in discourse, history, politics and culture (Riessman in Squire et al. 2008: 14). The position of researcher determines what is told, but interviewees also speak to other potential listeners and address future audiences (Squire et al. 2008). I was interested to know how my female respondents constructed themselves narratively during our interviews and what it was they wanted to tell me (and the readers of this book). I was interested in local narratives on women's lives and the structures of power that 'write' the lives of women in Farabako.

Story lines in Farabako

I asked the women to tell me about their life. I told them that I was interested in their health from the time they were young. Interestingly, the women did not speak much about their physical well-being; instead, they talked mostly about their social well-being. The women framed their narratives in terms of suffering and insecurity. The themes that recurred in the narratives were conflicts with their husbands and co-wives and subsequent conflict resolution, women staying in unhappy marriages for the sake of the children and women feeling insecure for not being taken care of.

Almost all of the narratives had a similar structure—the women started by telling me that they had been happy in their youth and in the first years of their marriage. Then something happened to make them feel insecure. For example, their husband died, they were abandoned or sent away by their husband, or there were conflicts with their husband and their financial situation deteriorated. After this event, they felt that they were no longer being taken care of and they spoke of suffering.

> I was happy in the first years of my marriage. It was after the death of my husband that I began to suffer. I worry if my children will have enough to eat. My problem is that I was given [in levirate] to a man who does not do for me what my first husband did for me; this makes me suffer. My deceased husband bought clothes and soap for me and my children, but at the moment all these costs are for me alone. Here it is very difficult for a woman who loses her husband. (Nakani Kante, 35 yrs)

> In my youth, before I was married, I had no difficulties whatsoever. My suffering started in the first years of my marriage. Last year, because of my suffering, I almost left to spend the rainy season at my father's. (Fatumata Kante, 30 yrs)

All women spoke of their social well-being and their social relationships with husbands, co-wives and affines were on the foreground in these narratives. Only one woman spoke specifically about physical ailments also. It is possible she spoke in this manner because she thought I expected it of her since I had taken her reproductive life history a few years previously. Here she sums up six of her nine pregnancies:

> The first time I was pregnant I was weak from coughing and I had painful feet, I even had difficulty walking. In my second pregnancy, I was not ill. During my third pregnancy, I had pain in my hips. During my fourth pregnancy, I had headaches; I vomited and was dizzy. In my fifth pregnancy, I had headaches, nausea and iron deficiency. In my sixth pregnancy, I first had a little pain in my abdomen, then strong pains and pains in my hips and feet. I could not work. I had problems with the birth of my first child. The other deliveries went without problems. I have six children who are living. Three children died. The death of my first child was due to a fever. Some people said that it was *kɔnɔ*, but I have no knowledge of children's illnesses. Two other children also died in this manner. (Mariamu Kante, 40 yrs)

I will now present Aminata's story. Her story brings together many of the themes present in the other women's narratives. This story is a composite of a life history interview conducted in 2011 in Aminata's natal village of Koumala, and previous interviews, informal conversations and participant observation when she still lived with her husband in Farabako, in 2009. I have chosen to tell her story because I had already come to know Aminata quite well before she told me her life history. Therefore, I was able to contextualize her narrative.

Aminata's story

> At the moment I suffer enormously. When I go to bed at night, I cannot sleep because I think of the child I left behind. It is a great loss to have a child and then have to leave him behind and to know that someone else is benefitting from that which is a mother's due. This is my dilemma and I do not know what to do. Since I arrived at my parents, no one has come to get me, though when I arrived here I was pregnant. If they had felt anything for me they would have sent someone to come and get me. Even if I don't go back, at least my parents would know that my husband's family does have feelings for me. ...Under these circumstances, I gave birth. After my delivery, I sent a message but no one from the family came to visit me. Even when the baby died no one came. It is this that makes me really suffer and proves to me that I am in a family that takes no responsibility. But nothing is lost, if it is my fate to return to my village then I will return, if fate decides differently I will go elsewhere.

In 2011, this is how Aminata Kante began telling me her story of troubles. We were in the compound of her older brother in Koumala, the small village where she was born. There were just the two of us in her room made of mud walls and a thatched roof. I sat next to her on her bed holding the tape recorder. I had asked her to tell me about her life and I told her that I was especially interested in her health. She told me about the problems with her husband. Expecting a narrative on physical well-being (my Western assumption of what 'health' is), I heard a narrative on social well-being, or in this case, the lack thereof instead. My translator had left the room to give us privacy, and Aminata just kept talking into the microphone. Although I only understood a few words, she talked without interruption for 30 minutes. She seemed grateful to be able to tell her story and it came pouring out along with significant pent-up emotions.

I first met Aminata in January 2009, in Farabako. She is the second wife of Madi Kante (see figure 3). Aminata is in her early twenties and has borne five children of whom three have died. When I met her, Aminata was very thin, as if she was not eating enough and wore threadbare clothes. She was well muscled from all the hard work she did every day. She had a nervous energy and

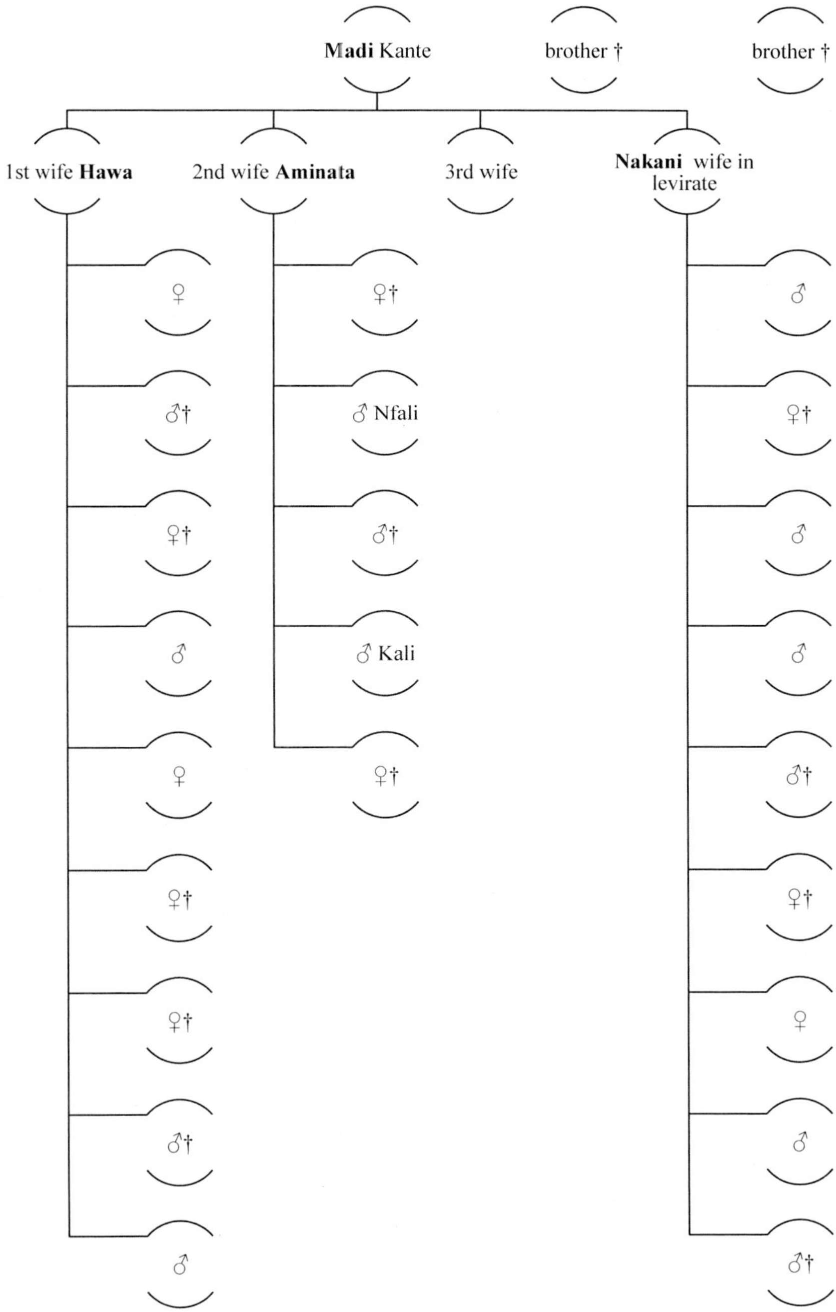

Figure 3. Family tree of Madi Kante, his wives and children

was constantly active, barely taking the time to sit down and breastfeed her son who was always fretting. She was always laughing and joking with everyone, including her husband's male guests. I enjoyed having her around, since her laughter was infectious. Her comportment was not as modest as most women in the village and others, including my translator, often spoke badly of her.

During my first visit in 2007, Aminata had not been in Farabako because of a conflict with her husband. Her husband Madi told me that Aminata was 'no good.' Later Aminata explained to me what had happened in 2007. 'If there is a sense of conflict among husband and wife, it is the children who suffer if they are ill and men refuse to pay.' Aminata experienced this conflict when her son Nfali was ill. She had had a fight with her new co-wife Nakani. Nakani had been given to Madi in levirate after the death of her husband, Madi's older brother. Nakani was unhappy with her match with Madi, but to refuse would have meant having to leave Farabako and her children behind. The fight between Aminata and Nakani had started over a dish for the funeral meal for Nakani's deceased husband. Aminata asked Nakani for a dish and Nakani said: 'Use your own dish.' When Aminata protested, Nakani said: 'That your anus may tear', which is a grave insult in Farabako. The shouting match culminated in Nakani taking a branch of wood from the fire and beating Aminata. Nakani broke and burned Aminata's leg. According to Aminata, Madi said that the fight was all her fault and he insulted her by saying: 'I will also break your ass.' When Aminata's son Nfali became ill, Madi was so fed up with her after the fight that he did not want to pay for the boy's medicine. This was the reason Aminata left with her son Nfali for her parents' village and her parents subsequently paid for the medicine. This was the first time she returned to her natal village—other times would follow.

Aminata stayed with her parents for two years. 'If a woman stays with her parents for a long time, then people will think that her parents love her and want the best for her—they defend her [honour] well.' 'If you are right, then there is no shame in staying with your parents,' according to Aminata. Aminata's parents wanted her to divorce Madi, because they did not want their daughter to be exposed to her co-wife's wrath. Madi's uncle went to Aminata's parents three times to mediate. The third time her parents agreed to let her go back to Farabako. Although Aminata was not happy to be back in Farabako again, she wanted to obey her parents. She wanted her 'parents' blessings'.

Back in Farabako (in 2009), Madi often insulted Aminata. She handled the situation by acting as if he had said nothing. 'If I let this bother me every time, then I would have no life.' Aminata knows that Madi does not love her and tries to find a way to manage this. But it is difficult, and there is jealousy because it is clear that Madi does love his first wife, Aminata's other co-wife Hawa. When I asked, 'is Madi sometimes nice to you?' Aminata answered: 'When he has money, he sometimes gives me a present.' Generally, Aminata steers clear of Madi because she feels ashamed that people see them fight so often. They seldom talk and there is little communication. Aminata wishes to be economically independent of Madi so that she does not need to ask him for anything.

In 2009, I witnessed several fights between Aminata and Madi. Her co-wives showed her no sympathy when there was a conflict. Aminata sometimes turned to me for support, as the next excerpt from my diary shows:

> 11 February 2009
> At 5.30 I wake from the crying of Kali, Madi and Aminata's little one-year-old son. The crying is so intense and does not stop, so I get out of bed to go take a look. Kali had not been feeling well yesterday, so I thought I should take a look. Aminata was busy lighting the fire for breakfast with Kali crying on her back. I managed to calm him down just by talking to him, and thus saw that he was not ill. I went back to bed. But Kali started crying again and now I heard that Madi had come outside and started yelling at Aminata. He then hit Aminata. Aminata ran out of the courtyard to the back of my hut and knocked on my window, crying loudly all the time. I opened the window and saw her huge frightened eyes and told her to come in. She came in and sat on my bed and cried and cried. Madi had hit her on back and on her arms. I tried to comfort her; she sat with me for ten minutes, then she went out to do her housework. Madi was there. I think he was angry that Kali had woken me. He told me that Aminata must give the breast to the child when he cries. Aminata said that she had already given the breast. By now the other women were up, Hawa and Nakani were present but did not interfere, or say anything. They did help Aminata with her work.
>
> This was a difficult situation. I sat on the edge of my bed thinking: was it my fault that Aminata got a beating? Was it because she had not prevented me from waking up? And does Madi (or anyone else) now have shame because I got mixed up in a private situation?

When I arrived in Farabako in 2011, Aminata had been sent away after yet another conflict. Because Aminata was one of my respondents with whom I had hoped to do a life history interview, I asked Madi if I could visit Aminata in her natal village where she had been living for the past six months. I told Madi that I did not want to interfere in family matters, but that I would like to see her. Madi told me that Aminata had threatened to put poison in his children's food. This was quite serious and thus a council of male family members had decided to send her away. I asked Madi if he wanted her to come back, and he answered, 'Sooner or later she will come back because of her two children.' After Madi gave me permission to go to Aminata's natal village, I carefully asked him if he wanted me to say something to Aminata's family when I visited her. He said I could tell them that if she promised never to speak of poisoning again, the negotiations between the families could commence. The next day, after an hour of dusty roads by motorcycle, my translator and I arrived in Aminata's natal village, and she told me her story:

> We cannot be loved by everyone, but also not rejected by everyone. It is in this situation that I find myself. Only God knows how I suffer except when I talk to someone. It is God who has chosen my fate. I think about the child I left behind. I am even afraid that my worries will kill me. I am angry with my conjugal family, but even more with my father's family because they have not tried to defend me. It is my co-wife [Hawa] who uses her charms to bring me into conflict with my husband. Today it is my older brother's decision that I will not return to the family of my husband. Even if they would send a delegation, I would not go back because of the suffering I feel there, because I do not want to die of suffering. If I had another husband, Madi would have another wife.
>
> My husband has let me suffer so much that only God knows how much. But every time I tell people this, they think I'm in the wrong—that I quarrel too much. No one understands me and no one wants to understand me. If a husband ruins his wife's name then she will not fit in the community. My husband ruined my name.
>
> My father is deceased and my mother is often sick, there is no one to defend me properly. Under the influence of the extended family, my older brother, who should defend me, has no longer taken responsibility for my affairs. My strategy now is to give the family of my husband one child, and I will keep this child I have with me [her youngest son Kali], he will never get this child.

Aminata goes on to explain the conflict that caused her husband to send her away:

> One day when I was pregnant I went to the fields with the children. I had taken porridge with me for my child. But Madi's children [by his other wives] ate it and this irritated me. When I returned home, I was angry with the children, especially N'Fa. I gave him a slap and he slapped me back, then I hit him. Madi then hit me and chased me out of the family. What made Madi especially angry was that I had told the children not to eat food that was not meant for them so as not to run the risk of being poisoned. My co-wife Hawa told Madi that I threatened to poison the children. Madi took this into consideration when deciding to send me away.
>
> I stayed with the family of Bubakar [the household head of another family] for one week. I decided then to return to my [natal] family. All the divination experts whom I had consulted told me that my co-wife was at the base of the conflict between Madi and myself. Madi refused to speak to the people that came to negotiate. Bubakar, with whom I was staying, also

> refused to support me because I had spoken of poisoning, even though it was a lie spread by Hawa. But I leave the judgment up to God. Madi hit me while I was pregnant. I told him that if I was lying that I would die during the birth. But thank God I came out of the delivery unscathed, which means that I was not lying, otherwise I would be dead.
>
> I would like to return to Farabako because I already have had children with Madi and I want to stay close to them. My parents must intervene before I can return. But for the moment my family has not received a single delegation of my husband's family to start the negotiations, and that is not a good sign.

After this interview I spoke to Aminata's older brother who said, 'a marriage is not a "grand boubou"'[79] (fudu tɛ dulɔkiba di); 'marriage is not a garment that you can take off and put on again, a marriage is about trust.' He went on to say that marriage is a relationship created by the family of the husband and wife, and only the family can end it. He was angry that Madi did not come to talk with him, but sent Aminata to her natal home on her own. We shared a meal and I left.

In representing Aminata's story, I have focused on the role of violence in Aminata's life as she tried to maintain her social ties. Her story illuminates linkages between violence, suffering and power; it shows the 'violence of everyday life'. I have told Aminata's story in detail because it illustrates many of the forces such as poverty and the patriarchal marriage system that limit not only her options, but also those of most women in Farabako. I will now describe the themes that Aminata's story has highlighted in more depth.

The suffering of insecurity

Aminata recounted her suffering in an unhappy and often violent marriage. Similarly, in the other life history interviews, the women in Farabako framed their life experiences in terms of suffering. The women all spoke of difficulties (*gɛlɛya*) and suffering (*tɔrɔ*). They suffered from the consequences of poverty and a heavy work burden. They suffered when their children died or when they themselves became ill. They suffered when their parents died or if they were widowed. They suffered from conflicts with their husbands and the jealousy of their co-wives. Women suffered if their honour was not defended. They suffered if their husbands did not provide for them and their children.

> My husband left, he abandoned me. I now take care of my children myself. How can you think that someone who is not taken care of has the same chances as someone who is well taken care of? I am not properly taken care of; this is why I suffer. (Kamisa Kante, 40 yrs)

[79] A garment worn by many men in West Africa.

Suffering is a recurring and expected condition in Farabako. Quantitative measures show how fragile their hold on survival is. Life expectancy at birth for women in Mali is 56 years. This is in large part due to the fact that in rural Mali one out of every four children die before their fifth birthday (WHO for 2009). In Farabako approximately a third of the children die before they reach five years of age. In Mali 78% of the population live on less than two US dollar a day (World Bank 2010). The average income in Farabako is less than one US dollar a day. But the experience of suffering cannot be felt in statistics. 'The 'texture' of affliction is perhaps best felt in the gritty details of biography' (Farmer 1997: 263), as the following quotations illustrate:

> The suffering I did when I was young was the result of the fact that my mother died when I was still young. When my mother died I had to leave school because no one could carry the financial burden. It is after this that I was married, here in Farabako, without bringing a dowry. The first year that I came here I had only one skirt. I came walking barefoot from my village in Guinea to here in Mali. When my mother died my brother had nothing. In this situation I married a man who was not rich and therefore I suffered. My luck was that the parents of my husband loved me and helped me a great deal; they gave me clothes. I have lost a total of six children and I have had two miscarriages. The death of my children was very hard on me and made me sad, especially the older children. Three of my children were still small when they died. The death of older children is very hard on a mother. My son who died from snakebite was four years old, he was in good health and the next moment he was dead and that was difficult to accept. Also the death of my youngest child was very difficult for me, he was three years old and meant a great deal to me also because he was a boy. (Nene Kante, 50 yrs old)

> Being abandoned by my husband has brought me grave financial problems. I suffer because I am poor and have no hope that that will change or that someone will help me. Look how often I have been lost; otherwise I would have been a fat woman by now. Poverty is worse than being burnt by lashes of a whip. If you are poor you are treated as a lazy good-for-nothing despite the fact you work as hard as you can. (Kamisa Kante, 40 yrs)

The common denominator of the women's stories of suffering was the insecurity they experienced if they felt that they were not being taken care of.

> How can we be happy if we have to take care of ourselves? (Nakani Kante, 35 yrs)

Happiness in their stories was often linked to feelings of security. The women spoke of being happy in their youth when they were still living with their parents. The first years of marriage were often happy. Happiness was also being well taken care of by their in-laws after marriage. Receiving clothes, shoes and food was often mentioned. Happiness was a husband or son who took good care of them. Happiness was also a year with a good harvest, 'a good day is a day that I eat well' one young mother told me.

The women spoke longingly of their parents and how their parents had taken care of them when they were young.

> I had few problems when I was young, when I lived with my parents. It is after my father died that the problems started. My father did everything for me and I have not had any one else that could do for me what he did, therefore I have suffered. (Narama Keita, 29 yrs)

The natal family was also a safe haven where women were taken care of when they had conflicts with their husbands. Sometimes the women left of their own accord after a fight or they left to avoid a conflict.

> It is only through patience and resignation that I can live in this difficult situation [of an unhappy marriage]. If my husband provokes me I sometimes leave him alone with the family. Last year I spent most of the rainy season at my father's because of my suffering. (Fatumata Kante, 30 yrs)

The women spoke of being happy if their husband and their husband's family took good care of them. Taking good care of them was always described in financial terms such as their husband paying for their clothes, medical bills and food.

> Before the birth of my son, I had a good relationship with my husband; he bought me clothes and shoes and he gave me presents. (Masitan Keita, 25 yrs)

> During one of my deliveries, my husband took care of me and took me to the clinic. He paid all the bills for me; this made me very happy. I will never forget this good deed of my husband. (Mariamu Kante, 40 yrs)

> The happiest time in my life was when the cousins of my husband were still alive; they gave me clothes and took care of me. They even built the three rooms I live in today. (Nene Kante, 50 yrs)

Many women expressed their unhappiness at not being well taken care of by their husbands. Traditionally, men should provide for the family. The husband should pay school fees, medicine, clothes for the children, the staple grain, and the daily ingredients for the sauce (*nasongo*). But, in practice men are not able to live up to this norm and more and more, women's earnings must cover male expenses (Brand 2000: 54). This led to a feeling of resentment (in the words of my translator: a 'sentiment de conflit').

> The men do little for the women, all they do is put the grain in the granary. The women do the rest, all the cooking and producing of children. The disinterest of the men for the women is the reason we do not talk. (Narama Kulibali, 30 yrs, February 2007)

This behaviour of not speaking was a woman's sanction for the men not living up to their role as a 'good husband'. Women were sometimes reluctant to speak to their husbands about their health or the health of their children. This sanction, however, contributed to a delay in seeking health care, as women in Farabako were dependent on their husbands for access to that care.

> There is an atmosphere of resentment here because men do not discharge their duty as providers; they do not buy clothes and such for us. The men show no interest in the women, therefore the women retreat into themselves and do not talk to the men. (Binetu Kante, 40 yrs, February 2007)

This atmosphere of resentment described by the women in Farabako, is similar to what Schulz (2011) found in urban Mali. Gender ideology assigns men and women to distinct and complementary spheres of productivity and complementary economic roles. Male authority is more ideological than material, since men have never been breadwinners. This was a French colonial norm that was never realised. As a consequence of diminishing job opportunities since the structural adjustment measures implemented in the 1980's, many households struggle to maintain their standard of living, and women are obliged to extend their activities beyond what is commonly seen as women's work. Husbands' growing inability to provide for their families and their simultaneous attempt to keep the upper hand in family decision-making processes, have led to a general atmosphere of disappointment and resentment, which adds to many women's sense of vulnerability (Schulz 2011: 101).

Many women in Farabako complained that men are no longer able to provide for the family and that the demise of collectivism is creating a heavier burden for them.

> Before, in our family, the men all worked together to take care of the family. But now, it is mainly the women that take care of the children, especially their clothes and other things. The fathers, the men, no longer have anything. (Nene Kante, 50 yrs)

> The last few months we have not eaten collectively because there are no longer any provisions. Everyone is only taking care of themselves. This

> situation places a heavy responsibility on the women. (Kamisa Kante, 40 yrs)

> I worry a lot about my children, especially about food for them because the collective meal is not enough and I have to go looking for food and that is what I find hard. (Nakani Kante, 35 yrs)

Not all men were unable to provide well for their households. There has been a marked differentiation since 2010 in Farabako. At that time, most families were struggling due to a bad harvest, however, one family prospered. This family had acquired the first (solar powered) television in Farabako. The women in this family did not speak of suffering. They were the only exceptions to the trope of no longer being taken care of. The mother of the most prosperous man in the village inverted the trope. She said she had suffered in the first years of her marriage, but things had improved in the village and now that her son took good care of her, she was happy.

> In the first years of my marriage there were not enough people in our family There were only three huts here in Farabako. […] I tell you, there were no women with more than two pieces of clothing; some women did not even wear a blouse, only a *fani*. […] The men worked on the land and we women chased away the birds and the monkeys, which is children's work. During this time there were no children and the women had to do this work next to their regular tasks. […] But slowly things improved and today we sleep in good rooms. […] At the moment we are happy, my son does everything for the family and we are content. […] We thank God that we have good rooms to sleep in, we have enough to eat and we no longer have to chase away the birds and monkeys. (Nandabi Kante, 70 yrs)

The wife of this same man was happy in her youth and also happy now because she had adjusted to the rules of marriage and her husband took good care of her.

> I was happy when I was young; I participated in theatre productions in the region. […]. I was popular and indispensable. […] The fear of my father was that my popularity would attract enemies.. […] I followed my father's instructions, stopped performing and got married. […] Now that I am married, I feel stress because I am subjected to the rules of marriage and I do not have my freedom as I did when I was single, I am often obliged to accept the will of the family and my husband and that gives me stress.[…] When I am with my husband I follow his rules.[…] Since our marriage there are no problems between me and my husband and he does a great deal for me. (Mariamu Kante, 40 yrs)

These two women were the exception. The other women protested that they were not being taken care of.

Patriarchal blackmail
All women, including Aminata, emphasised the importance of children in their marriage. A girl becomes a woman when she has children. Having children is a crucial part of personhood for women (and men) in Farabako. A woman without progeny is 'lost'; she has no one to take care of her in old age and no one to succeed her. Women considered producing children as the validation of their marriage into their conjugal family.

> The objective of marriage is to have children and I have had children and therefore I am happy with my marriage. (Mariamu Kante, 40 yrs)

Children are necessary to work the land and as security in old age. Children are the future of the patrilyny. Sanctions were harsh for women who did not produce (male) children as is illustrated in the following Malinke song: [80]

Malinke Song

Wolobali	The infertile woman
Wolobali ka fana	The infertile woman is deceitful
Son tɛ wolola la	The fertile woman has no faults
Wolobali kɔrɔ ka fana	The old infertile woman is deceitful
Son tɛ wolola la	The fertile woman has no faults
Den wolobali ye jalon di	The woman that does not give a child is an adulteress
Son tɛ wolola la	The fertile woman has no faults
Den wolobali ye jalon di	The woman that does not give a child is an adulteress
Fo n'bada kelen kɛ	I need to make one

Malinke mothers are said to sing this song to their daughters to express the imperative of having children to be above suspicion of adultery and to stay in the good graces of their husbands (Keita 2005). Several women in Farabako who had no (male) children were accused of adultery and their reputation and their honour were damaged.

> I had difficulties because I had had three daughters and my father-in-law was not satisfied because he wanted grandsons. My father-in-law said that he could not thank a [son's] wife who did not have boys, and that he was not

[80] My translation.

> happy with me. I then prayed to God to give me sons, and since then I have had sons. (Mariamu Kante, 40 yrs)

> The three children that came after my son Maramuri, died, one after the other and this situation led to great difficulties between my husband and me. This almost led to a divorce… Here 'en brousse' [in the countryside] if your children die, the husband thinks that you are the cause, because you have committed adultery or because you have transgressed the social norms. (Nandabi Kante, 70 yrs)

> [After the abortion] my husband was angry with me and accused me of killing his child and he threatened to divorce me. People accused me of adultery because, after the death of my former husband, I was given to a man with whom I have a bad relationship. In such a situation people quickly see you in a relationship with other men. (Nakani Kante, 35 yrs)

Children belong to the family of the father. As we saw in Aminata's story, if a couple separates, the woman must leave the village and leave her children behind with her husband's family. If a woman becomes widowed she is given in levirate to her deceased husband's brother (if she has no adult sons to take care of her). If she refuses to marry him, she must leave her children behind with him and leave the village. Only children who are still breastfeeding are allowed to stay temporarily with their mother. Many women stay in unhappy marriages so they don't lose their children.

> I have children and I cannot leave them, otherwise I would have left a long time ago. (Fatumata Kante, 30 yrs)

> I stay here in this family because I have children; because it is difficult to leave a man you have children with, even if he no longer loves you. (Masitan Keita, 25 yrs)

Children are the future of the patrilyny, but also the cement that keeps a marriage together.

> I don't want a divorce because I want to stay close to my children. I am optimistic that my husband will return, because I have had his children; a woman always keeps her husband if she has borne his children. (Kamisa Kante, 40 yrs)

The patrilineal and patrilocal marriage system in Farabako is such that women cannot leave an unhappy marriage without losing their children. Therefore, conflict resolution was of the utmost importance, as the story of Aminata illustrated.

Conflict and conflict resolution: Keeping the social fabric intact

As we have seen in Aminata's case, the private interviews were a platform for the women to speak about the difficulties they had experienced in their (polygamous) marriages, among other topics. Women described conflicts with their husbands and their co-wives. They spoke of feeling humiliated, being insulted and the hurt of not being defended by their family. They referred to their husband's lack of interest in them. The women spoke of the patience and resignation necessary to cope with these conflicts.

Conflicts with husbands

The women also talked of conflict resolution by mediation by their parents and other family members. As in Aminata's case, conflict resolution often consisted of the women leaving their compound and going to a mediator or to their parents in their natal village.

> My husband chased me out of the family, but luckily, otherwise you would not have found me here, Kali Kante [a male family member] intervened to keep me here. It was a child of [the adjoining compound] who burned my plate in the fire. I was angry with him and I shouted at him. My husband reacted by insulting me gravely and banishing me from the family. I was very humiliated, I cried almost all day and could barely eat because of the misery I felt. It was the insults that hurt me most… Now things are better, there is no longer a problem between us and we get along fine. (Hawa Kante, 35 yrs)

> My husband is very bad. He constantly causes situations that hurt me. One day, there was a stranger in the village who gave me rice to prepare for him. I went to give him his rice and when I came back my husband hit me so hard that he wounded me. He was angry that I had done that and ordered me never to prepare food for that type of person. He hit me without warning, this I did not accept. This time was very difficult for me. Madi [her husband's cousin] kept me with him for fifteen days. If Madi had not intervened we would have been divorced. (Fatumata Kante, 30 yrs)

> One day I asked my husband to buy shoes for me, which he refused. But I caught him in the act of buying shoes for his girlfriend. I told this to his family. He then got very angry with me and insulted my parents; that is why I left for my parents. It was Adama [her husband's cousin] who came to my father to end the conflict but the negotiation was not easy; it was my husband who had insulted my parents. The delegation tried four times to negotiate with my parents but only the fifth time did they come to an agreement; there was even a threat of a divorce. My parents themselves had asked for a divorce, but thanks to the negotiations things worked out. (Masitan Keita, 25 yrs)

Being able to go back to one's natal family can be viewed as a form of autonomy for women *vis a vis* their husband. Returning to one's natal family can be construed as a temporary sanction against one's husband. Mobility in conflict resolution can also function as a safety valve (cf. Brand 2000: 295). By a woman's action in leaving her husband and going to her natal village, the harmony in the village is restored and conflict mediation can commence. This sanction is usually temporary, although the sojourn away from home can be quite lengthy, as we have seen in the case of Aminata who stayed with her parents for two years before her return was negotiated to everyone's satisfaction. In the end, a marriage is a contract between the two families and the woman's family will negotiate her return.

Conflicts with co-wives

Women's emotional and material insecurity is exacerbated by polygamous marriage arrangements. Women are often anxious that their husband will take a second wife leading to arguments over the allocation of resources. Many women, including Aminata, expressed feeling discriminated against because their husband did not take equally good care of all his wives, and this led to a feeling of insecurity.

> Since my co-wife arrived, my husband has been good to me. But when my labour pains started and the old women advised him to take me to the doctor, he answered that he had no money. When my co-wife was pregnant they advised him that her delivery should take place in a clinic; he followed this advice. This discrimination caused me much pain…I felt as a kind of survivor at that time because I could have died had there been complications. (Kamisa Kante, 40 yrs)

Some women expressed feelings of jealousy and hurt because their husband loved their co-wife more than them.

> My husband favours my co-wife above me, I do not mind this so much, but the fights are hard on me. If my co-wife does something stupid, he does not mind because he loves her; if it is me, he does mind. (Masitan Keita, 25 yrs)

Despite the difficulties of a polygamous household, all women emphasised the necessity of a co-wife to help with the housework and in taking care of the children.

> I am the first wife. Since the second wife arrived she has always respected me, she gives me water to wash with and she washes my clothes and also my children. There is not a single problem between us, it is the same with

> the third wife. If one is sick the others take care of her and her children. (Mariamu Kante, 40 yrs)

> If I could choose, I would choose to have a co-wife because if I die, then I know she will take care of my children. (Kamisa Kante, 40 yrs)

The women's stories affirmed the family values and the structures of the patriarchal system. However, at the same time, these stories expressed complaints that these structures were no longer working to care for the women and their children. The women positioned/constructed themselves as good wives, who were victims of poverty and unhappy marriages. They wanted me to know that they had suffered an injustice they could not escape—only resign themselves to it. They told me of their hard work keeping the weave of their social fabric intact in the context of changing gender relations.

Gender-based violence, social ties and insecurity

I have told Aminata's and the other women's stories because they shed light on the structural violence of grinding poverty and sexism/patriarchy. Interpersonal gender-based violence is defined here as any act of force or coercion directed at an individual woman that causes harm and suffering, and serves to reinforce a woman's subordinate position. As such, this form of violence reflects power imbalances inherent in a patriarchal society (Richters 1994; Hof and Richters 1999). The violence goes beyond the physical to include assaults on self-respect and personhood. Violence is not a term the women used during the interviews. This is not surprising, as hierarchies (and oppression) are naturalized into a common-sense discourse shared by the dominant and the dominated alike. The words the women used were: suffering, conflict, beaten until wounded, hit while pregnant, chased out of the family, insults that hurt, the pain of being treated like a good-for-nothing, injustice, feelings of mortification and shame.

Aminata's story illustrates some of 'the mechanisms through which large scale forces crystallize into the sharp hard surfaces of individual suffering' (Farmer 1997: 263). It shows power micro-dynamics whereby she did not so much resist subordination to her husband's family, but rather accommodated it. The 'everyday violence' that Aminata experienced was implicit, legitimate and routinized; it was inherent in the patriarchal marriage system. Aminata, and many others like her, had to accept (what I call) violence in order to stay in the family and keep their children. The women had to accept the physical violence of being beaten, as well as the psychological violence of fear of reprisal for failing to conform to expected behavioural norms, loss of honour and/or loss of their children. As Scheper-Hughes and Bourgois have stated: 'The family is one of the most violent of social institutions' (2004: 3).

Studies have shown that social capital in the form of a large social network often correlates with improved health outcomes (Nguyen and Peschard 2003; Adams et al. 2002). The rationale is that a close-knit social network may be more effective in coordinating action to support therapy management, and that social isolation may be detrimental to physical and social well-being. The social networks of women in Farabako were comprised almost solely of kinship ties—the basis of social organization in Farabako. The collective of the African extended family has often been romanticized as a place of solidarity, while the kinship group is also marked by the tensions and oppression that create its dynamic. One must contextualize social capital and look at the local dynamics of reciprocity and exchange to see how social ties result from asymmetrical relations of power (Nguyen and Peschard 2003). Social capital can have a 'dark side'; networks may function efficiently, but can nevertheless be regarded as socially or morally undesirable (Baron et al. 2000: 31).[81] A woman's social ties, such as within an extended family, can have a beneficial effect on her physical well-being while at the same time be a source of suffering. It is my contention, that in Farabako, in a context of extreme poverty and a sexist social and moral order, violence against women is used to secure family solidarity, and that this takes a psychological and physical toll on the women. From a feminist perspective this is the dark side of social capital in Farabako.

After listening to Aminata's and the other women's stories, one wonders if accommodating gender-based violence may be the price women have to pay to stay in the collective of the patrilineal kin group. And might I go so far as to hypothesize that coercion is the basis of social capital in Farabako, because it secures the women (through their children) in a patrilyny? Larger social networks may correlate with better physical well-being, but we must look at the (gender) violence necessary to keep family ties intact and the effect this has on women's social well-being.

The stories of women in Farabako show the conflict and conflict resolution in the day-to-day hard work of keeping the weave of the social fabric intact. But first and foremost, the women's stories were about their feelings of insecurity and suffering. When I asked the women of Farabako to speak of their health, they spoke of feeling insecure. For most women and men in Farabako insecurity is the norm, a permanent feature of their lives.[82] They live, and always have lived in a context of severe poverty, but now social change in the form of increasing individualization and differentiation and the increasing dependency on money[83] has put a strain on gender relations. Money is needed now more

[81] The Mafia, for example.

[82] Similarly, in their work among pastoralists in central Mali, De Bruijn and Van Dijk have described their respondents' feelings of being lost, totally dependent on circumstances and emotionally, physically and existentially insecure. They argue that insecurity is a 'total experience', not confined to one life sphere or another, but rather integrated in their lives and in their society (De Bruijn and Van Dijk 1995: 116).

[83] See Boserup's (2007 [1970]) work on the negative effects on women from the penetration of capitalism in subsistence economies.

than ever, because villagers take part in the money economy. But in Farabako, men and women face a lack of work opportunities outside subsistence farming. Women have limited or no independent income. Men's growing inability to provide for their families leads to a pervasive atmosphere of disappointment and resentment, which contributes to women's sense of vulnerability.

The agency of lament

Conceptualizing suffering only as the product of a social order would represent the women of Farabako as victims of social forces, rather than as agents in their own lives. As we have seen, Aminata was able to convey her feelings of injustice and insecurity. She felt the injustice of being treated badly by her husband and co-wives, having to leave her child behind and having her reputation ruined. Aminata spoke of the injustice and insecurity of not being taken care of by her husband. Aminata did what she could—she turned to her parents for help, hoping they would defend her honour. She made an oath to God to clear her name. She vowed to keep the younger of her two children. She spoke of justice as necessary for reconciliation. But, in all her anger and rebelliousness, in the end Aminata will most likely return to her unhappy marriage to be with her children. She, as many women in Farabako, accepts suffering. Accepting suffering is a form of agency. Agency is not only about resistance to the restraints and dominance of (patriarchal) structures, rather agency is how women make themselves into the kinds of persons who fit into those structures (cf. Mahmood 2005). A woman's accepting subordination to males, affines and elders is a condition for being recognized as a virtuous member of the community. Accepting suffering reasserts patriarchal ideology, but at the same time can be part of the project of working on oneself to become a good woman. In this way, women's stories do not simply reflect a particular social context, but rather they constitute it.

Personal narratives are performative and they make and reshape (gender) relations. The women's narratives can be viewed as a performance and read as a lament. So what does a narrative full of lamentation do? I argue that speaking of suffering is part of being a good woman in Farabako. Melhuus (1997) describes suffering as a female virtue and as part of women's moral discourse. Suffering heightens self-esteem. The point is not to suffer, but rather to frame your life in terms of suffering. This seems to be the case in Farabako also.

I believe that another reason that the women of Farabako speak of suffering so abundantly is to evoke pity from the listener. If someone takes pity (*hinɛ*) on you, then they will be more inclined to help you in times of difficulty. We have seen (in chapter 4) that pity is an important factor in a woman's social network. 'Taking pity' was the term used to describe reciprocity between two people who liked each other. Women sustained their ties not through financial means, but rather by taking pity on each other. Evoking pity is accepted behaviour in Farabako, whereas asking outright for help is considered shameless. The women's lamentations were performed for me (and the readers of this book), possibly in the hope that we could help them decrease their insecurity.

Conclusion

The narratives of the women of Farabako made me shift my focus from illness to suffering (cf. Kleinman, Das and Lock 1997). The women did not primarily speak of their physical well-being, but rather of feeling insecure. They had lost their sense of safety in the world including a basic trust that they would be taken care of. Women spoke about their health in terms of suffering due to feelings of insecurity in a context of vulnerability. Social change in the form of individualization had aggravated their suffering—they were no longer taken care of. For the women of Farabako, security is a prerequisite for physical and psychological well-being. Social capital is often presumed to contribute to people's health. This also applies to Farabako. However, the maintenance of social capital by women also had a negative effect. In these narratives, the women spoke of the (physical and psychological) 'everyday violence' needed to keep their social ties intact.

Throughout this book, when writing about marriage, I have privileged the social ties between husbands and wives. Initially this was influenced by my Western bias towards marriage as a partnership between two individuals rather than a relationship between families. Subsequently, it became clear from my female respondents' narratives that their marriage relationships are shifting; the role of the husband in taking care of a wife is becoming more prominent (compared to the role of other family members such as parents-in-law).

In life history interviews, women emphasized the role of their husbands when speaking about being taken care of. Generally, only elderly women spoke of how they were well taken care of by their in-laws and later by their sons. It is the norm that adult sons should take care of their (widowed) 'mothers' (including co-wives of their biological mother). Yet in Farabako there were several cases of widows whose adult sons did not take care of them, but rather these widows were given in levirate to a 'brother' of their deceased husband. One case is Nakani, whose story is told in chapter 5. Nakani was not taken care of by her adult son (the son of her former co-wife) who had a wife and children of his own; rather, she was taken care of by her husband's brother. There seems to be more pressure on men in their role as husbands than in the past. A woman's position has become more vulnerable now that she is increasingly dependent on her husband for her well-being. My point here is that my focus on the husband-wife relationship within a marriage is not only my Western bias, but is due to a change in marriage relations taking place recently in Farabako.[84]

[84] Research on modern day levirate constructions is necessary to corroborate these findings as many of my respondents still had young children and no adult sons to take care of them. It appears that the husband-wife relationship is changing in Farabako as it has in Bamako where more people live in nuclear families.

For my female respondents, being-taken-care-of was their language of well-being. In Farabako, insecurity is an indicator of ill-being and should be taken into account in the planning and implementation of public health programs geared to reduce maternal and child mortality. When studying therapy management, it is not sufficient to focus only on illness, rather one must also focus on insecurity within the household. A mother's emotional and material insecurity can lead to feelings of powerlessness and ill-being, which in turn can lead to passivity in the therapy management of her child's illness episode. I will expand on this further in chapter 11.

The women in Farabako framed their life experiences in terms of suffering. Their suffering was a 'social suffering', caused by the societal forces that they were exposed to, but had little control over (cf. Kleinman, Das and Lock 1997). Central to this chapter were the effects of the structural violence of poverty and patriarchy, and how these effects were expressed by the women articulating and accepting suffering. In the following chapter, I reflect on the suffering of the women in Farabako, not simply as a product of misfortune, but also as a manifestation of injustice (cf. Fassin 2010); an injustice that needs to be addressed in the context of promoting mother and child health.

10. MEDICAL ETHNOGRAPHY AS AN ETHICAL TRAJECTORY

In this chapter, I reflect on the ethical trajectory of my research. In the previous chapters, the focus was on the local moralities in health and health care. This chapter focuses on the role of morality in ethnography. I start with a description of the debate on moral anthropology that began in the 1990s and has recently been renewed to answer the question: should anthropology be moral, and if so, how? I next suggest a starting point for a feminist anthropology of moralities. I continue by describing how my Western-feminist-biomedical assumptions travelled to Farabako and the friction they encountered there. Finally, I reflect on how best to represent the suffering of the women of Farabako—in a language of compassion or a language of human rights. The choice of the language of representation can affect the policies and programs that promote mother and child health.

A moral anthropology

In the course of this research, I have wished to position myself squarely on the side of human suffering, or 'to work towards an anthropology of affliction and not simply an anthropology of medicine' to use Scheper-Hughes' words (1990: 196). I felt a great deal of sympathy with Scheper-Hughes' quite personal account of political engagement in *Death without weeping: The violence of everyday life in Brazil* (1992). I consider ethnographies such as the one by Scheper-Hughes which delve into the lives of people and are not afraid to take up issues relating oppression and social crisis to everyday interpersonal violence to be essential for a responsible anthropology.

Scheper-Hughes' (1995) argument is that cultural relativism, in the form of moral relativism, is no longer appropriate in the world we live in. According to Scheper-Hughes, there is no objectivity that stands outside a moral position. Power operates through hegemonic constructions of social reality and makes 'natural' the arrangements that perpetuate social inequalities such as the widespread neglect of children, women, and the poor. She argues that anthropologists are also susceptible to such hegemonic views of the world and that their reactions have been to take the detached pose of indifference and call it 'objectivity'. Scheper-Hughes believes that if anthropology is to be worth anything at all, it must be politically committed and morally engaged.

D'Andrade (1995) argues that Scheper-Hughes' use of the moral model of oppression is an oversimplification and leads her away from a search for realistic solutions and toward an approach in which 'witnessing' becomes an end in itself. The moral model does not explain much; it simply condemns discrimination as oppression. It does not tell us why discrimination is worse in a particular time or place. The moral model has no theory of good power or good inequality, and so must simply condemn without understanding the operation of a social system. Also, the model is almost entirely negative; it creates a climate of denunciation and rage. The moral model is ethnocentric and advocates equality (the escape from inequality) and freedom (the release from oppression). These are Western values and describing and denouncing oppression is not enough. D'Andrade argues that anthropology's claim to authority should rest on knowing empirical truths about the world, and he calls for an objective model of moralities that is distinct from the moral model (as used by Scheper-Hughes).

D'Andrade wants to keep objective and subjective goals separate so that moral assessments can be achieved after carefully weighing the facts. D'Andrade makes a distinction between empirical knowledge (out there) and a moral position (adopted by the anthropologist). I disagree. In his attempt to separate the scientific from the moral, D'Andrade seems to avoid the issue that all the models devised to collect and evaluate empirical evidence are ultimately based on implicit moral criteria. I argue that research involves active engagement with respondents. Even the most invisible anthropologist is an active presence, in spite of herself. Research should be carried out in a manner that protects the findings from a political and moral bias to the greatest possible degree, but this does not mean that it should be (or can be) conducted in a moral and political vacuum. Morality, in the form of culturally constructed values and preferences, influences the definition and selection of researchable projects. What we choose to study (or not to study) in the name of anthropology is a political and moral decision; for example, 'the oppressed' are a morally approved research subject.

D'Andrade protests against social scientists who hold a moral model of anthropology that sacrifices objectivity for moral engagement. Scheper-Hughes protests against those who refuse moral and political engagement. Their stances are a contrast between an objective 'white coat' and a militant 'barefoot' anthropology, yet they both write about the adequacy of anthropological research (Nader 1995: 426). I believe that the perspective of moral anthropology is not necessarily wrong, but rather it is theoretically weak. Engagement demands analysis; however, neither Scheper-Hughes nor D'Andrade directly addresses how the anthropologist's morality should interact with the morality of cultural others; for this, we must turn to the debate between Fassin and Stoczkowski.

An anthropology of morals

Fassin (2008) describes the tension between cultural relativism, which tolerates a variety of moralities, and the moral conviction about universal values that are worth fighting for. He sees a blurred distinction between ethical indignation and critical thinking (Fassin 2008: 342). In his attempt to reconcile the pros and the cons of a moral agenda in the social sciences (as illustrated in anthropology by the debate between Scheper-Hughes and D'Andrade), Fassin pleads for an anthropology that takes moralities as objects of study. Fassin suggests that moral anthropology should be one that studies moral issues in society and simultaneously the moral assumptions underlying the research. He does not endorse Scheper-Hughes' argument for an anthropology that proposes its own morality—that of the anthropologist. Anthropologists are always confronted with a series of moral issues that are often crystallized by their presence in field situations. Fassin (2008) disagrees with D'Andrade (1995) that it is possible to separate the scientific from the moral. The anthropologist cannot avoid taking a moral position and should not escape the moral position she adopts. Fassin argues that it is epistemologically and politically imperative to question the values and judgments that underlie our work.

Fassin calls for a critical analysis that attempts to understand moral issues in a cultural and historical context. An anthropology of morals should analyse where and why social agents locate the good and the bad. Fassin argues that morals should become a legitimate object of study for anthropology, just as politics and medicine. Hence, an anthropology of morals should no more promote values and do good, than political anthropology should support political parties or medical anthropology propose medical treatments. An anthropology of morals should make the way judgements on good and evil are formed, justified and applied in various societies and contexts both explicit and understandable (cf. Zigon 2008). To do this, the anthropologist must make an effort to explicate and explore her moral prejudices. Thus, Fassin proposes to take the anthropologist's moral values and practices into account to understand the impact of her moral options on the production of academic knowledge. 'The only rigorous attitude towards moral issues is a permanent questioning of the "moral grounds" of our understanding of societies and their moralities' (Fassin 2008: 342).

A common assumption underlying a moral anthropology such as Scheper-Hughes proposes, is that knowledge production is always compatible with ethical commitment. However, epistemological values that are fundamental for the study of society, such as objectivity, are not the same as the moral values necessary for action to reform that society. For Stoczkowski (2008), anthropological research necessarily mobilizes a system of values carried by the anthropologist, although sometimes unconsciously. Moral values and epistemological values coexist and sometimes conflict. The anthropologist must be aware of this, and must analyse the epistemological challenges of moral judgements at work in everyday scientific practice. According to Stoczkowski, ' moralities used spontaneously separate us from an epistemologically sound science, while moralities made explicit and transformed knowingly into a heuristic tool reunite us with it' (2008: 354). Here Stoczowski agrees with Fassin that once made explicit, the observer's moral standpoint ceases to be an awkward problem, a source of an epistemological dilemma and a constant threat to objectivity. On the contrary, the observer's moral standpoint becomes a legitimate research tool that can shed light on how our particular system of morals helps us to understand moralities in the lives of the people we study (or sometimes prevents us from understanding).

Whereas Fassin claimed a direction for studies in political and moral anthropology, and Stoczkowski stressed the epistemological dilemmas that moral stances in anthropology cause, they both share the conviction that anthropology should not be moral in the sense of promoting the good. They both argue for an anthropology of morals; moral values should be objectified (made the object of study) on the side of the observed and of the observer. Zigon (2007, 2010) agrees with this standpoint and has conceptualised a theoretical framework for an anthropology of moralities (see chapter 4) with reference to both Fassin and Stockzkowski.

Fassin and Stoczkowski conclude their debate by agreeing that only when anthropologists become reflectively aware of their own moral positions and assumptions can anthropology safely investigate local moralities. Thus, the question is not: should anthropology be moral? Rather, the question is: what is it that counts as morality in the various social worlds we and our respondents inhabit, and what are the processes by which this morality comes to matter?

Translating this approach to my research, I realised that to attempt to understand the role of the local moral discourse of shame and the local medical moral discourse for the health of women and young children in Farabako, I needed to examine both the local moral discourse *as well as* my Western feminist and biomedical assumptions as the object of my study. My Western medical-ethical assumptions did not travel well. The implementation of biomedicine in Farabako and my anthropological research was an 'ethical moment'; a moment when both my respondents and I had to step out of our unreflexive states to communicate and negotiate medical and moral/gender discourses. In approaching medical ethnography as an 'ethical moment', I hope to have demonstrated that becoming aware of one's assumptions is a useful ethnographic tool in medical anthropological research.

Towards a feminist anthropology of moralities

In my view, a feminist anthropology of moralities is one in which agency is first detached from politics, subsequently analysed, and then used to understand how and why women embody inequality and how inequality is reproduced (cf. Zigon 2008). A feminist anthropology of moralities should go beyond describing various modalities of agency and attempt to show how moral and ethical assemblages contribute to legitimizing existing social inequality (cf. Richters 1991). A feminist anthropology of moralities should examine which subject positions are open to women within a particular discourse, and what significance subordination holds for them (cf. Mahmood 2005).

Anthropologists have argued that all cultures and societies are founded upon relations of gender inequality, and the task of the anthropologist is to show how culturally specific systems of inequality are constructed, practiced and maintained (Strathern 1988; Collier and Yanagisako 1989). There is no single arrangement of gender inequality within a culture, rather various arrangements of gender inequality coexist. Specific forms of gender inequality are the product of specific discursive formations, such as the discourse of shame. To evaluate the violence that particular systems of gender inequality enact on women, one must analyse the work that discursive practices perform in making specific kinds of subject positions possible. It is not enough to simply point out, for example, that a discourse of shame serves to legitimize women's subordination. Rather, it is only by exploring the discourse of shame in relation to the practical engagements in which it is embedded, such as health care seeking, that we can come to understand the significance of subordination to the women who embody it (cf. Mahmood 2005: 167).

The morality of biomedicine in friction

I went to do good. I went to Farabako thinking I could help by bringing Western biomedicine to the village. I would do the villagers a service by setting up a maternity clinic and training local midwives. In the course of my research, I realised that I had gone into the field with many (moral) assumptions that I was not fully conscious of at the start.

It was my assumption that women in countries with high maternal and child mortality, such as Mali, need salvation and that implementing biomedicine could improve mothers' and children's health (under the assumption that biomedicine is superior). From my feminist viewpoint, I assumed that women in Mali lived in an oppressive patriarchal society, and that oppression was bad. Building on these assumptions, I set out to unmask the symbolic hegemony that hid or legitimized that oppression. As an anthropologist I would conduct fieldwork not only in order to observe society, but also to defend the rights of the oppressed including women, children, the sick, and poor people. My main mission would be to testify, defend and lavish the benefits of science on those in need, and as a midwife to also take care of them. Ideally, my medical and anthropological knowledge would help improve their health and decrease gender inequality in health.

However, during my fieldwork, my engagement did not help me to understand the health situation of women and their children in Farabako, and my 'witnessing' of their troubles did little to improve their health. In the first instance, my engagement, based on (often unconscious and unspoken) moral and biomedical assumptions, often got in the way of my understanding. This has become clear throughout this book. But reflecting on the friction my assumptions encountered, turned out to be productive in coming to an understanding of therapy management in Farabako.

I set out to undertake a participatory action research and I assumed that together with the villagers of Farabako I could bring about change—an improvement in their health and that biomedicine was the necessary means with which to do this.

I had entered the field with anthropological knowledge of 'indigenous medical systems' and an awareness of the existence of various medical discourses. But, because my task was to set up a maternity clinic, I had to let biomedical assumptions dominate my thinking. This meant that I made many unconscious comparisons; for example, comparing 'traditional beliefs' and 'Western knowledge'. I believed that if I understood the health beliefs and health-seeking behaviour of pregnant women and young mothers that I could use this knowledge to better implement Western biomedical health care. In hindsight, my helpfulness could be understood as a form of domination and my belief in the necessity of Western medicine for alleviating Farabako's ills as (an unconscious) 'development' ideology. The morality implicit in biomedicine became explicit in the maternity clinic of Farabako.

Equipped with medical anthropological concepts, I set out to research the meaning women gave to their health and the social meaning of health and illness within a therapy management group. However, in attempting to reconstruct illness episodes from the point of view of indigenous medical knowledge, I was often unable to let go of my own biomedical theory of knowledge. In the maternity clinic, I was initially transforming my respondent's information into biomedical facts to be able to give what I perceived to be a proper treatment (see also Richters 1991: 135). Underlying my attempt to understand indigenous medical theory, was my biomedical assumption (at the time unspoken and unconscious) that the 'real' cause of illness is to be found at a cellular level. For example, it took quite a while before I could let go of the assumption that malnutrition was about protein and energy deficiency. My anthropological background had convinced me of the importance of the social in health, but my biomedical background kept getting the better of me. In biomedicine, the patient is examined as a biomedical object outside of the social context.

During the first phase of this research, I gained insight into local ideas of patho-physiology, local taxonomies and the social and cultural context of pregnancy and illness. This work was not value-free. Initially, the Western metanarrative of development was the basis for my interpretation of local meaning. Using ethnomedical models of illness to attempt to increase clinical efficacy in the maternity clinic was really nothing more than an extension of the biomedical model of health. Translating cultural information into 'natural' information is reductionism. For example, after working in the maternity clinic with the local midwives and conducting many interviews, I had information on local nosology. I could tell you that *kɔnɔ* is a bird-witch that eats children, and that *kɔnɔ* is also an illness category in Farabako. *Kɔnɔ* is a category that corresponds to my biomedical category of convulsions due to severe infection.

Having this information facilitated the biomedical treatment of sick children who came to me in the clinic. But this information was not enough to understand health in Farabako. *Kɔnɔ* was an illness category the mothers of Farabako used often in interview settings, but when speaking spontaneously about their health and the health of their children they spoke about shame and the suffering of insecurity. It became apparent to me that shame (*maloya*) counts as morality in Farabako, and that therapy management is a process by which this morality comes to matter.

The grounded theory method of returning to the field several times facilitated reflection on my moral and biomedical assumptions. I was able to use this awareness as an ethnographic tool to better understand health and health care in Farabako. My research approach changed from a moral participatory action research geared to improving the health situation in Farabako, to a study of local moralities in the therapy management of children's illnesses.

I have taken moralities as an object of study without letting go of my feminist principles. I have looked at the significance that subordination to moral discourse has for women and the role moral discourse has in perpetuating inequality. I have analysed passivity as a modality of agency, within the moral discourse of shame, rather than as a sign of oppression.

I argue that shame works as an intersubjective logic that maintains inequality. Institutional shame originates from and supports hierarchy; women are ranked lower than men and their reputations are men's responsibility. This inferiority is embodied by the women and leads to inertia. The public discourse of shame enforces this with extensive prohibitions for women. Women must have a modest demeanour, not speak out of turn and not take initiative. This can lead to a mother's passivity in the face of child mortality (more on this in the next chapter).

I have examined which 'technologies of the self' women in Farabako use to constitute themselves as moral subjects (cf. Foucault 1994d). It has become clear that women's submission to certain forms of authority can be a condition for achieving their potentiality and that having shame is a 'technique of the self' aimed at comfortably inhabiting a moral discourse (cf. Mahmood 2005). The significance that this subordination has for women is that they will be seen as 'good women'. A woman who 'has shame' will be considered a trustworthy woman and this enhances her social capital and that of her husband and this increases her chances of her receiving help if one of her children becomes ill.

The various modalities of agency that operate in the negotiations of Farabako's patriarchal system have been examined. I have looked at suffering and survival and how women survive within a system of inequality. I have shown that accepting suffering is a form of agency geared to keeping the social fabric intact and thus contributes to the well-being of the women's children.

The language of representation

Throughout this book, I have struggled with the question of how to represent the women of Farabako and what they call their suffering. I reject the relativist view that suffering is acceptable when it is an established way of life. I could use a humanitarian approach and mobilise sympathy for the poor women and children of Farabako using a language of compassion rather than justice. Humanitarianism is the language of (political) solidarity and moral justification; it is the language of moral anthropology that I started out with. However, this would portray the women as innocent victims of the oppression of patriarchy. To represent the women as not having the capacity to create their own future would be wrong (cf. Wilson and Brown 2009). In the language of humanitarianism, life is sacred and suffering is valorised; the faceless 'other' is a victim of misfortune to whom we have an obligation to help. However, this is a moral simplification and social reality is quite complex. I do not want my account to contribute to the 'catastrophization of the social world' (Fassin 2011: 180) thereby, contributing to further 'compassion fatigue' (Moeller 1999) with yet another account of the poor women and children of Africa.

Suffering is not simply a product of misfortune as humanitarianism intimates, but also a manifestation of injustice. An alternative to the humanitarian approach would be to use a human-rights approach. Human-rights language portrays suffering as the violation of human rights, and human rights as a prerequisite for health. However, this is a language of entitlements and legal justification built on Western moral assumptions. Rights-based language can distort the nature of individual and social suffering by 'translating "thick" moral (and political) problems into "thin" legal representations' (Richters 2004: 166). The human-rights approach often focuses on individuals, giving them a face, yet disengaging the self from the social. And as has become clear in this book, to understand health in Farabako, we need a socially embedded understanding of the self (cf. Richters 2004: 170).

So, how to represent the suffering of the women of Farabako without turning them into faceless victims and disengaging them from their social context? I have attempted to understand the human condition in Farabako without reducing it to an abstraction by contextualizing suffering (cf. Wilson and Brown 2009). I have analysed the effects of domination expressed through suffering. I have shown how women actively inhabit moral and gender discourse rather than portraying them as vulnerable victims of patriarchy.

I argue that in Farabako, existential factors are even more crucial in womens' suffering than cultural ones or questions of human rights (cf. Jackson 2005: 175). Suffering in Farabako is a condition of ill-being caused by a lack of ontological security generated by poverty and gender inequality.

Arriving at the end of my ethnographic journey, I have come to appreciate the relevance of Jackson's (2005) existential anthropological approach for my (method of) analysis with a focus on modes of 'being in the world', intersubjectivity[85] and reflexivity. Jackson (2005) argues for a methodological relativism using the practice of putting oneself in the place of the other, an 'openness to submitting one's assumptions to the test of dialogue and debate'. I have become deeply involved in the local and particular life worlds of the women and children of Farabako. I have reached forms of understanding through engagement rather than detachment, thereby 'creating the social conditions under which coexistence is possible' (cf. Jackson 2005: 178). I have represented the process of searching for a common ground of understanding between my respondents and me.

Conclusion

In the course of this research, my attention has moved from a medical approach to health with a focus on individual determinants of health to a more public health approach that also considers the societal determinants of health. Where I was first looking for biomedical 'facts' of pregnancy outcome and children's illnesses, I soon found that the seeming passivity of mothers in the face of child mortality was an issue in therapy management that needed in-depth study, and my focus changed to shame and suffering.

This research has moved from a clinically applied medical anthropological approach (social science *in* medicine) to a critical medical anthropological approach (social science *of* medicine). My focus moved beyond health care seeking and health beliefs and towards medical moralities and ethics—both my respondents' ethics and mine. My approach shifted from a moral anthropology towards an anthropology of morals. My struggle, as a midwife and anthropologist, has been how to position myself practically, politically and ethically towards medical modernisation. It has been an ethical trajectory of becoming reflexively aware of my own moral assumptions and using this awareness as an ethnographic tool.

I have taken an approach of being involved rather than detached, and in this sense my approach was a moral one. I still wish to position myself squarely on the side of human suffering. I want to delve into the lives of the women of Farabako to take up issues relating to their subordination (cf. Scheper-Hughes 1995), while realising that describing and denouncing oppression is not enough (cf. D'Andrade 1995). This book is not a moral ethnography that proposes my own morality, but an ethnography that studies moral issues in society and, at the same time, studies the moral assumptions underlying the research (cf. Fassin 2008; Stoczkowsi 2008; Zigon 2010). I have taken a feminist approach by showing how moralities, such as the discourse of shame, can contribute to legitimizing existing social inequality in Farabako. Zigon's theoretical frame-

[85] Van der Geest, Gerrits and Singer Aaslid (2012) argue that subjectivity becomes an obstacle to understanding the other if it is not taken to the next step—intersubjectivity, a convincing analysis of how knowledge and insight that can be shared between individuals. By studying this process, subjectivity can lead to better ethnography (p.6).

work for an anthropology of morals was a useful heuristic tool to do this.

In this chapter, I have shed light on my own ethical trajectory and the string of 'ethical moments' within my medical ethnographic research. In the following chapter, I use the insights gained in these ethical moments to come to a conclusion on the importance of local moralities in health and their role in therapy management.

11. THE LANGUAGE AND LOGIC OF WELL-BEING

This book has been about mothers 'in the middle of nowhere' and, in particular, their role in the therapy management of their children's illnesses. The observation that mothers in Farabako sometimes seemed to 'do nothing' when their children were ill initiated the trajectory of this research. I have studied their seeming passivity as agency. I found that for these mothers, agency could be geared towards non-action, because to take action may be perceived as shameless behaviour for a woman. While avoiding shameless behaviour may succeed as a strategy to avoid social risk, I argue that it limits mothers in accessing the (biomedical) health care that could potentially reduce child morbidity and mortality. The root of what I originally perceived as passivity lies in the vulnerability context in which the women of Farabako live. I have singled out poverty and the moral discourse of shame as key determinants of this context.

In this chapter, I begin by summarizing the factors that influence mothers' agency in the therapy management of their children's illnesses in Farabako. Subsequently, I complement my previous explanations by using a more existential approach to therapy management. I explore the relationship between the important themes that were presented and discussed in this book including: a lack of security, shame and suffering. I posit that women's suffering is an expression of the lack of ontological security in the context of vulnerability. Where in chapter 9, I highlighted security as a key concept in the language of well-being women used in their life histories, I now theorise that trust is also an important factor contributing to women's well-being. Next, I argue that in Farabako shame is enabled by structural inequality, while at the same time shame is the embodiment of this inequality. Then, I examine how shame allows a woman to bear suffering in what is locally perceived as the proper manner. I theorise that shame works as an important intersubjective logic in health seeking. I conclude by arguing that health care workers and policy makers must understand the language and the logic of patients' therapy management as a first step to make health care interventions successful.

Non-action in therapy management

Powerlessness and ill-being are characteristic of people living in poverty anywhere in the world (Narayan 2000: 21). While women do not speak about powerlessness as such, I find powerlessness is a relevant concept to analyse their situation. Some of the dimensions of powerlessness and ill-being that emerged from the stories of the women of Farabako are that their livelihoods and assets were precarious, seasonal and inadequate. The village is isolated and not serviced by the government or NGO's. The women's bodies were hungry, exhausted and ill. Gender relations were troubled and unequal. Women suffered from a lack of security and their capabilities were limited because of a lack of information, education, and confidence.

Methodologically, it is difficult, if not impossible, to produce a systematic analysis of child mortality and the struggle for existence in Farabako. We can never grasp all the factors at play in the health behaviour of therapy group members or all the repercussions that follow from that behaviour. However, I do believe that it is possible to give a glimpse of what is at stake for women in Farabako when their children become ill.

In this section, I summarize the factors that lead to mother's powerlessness in accessing (biomedical) health care when their children become ill using a hypothetical case of a young mother named Kajatu (see Figure 4). The case illustrates what typically happens when a child becomes ill in Farabako. This case is based on the many interviews with mothers, fathers and healers in Farabako as well as participant observation in and around the maternity clinic. While this case focuses on the therapy management of children's illnesses, many of the same factors also play a role in the therapy management of pregnancy.

> If her child becomes ill, Kajatu gives traditional medicine to the child, asks advice from her mother-in-law, consults traditional healers (*musokɔrɔbaw*, *somaw*, or herbalists) and/or takes her child to a doctor in a neighbouring village. It is difficult for her to get to a doctor at a health clinic due to the geographical isolation of the village, her lack of income and the difficulty she experiences in asking for help and money to get there. Kajatu perceives biomedical care as just one of the options she can choose from, the most expensive, but not necessarily the superior option. She has learned that childhood illnesses that have supernatural causes such as *kɔnɔ* (caused by a bird-witch that eats children) or *siran* ('fear', an illness caused by sorcery) are treated more effectively by traditional healers than by a doctor. Kajatu, as most other mothers in Farabako, has had no schooling and she lacks biomedical knowledge of disease and disease prevention. For example, Kajatu says that she does not know the cause of malaria. Her children do not sleep under mosquito nets. Local medical knowledge is secret and is seen to be dangerous, for this reason, acquiring knowledge on children's illnesses and their treatment was not something that occupies her. This is the terrain of the elderly women and traditional healers. Giving information on children's illnesses to this mother would not necessarily inspire confidence in the proposed treatment. She expects a good healer to assure her that everything will be all right and that her child will recover.
>
> Unsanitary living conditions, food insecurity and endemic infectious diseases expose Kajatu's children to disease and the risk of death on a daily basis. Some illnesses such as (uncomplicated) malaria are so frequent (her

young children have several bouts of malaria a year) that she perceives them to be more of a way of life, or an acceptable risk, than an illness needing immediate treatment. Of the eight children she will bear, three will die before they reach the age of five. Kajatu has a certain 'fatalism' when one of her children becomes ill. She has a resigned acceptance that events should be allowed to take their course. Causes of illness are not simultaneously seen as causes of death. Death is not caused by illness; rather death is caused by God. One can become ill from natural or supernatural causes, but one dies because it is God's will. Kajatu told me: 'You [LH] keep searching for a cause, but here with us it is God'.

Kajatu often did not feel capable or entitled to take action when one of her children was ill, especially in the early years of her marriage. She had married at age fourteen and was a mother at age fifteen. She had had no reproductive choice and she had no (biomedical) knowledge of contraceptives. As a young wife, she occupied a low position in her husband's household. She had almost no personal income, and was dependent on her husband and his family. Limited social capital meant that there were only a few people she could ask for financial assistance, and a moral discourse of shame (*maloya*) made it difficult for her to ask for help. She did not see it as her task to plan a course of action if her child was ill; rather this was her husband's and mother-in-laws's job. So she often waited for others to take action. She did not take the initiative. To keep her limited social capital intact she refrained from shameless behaviour and accepted suffering.

In summary, a mother in Farabako reacts passively in the face of her child's mortality because she is often very young and inexperienced, and has a lack of biomedical and local medical knowledge. It is difficult for her to access biomedical health care. She sees biomedicine as an (often prohibitively) expensive alternative to local treatments. She has little to no money of her own, and she has few people she can ask for (financial) help. In certain cases, shame hinders her from seeking health care. She waits for her husband or her mother-in-law to take action when her child is ill; she has shame in taking the initiative.

Although I have tried to understand mothers' health seeking behaviour in Farabako by contextualising it, this is still an analysis made to fit my conceptual model of the vulnerability context. When women in Farabako spoke of their health and the health of their children, they did not speak in terms of physical ailments, exposure to risk, capability to cope or powerlessness (these are all my terms), but rather in terms of suffering. They spoke of the shame of poverty and the fact that they and their children were not well taken care of. The women used a language of social ill-being. They experienced poverty as illness; their suffering was a 'social suffering' caused by the societal forces that they were exposed to, but had no control over (cf. Kleinman, Das and Lock

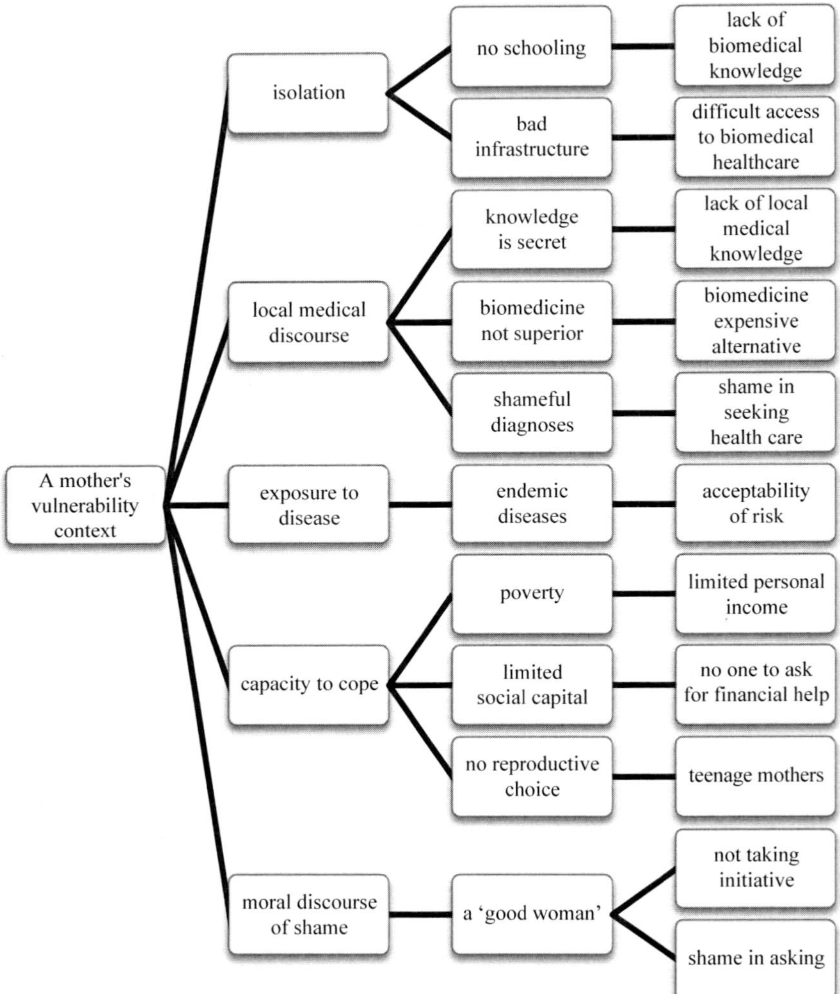

Figure 4. A mother's vulnerability context: factors influencing non-action in therapy management

1997). Their language was one of not-being-taken-care-of, shame and suffering. I will now continue by examining the relationship among these three concepts and their influence on therapy management. I postulate that in Farabako therapy management lies at the intersection of shame, suffering and not-being-taken care-of.

Ontological insecurity

In Farabako, women defined well-being as being-taken-care-of. This included a material well-being (often expressed as having enough clothes and shoes for the children), a social well-being (being able to care for their children, having self-respect and good relations in the family and community) and having security (often financial security, food security and confidence in the future).

Conversely, descriptions of ill-being in Farabako focused on: material lack and want (of food, livelihood, assets, and money); bad relations within the family; insecurity, worry, fear and low self-confidence; and helplessness and frustration. Both women and men referred to the deterioration of their social well-being. They recounted, with nostalgia, a time when moralities that secured social cohesion (such as *maloya* and *badenya*) were observed. The women spoke in terms of no longer being taken care of as well as having difficulties (*gɛlɛya*), suffering (*tɔrɔ*), and shame (*maloya*).

Women could no longer trust that they would be taken care of. I interpret their stories as expressing a longing for ontological security. Giddens (1991) defines ontological security as a person's fundamental sense of safety in the world. Ontological security is a 'sense of invulnerability' that blocks out dangers in favour of a generalised attitude of hope derived from basic trust (Giddens 1991: 40). Trust is the basis of ontological security. Trust works as a 'protective cocoon' and 'brackets out' potential occurrences that produce a paralysis of the will, or feelings of engulfment if the individual were to seriously contemplate them (Giddens 1991: 3).

The day-to-day maintenance of habits and routines helps to bracket out questions about ourselves, others and the material world that have to be taken for granted to continue with everyday activity. This unreflexive habitus is a crucial safeguard against threatening anxieties. I argue that in Farabako women do not trust that they will be taken care of by their husbands and affines and this in turn leads to a lack of ontological security. Lack of trust makes it difficult for mothers to bracket out the ever-present threat of hunger and dangers such as their children's exposure to disease. They have lost their sense of safety in the world. This is similar to what happens in an 'ethical moment' (chapter 5). In an ethical moment people are forced out of their zone of existential comfort and unreflexive moral habitus becomes reflexive (Zigon 2008). In the vulnerability context of Farabako, women feel they are no longer well taken care of and this leads to suffering. In Farabako, ontological insecurity is the suffering of not being taken care of; it is the suffering of vulnerability.

As has become clear throughout this book, the language of biomedicine has been of limited usefulness in understanding well-being in Farabako. The biomedical vocabulary of disease and death can even deflect analysis and response away from the underlying societal conditions of which morbidity and mortality are expressions, as we saw in the case of malnutrition in chapter 8. It may be more productive to (temporarily) let go of this biomedical conceptual foundation with its focus on individual health behaviour, and develop a language of ill-being that can be used in societal level analysis.[86]

The language of ill-being in Farabako is suffering, lack of ontological security and shame. This language of dismay may offer a more valid means of describing what is at stake, rather than the usual terminology of disease and death used in government and NGO health programs and policies. The language of ill-being collapses dichotomies of individual and social levels of analysis, health and social problems. The language of ill-being shows the 'permeability between borders of moral imagination, bodily affect and social processes' (Kleinman, Das and Lock 1997: xi). This language shows the socially embedded understanding of the self and of ill-being in Farabako.

The embodiment of inequality

The women of Farabako emphasised that poverty and not being taken care of, are the basis of shame. I argue that poverty and gender inequality, enable, maintain and magnify the moral discourse of shame. *Maloya* is an expression of the embodiment of the structural inequality of poverty and patriarchy (cf. Fassin 2003).

As we have seen, women's over-all (financial) dependence on a husband's family and their subordinate position within the household, make the discourse of shame a significant factor in therapy management in Farabako. Women suffered the shame of not being taken care of by their husbands, and women had shame in taking initiative by asking for the necessary (financial) help to access (biomedical) health care. Poverty enables and maintains the discourse of shame that contributes to mothers' powerlessness in therapy management.

In contrast, in the country's capital Bamako, women have more possibilities to participate in income-generating activities; they are less poor and have a certain amount of (financial) autonomy. In Bamako, women also spoke of the importance of *maloya*, but much less frequently than in Farabako. There is a less strict gender division of labour and space in Bamako. There, men and

[86] A language of ill-being describes and incorporates societal values. The question remains how to translate this language of ill-being, with its vocabulary of insecurity, shame and suffering, into health care policy and projects. Mann (1997) argues that the language of human rights is useful for expressing, considering, and incorporating values into societal level (public health) analysis and response. Mann states that (bio)medicine has chosen ethics as its language of analysis of individual health behavior. Public health, because it is centrally concerned with the structure and function of society, should use human rights as a language useful for guiding societal level analysis and response.

women slept together with their small children in one room. It was not considered shameless behaviour if men and women talked together in public and this facilitated their communication over health matters. Mothers and fathers in Bamako often had mobile telephones so mothers could easily consult their husbands on which course of action to take when a child became ill, even if their husbands were absent. Mothers in Bamako had much easier (financial and physical) access to biomedical health care facilities. These mothers seldom spoke about *maloya* when speaking about their own health and that of their children.

As the case of Bamako shows, a reduction in poverty can lead to less powerlessness and more agency for women as well as a diminished importance of *maloya*. Societal change is only possible if women's position of powerlessness inherent in poverty is reduced. Only by reducing poverty (MDG 1) will the maternal and child mortality (MDG's 4 and 5) in Farabako decrease.

From a Western feminist perspective, women's lack of security and children's vulnerability to disease and death is fundamentally connected with gender inequality. The success of a health care project in Farabako is inherently limited in the absence of societal changes that would strengthen women's ability to negotiate biomedical discourse by promoting and protecting women's rights. As long as girls have little education, become pregnant at a young age and are financially dependent on their husbands, child mortality most likely will not decrease. Mann (1997) argues that the extent to which human rights are realised may represent a better and more comprehensive index of well-being than traditional health status indicators. For example, if women in Farabako had more reproductive rights,[87] this could help to reduce child mortality. I argue that these 'universal' rights would need to be contextualised and translated into the language of well-being in Farabako. Focusing on one or more reproductive right, and not on the totality of reproductive rights would have limited effect. For example, if young women had education on contraceptives and the freedom to use them, they would probably have fewer teenage pregnancies, and this would reduce child mortality. However, this does not mean that these girls would have a greater sense of well-being. The language of well-being in Farabako is security within a family; it is the trust that a woman will be taken care of, and one way she can secure her place in her husband's family is by producing progeny as quickly as possible.

For women in Farabako, the basis of security is the trust that one will be taken care of by one's husband's family. This feeling of trust and security is thus linked to gender inequality within a patriarchal marriage system. Being-taken-care-of gives a feeling of well-being and thereby, reproduces (unequal) gender relations. Inequality is reproduced in being-taken-care-of.

---

[87] Reproductive rights are a cluster of rights, including the rights to health, bodily integrity, privacy, information, education, and equal rights in marriage and divorce.

The intersubjective logic of shame

Understanding the language women use to describe their health is an important part of understanding therapy management. The next step is to understand the logic that mothers use in the therapy management of their children's illnesses.

The meaning of human existence cannot be reduced to cultural rules or natural forces, rather it is found in what Arendt calls 'the subjective in-between' (1958: 183). This is the intersubjective space between people—the network of interpersonal relationships. From this point of view, culture is not a static set of customs, beliefs and meanings, but rather a 'potentiality' that is realised and experienced in our interactions with others as well as in our relationships to the material world (cf. Jackson 2005: xiv). In other words, our being is conditional on our interactions. The same can be said of health; it is a potential that is realised in our interactions with others. For example, my sense of a situation, say, my way of looking at the symptoms (of what I call) malnutrition, is negotiated by my respondent's (often differing) sense of the same situation and this negotiation leads to giving significance to illness. This negotiation of medical discourses happened in the intersubjective space or, what Richters (2011) calls, the 'social synapse' between my respondents and me in the maternity clinic. This same process goes on at the household level, where child health and illness is given significance within the interpersonal relationships of the mother and her therapy management group.

Critical moments in one's life are moments when something significant happens and moral questions of right and wrong become important while forms of reason other than rationality often come into play; for example, love, respect, dignity, and well-being (Jackson 2005). I argue that in Farabako shame works as a form of reason, as an intersubjective logic that comes into play on many occasions. One such occasion is when a woman's health or that of her child is at stake. Intersubjective logic is the logic that informs everyday patterns of social interaction; it is a logic of belonging and of social well-being. According to the intersubjective logic that operates within the discourse of shame, conformity, forbearance, resignation and humility may be more effective in handling difficult or oppressive situations than active resistance and wilful self-definition. To yield to the will of others may increase one's sense of significance. Shame (*maloya*), as we have seen, expresses both a virtue and the means through which virtue is acquired. Having shame is a sign that a woman is virtuous and at the same time having and performing shame is a means for a woman to become and to actually feel virtuous (cf. Mahmood 2005). Having shame is an act of developing the self's potential, a way of becoming who one wants to be. *Maloya* could be considered emblematic of passivity and inaction, but *maloya* does not mark reluctance to act, rather it is a constructive project. *Maloya* is a site of considerable investment, struggle and achievement. In this way, submission to certain forms of patriarchal authority by 'having shame' is a condition for achieving one's potential of being a 'good woman'.

A woman who does not have shame is damaging to her husband's family's reputation and by extension her husband's social network. This can have grave consequences in the context of vulnerability in Farabako. The sanction for a woman's shameless behaviour is public ostracism, insults, loss of respect and threat of divorce. In cases of divorce, the mother must leave her children behind with her husband. In this way, a child's future can be seen as dependent upon the mother's moral behaviour, maybe even more so than on education, nutrition or health care. The intersubjective logic operating within the moral discourse of shame led mothers in certain instances to decide not to seek health care for themselves or their children. 'Having shame' can be more important than seeking health care for a child who is ill.

The relationship between suffering and the discourse of shame is that *maloya* allows a woman to bear the suffering correctly. 'Having shame' is not the ability to rise above the suffering, but rather it is the manner in which suffering is lived, as a 'good woman'.[88] *Maloya* works as an intersubjective logic in dealing with suffering.

In summary, the language of ill-being in Farabako is one of not-being-taken-care-of, suffering, and shame. Women suffer due to a lack of ontological security because they are not taken care of. Shame is an expression of the embodiment of the structural inequality of poverty and patriarchy. Shame works as an intersubjective logic in dealing with suffering. Therapy management takes place at the intersections of these processes.

Recommendations: Beyond culture

It is important for health care workers in isolated impoverished places like Farabako to understand the factors leading to mothers' powerlessness and their related seemingly passive behaviour in the face of child mortality. To do this, health workers must learn the language of ill-being that their patients use and they must fathom the intersubjective logic at work in therapy management.

This book has demonstrated that, to understand therapy management, it is not enough for biomedical health care workers to be aware of the interpretations the 'other' gives to health and illness. To improve cultural competence in health care, health care workers, especially, but not only when working in countries other than their own, should be trained to become aware of their own medical assumptions. By becoming aware of their own (bio-)medical assumptions, they will be more equipped to understand their patients' medical assumptions. This will make it possible to find a common ground where patients and healers move towards speaking the same language and work out ways in which health care can be improved.

Understanding the role of local moralities in health is crucial for imple-

[88] This is similar to the Egyptian concept of *sabr* (patience) as described by Mahmood (2005: 172).

menting biomedical health care and lowering child mortality in out-of-the-way places such as Farabako. This ethnography can contribute to developing a new language of health and well-being, not only regarding clinical care, but also in public health policy and programs. A language of health care must take feelings of insecurity and powerlessness as indicators of ill-being into account when planning and implementing public health programs geared to the reduction of maternal and child mortality.

However, even if we find an appropriate language of well-being and understand the intersubjective logic of therapy management, child morbidity and mortality can only be significantly reduced if structural inequality is tackled. Gausset (2001), in his study of European approaches to AIDS in Africa, argues that Western assumptions about what is best for the global South are wrong. The assumption that African cultural practices are the principal barriers to health care development programs reflects enduring Eurocentric assumption that African 'culture' is an obstacle to development. The implication is that Western science can save Africans from themselves (cf. Jackson 2005). In fact, Gausset observes that controlling AIDS in Africa demands exactly the same resources and the same improvements that are demanded in the West. I agree with Gausset. The major health problems for children in Farabako, such as malaria, pneumonia and measles are also not specifically African, but are similar to the problems existing (or that have existed) in Europe or America. An improvement in maternal and child health demands the same resources and improvements in infrastructure, health education and health insurance, etc. as in the West. In other words, improvement in maternal and child health demands improvement of the vulnerability context. Alleviation of poverty is the most urgent intervention. In Farabako, the phenomenon of mothers' passivity in the face of child mortality is influenced by the 'cultural' discourse of shame, but 'culture' is not the main obstacle to (biomedical) health care seeking. I argue that poverty, as a key factor in the vulnerability context, is the main obstacle. Poverty enables and maintains the discourse of shame that contributes to mothers' powerlessness in therapy management.

Suggestions for midwifery practice and further research

My initial ethnographic grounded theory approach led me to study the social phenomenon of 'having shame' and powerlessness in the face of health adversity. I have given an analysis of how women practice therapy management in Farabako, while paying attention to how people are positioned within a therapy management group and society. While I now acknowledge the importance of ontological insecurity, the embodiment of inequality and the intersubjective logic of shame in therapy management, I have only just begun to understand what it is like for women to be in a position of powerlessness. Further research with an existential approach is needed to understand how women experience their role in therapy management.

This ethnography has contributed to a feminist anthropology of moralities. I have first detached agency from politics and subsequently analysed and then used agency to understand how and why women embody inequality and how inequality is reproduced. I have shown how moral and ethical assemblages contribute to legitimizing existing social inequality. I have looked at which subject positions are open to women within a certain discourse, and what significance subordination holds for them. I have contextualised suffering. This helped me to understand women's language of ill-being. Further research is necessary to examine how to translate this language of ill-being into a language that can be used in health care policies and programs.

This book has been about the travelling of my biomedical assumptions and Dutch midwifery practice from the Netherlands to a small village in Mali. Let me now travel back home. In my work as a midwife in the Netherlands before going to Mali, I had already remarked on the gender dynamics at play between the pregnant women and their husbands in my practice. My field work in Mali has made me reflect on my previous experiences as a midwife and how to interpret the therapy management of pregnant women in the Netherlands.

Therapy management as a concept is not only relevant in attempting to understand health and health care in isolated areas in Africa; it is a concept equally applicable to Western populations. Understanding the importance of cultural assumptions and values, social roles and institutions, gendered power relations and economic circumstances in how pregnancy and illness is responded to, can help midwives and other health care workers in the West to approach pregnant women not only as individual agents. Pregnant women can be approached as part of a therapy management group that involves husbands and other significant therapy group members in a dialogue on what they all consider to be the best care for the pregnant woman. This can result in a health care for pregnant women that accounts for the importance of social well-being and the role of moralities in health. As an anthropologist, I would be interested to study which factors are central to therapy management of pregnancy and birth among native as well as migrant women in the Netherlands.

This research has shown the importance of becoming aware of one's medical and moral assumptions and those of the patient in finding a way to communicate effectively. Further research on the negotiation of medical and moral discourse in Dutch midwifery practice could contribute to improving the level of care. In the Netherlands, communication between pregnant women and health care providers is a process of shared decision-making, under the assumption that pregnant women have the knowledge and confidence to do so. However, Jonkers et al. (2011) found that many migrant women, in contrast to the pro-active native Dutch women, had a 'reticent mindset' that hindered them from having effective involvement for obtaining the necessary care and decision-making about that care. Migrant women did understand the health information, but lacked the appropriate communication strategies to adequately interact with Dutch caregivers. In certain cases, this led to substandard care in treating severe obstetrical complications (Jonkers et al. 2011). It would be interesting to research this 'reticent mindset' further, not as a cultural given, but rather as originating in friction between medical and moral discourses within therapy management.

Conclusion

This ethnography has shown that understanding local moralities is a prerequisite for understanding therapy management. I have elaborated a method of not privileging my (biomedical and moral) viewpoint over that of 'the other', but rather comparing my position to local medical and moral discourse. This was a useful ethnographic tool to show our (my respondents' and my) search for a common understanding of what good therapy management should be.

In Farabako, by demonstrating shame, women created a way of existing and co-existing within the context of vulnerability. In Farabako, shame works as an intersubjective logic in dealing with the potentialities of child disease and death. 'Having shame' allows a woman to correctly bear the suffering induced by insecurity.

REFERENCES

Adams, Alayne, Sangeetha Madhavan, and Dominique Simon. 2002. 'Women's Social Networks and Child Survival in Mali' *Social Science & Medicine* 54 (2): 165-178.

Allen, Denise Roth. 2004. *Managing Motherhood, Managing Risk: Fertility and Danger in West Central Tanzania* Ann Arbor, University of Michigan Press.

Andrews, Molly, Shelley Day Sclater, Corinne Squire, and Maria Tamboukou. 2004. 'Narrative Research' in: Clive Seale, Giampietro Gobo, Jaber Gubrium and David Silverman (eds.). *Qualitative Research Practice* London, Sage: 109-124.

Arendt, Hannah. 1958. *The Human Condition* Chicago: University of Chicago Press.

Arnfred, Signe. 2003. *Re-Thinking Sexualities in Africa* Uppsala, Nordic Africa Institute.

Bähre, Erik. 2007. 'Reluctant Solidarity: Death, Urban Poverty and Neighbourly Assistance in South Africa' *Ethnography* 8 (1): 33-59.

Bailleul, Charles. 2000. *Dictionnaire Bambara-Français* Bamako, Editions Donniya.

Baro, Mamadou, and Tara Deubel. 2006. 'Persistent Hunger: Perspectives on Vulnerability, Famine, and Food Security in Sub-Saharan Africa' *Annual Review of Anthropology* 35: 521-538.

Baron, Stephen, John Field, and Tom Schuller. 2000. *Social Capital: Critical Perspectives* New York, Oxford University Press.

Biehl, Joao, Byron Good, and Arthur Kleinman (eds.). *Subjectivity: Ethnographic Investigations* Berkeley, University of California Press.

Bird, Charles S., and Martha B. Kendall. 1987. 'The Mande Hero' in: Ivar Karp (ed.). *Exploration in African Systems of Thought* Bloomimgton/Indianapolis, Indiana University Press: 13-26.

Bledsoe, Caroline. 1995. 'Marginal Members: Children of Previous Unions in Mende Households in Sierra Leone' in: Susan Greenhalgh (ed.). *Situating Fertility: Anthropology and Demographic Inquiry* Cambridge, Cambridge University Press: 130-153.

Bledsoe, Caroline, Douglas Ewbank, and Uche Isiugo-Abanihe. 1988. 'The Effects of Child Fostering on Feeding Practices and Access to Health Services in Rural Sierre Leone' *Social Science & Medicine* 27 (6): 627-636.

Bleek, Wolf. 1981. 'Avoiding Shame: The Ethical Context of Abortion in Ghana' *Anthropological Quarterly* 54 (4): 203-209.

Boonmongkon, Pimpawun, Mark Nichter, Jen Pylypa, Niporn Snahajariya, and Soiboon Saitong. 2002. 'Women's Health in Northeast Thailand: Working at the Interface between the Local and the Global' *Women & Health* 35 (4): 59-80.

Boserup, Ester. 2007 (1970). *Women's Role in Development* London, Allen and Unwin.

Bourdieu, Pierre. 1966. 'The Sentiment of Honour in Kabyle Society' in: John George Peristiany (ed.). *Honour and Shame: The Values of Mediterranean Society* Chicago, University of Chicago Press: 191-242.

———. 1986. 'The Forms of Capital' in: John Richardson (ed.). *Handbook of Theory and Research for the Sociology of Education* New York, Greenwood: 241-258.

———. 1990. *The Logic of Practice* Stanford, Stanford University Press.

———. 2001. *Masculine Domination* Stanford, Stanford University Press.

Brand, Saskia. 2000. *Mediating Means and Fate: A Socio-Political Analysis of Fertility and Demographic Change in Bamako, Mali* Leiden, Brill.

Breedveld, Anneke, and Mirjam de Bruijn. 1996. 'L'Image des Fulbe: Analyse Critique de la Construction du Concept de « Pulaaku »' *Cahiers d'Études Africaines* 36 (144): 791-821.

Brown, David, Christopher Brown, and Scott Desposato. 2008. 'Who Gives, Who Receives, and Who Wins? Transforming Capital into Political Change through Nongovernmental Organizations' *Comparative Political Studies* 41 (1): 24-47.

Bruijn, Mirjam de, and Han van Dijk. 1995. *Arid Ways: Cultural Understandings of Insecurity in Fulbe Society, Central Mali* Amsterdam, Thela.

Bruner, Jerome. 1990. *Acts of Meaning: Four Lectures on Mind and Culture* Cambridge MA, Harvard University Press.
Bryce, Jennifer, Kate Gilroy, Gareth Jones, Elizabeth Hazel, Robert Black, and Cesar Victora. 2010. 'The Accelerated Child Survival and Development Programme in West Africa: A Retrospective Evaluation' *The Lancet* 375 (9714): 572-582.
Butt, Tanveer, Bruce McCarl, J. Angerer, P. T. Dyke, and J. W. Stuth. 2005. 'The Economic and Food Security Implications of Climate Change in Mali' *Climatic Change* 68 (3): 355-378.
Camara, Brahima. 2010. 'L'Imaginaire du Chasseur au Pays Mandingue' in: Cristiana Panella (ed.). *World of Debts: Interdisciplinary Perspectives on Gold Mining in West Africa* Amsterdam, Rozenberg: 111-126.
Caplan, Patricia (ed.). 1987. *The Cultural Construction of Sexuality* London, Tavistock Publications.
Castle, Sarah. 1993. 'Intra-Household Differentials in Women's Status: Household Function and Focus as Determinants of Children's Illness Management and Care in Rural Mali' *Health Transition Review* 3 (2): 137-157.
———. 1994. 'The (Re) Negotiation of Illness Diagnoses and Responsibility for Child Death in Rural Mali' *Medical Anthropology Quarterly* 8 (3): 314-335.
Charmaz, Kathy. 2006. *Constructing Grounded Theory: A Practical Guide through Qualitative Analysis* London, Sage Publications Ltd.
Clandinin, D. Jean (ed.). 2007. *Handbook of Narrative Inquiry: Mapping a Methodology.* Thousand Oaks CA, Sage Publications.
Collier, Jane, and Sylvia Yanagisako. 1989. 'Theory in Anthropology since Feminist Practice' *Critical Anthropology* 9 (2): 27-37.
Cox Macpherson, Cheryl, and R. Connolly. 2002. 'Enough is enough?: Disclosure in Cross-Cultural Research' *IRB: Ethics and Human Research* 24 (3): 7-9.
D'Andrade, Roy. 1995. 'Moral Models in Anthropology' *Current Anthropology* 36 (3): 399-408.
Delor, François, and Michel Hubert. 2000. 'Revisiting the Concept of "Vulnerability"' *Social Science & Medicine* 50 (11): 1557-1570.
Dettwyler, Katherine. 1986. 'Infant Feeding in Mali, West Africa: Variations in Belief and Practice' *Social Science & Medicine* 23 (7): 651-664.
———. 1989. 'Styles of Infant Feeding: Parental/caretaker Control of Food Consumption in Young Children' *American Anthropologist* 91 (3): 696-703.
———. 1994. *Dancing Skeletons: Life and Death in West Africa* Prospect Height IL: Waveland Press Inc.
Diallo, Assitan. 2004. 'Paradoxes of Female Sexuality in Mali: On the Practices of Mogomaka and Bolokoli-Kela' in: Signe Arnfred (ed.). *Re-Thinking Sexualities in Africa* Uppsala, Almqvist & Wiksell Tryckeri: 173-194.
Douglas, Mary. 1986. *Risk Acceptability According to the Social Sciences* London, Routledge and Kegan Paul Ltd.
Engle, Patrice, Margaret Bentley, and Gretel Pelto. 2000. 'The Role of Care in Nutrition Programmes: Current Research and a Research Agenda' *Proceedings of the Nutrition Society* 59 (01): 25-35.
Farmer, Paul. 1997. 'On Suffering and Structural Violence: A View from Below' in: Arthur Kleinman, Veena Das and Margaret Lock (eds.). *Social Suffering* Berkeley, University of California Press: 261-284.
Fassin, Didier. 2003. 'The Embodiment of Inequality: AIDS as a Social Condition and the Historical Experience in South Africa' *EMBO Reports* 4: S4-S9.
———. 2008. 'Beyond Good and Evil? Questioning the Anthropological Discomfort with Morals' *Anthropological Theory* 8 (4): 333-344.
———. 2011. *Humanitarian Reason: A Moral History of the Present* Berkeley, University of California Press.
Fassin, Didier, and Wiktor Stoczkowski. 2008. 'Should Anthropology be Moral? A Debate' *Anthropological Theory* 8 (4): 331-332.
Feierman, Steven, and John Janzen. 1992. *The Social Basis of Health and Healing in Africa* Berkeley, University of California Press.
Fessler, Daniel. 2007. 'From Appeasement to Conformity: Evolutionary and Cultural Perspectives on Shame, Competition, and Cooperation' in: Jessica Tracy, Richard Robins

and June Price Tangney (eds.). *The Self-Conscious Emotions: Theory and Research* New York, The Guilford Press: 174-193.
Finerman, Ruthbeth. 1995. '"Parental Incompetence" and "Selective Neglect": Blaming the Victim in Child Survival' *Social Science & Medicine* 40 (1): 5-13.
Finkler, Kaja. 2008. 'Can Bioethics be Global and Local, or must it be both?' *Journal of Contemporary Ethnography* 37 (2): 155-179.
Foster, George. 1976. 'Disease Etiologies in Non-Western Medical Systems' *Journal of Contemporary Ethnography* 78 (4): 773-782.
Foucault, Michel. 1990. *The History of Sexuality, Vol. 2: The Use of Pleasure* New York, Vintage.
———. 1994a. 'Technologies of the Self' in: Paul Rabinow (ed.). *Michel Foucault: Ethics, Subjectivity and Truth. Essential Works of Foucault, 1954-1984* London, Penguin Books: 223-252.
———. 1994b. 'On the Genealogy of Ethics: An Overview of Work in Progress' in: Paul Rabinow (ed.). *Michel Foucault: Ethics, Subjectivity and Truth. Essential Works of Foucault, 1954-1984* London, Penguin Books: 253-280.
———. 1994c. 'Polemics, Politics, and Problematizations: An Interview with Michel Foucault' in: Paul Rabinow (ed.). *Michel Foucault: Ethics, Subjectivity and Truth. Essential Works of Foucault, 1954-1984* London, Penguin Books: 111-119.
———. 1994d. 'The Ethics of the Concern for Self as a Practice of Freedom' in: Paul Rabinow (ed.). *Michel Foucault: Ethics, Subjectivity and Truth. Essential Works of Foucault, 1954-1984* London, Penguin Books: 281-301.
Gage, Anastasia. 2007. 'Barriers to the Utilization of Maternal Health Care in Rural Mali' *Social Science & Medicine* 65 (8): 1666-1682.
Gammeltoft, Tine. 2006. '"Beyond Being": Emergent Narratives of Suffering in Vietnam' *Journal of the Royal Anthropological Institute* 12 (3): 589-605.
———. 2008. 'Childhood Disability and Parental Moral Responsibility in Northern Vietnam: Towards Ethnographies of Intercorporeality' *Journal of the Royal Anthropological Institute* 14 (4): 825-842.
Gausset, Quentin. 2001. 'AIDS and Cultural Practices in Africa: The Case of the Tonga (Zambia)' *Social Science & Medicine* 52 (4): 509-518.
Geschiere, Peter. 1997. *The Modernity of Witchcraft: Politics and the Occult in Postcolonial Africa* Charlottesville, University of Virginia Press.
Giddens, Anthony. 1991. *Modernity and Self-Identity: Self and Society in the Late Modern Age* Cambridge, Polity Press.
Gilmore, David D. (ed.). 1987. *Honor and Shame and the Unity of the Mediterranean* Washington, American Anthropological Association.
Goddard, Victoria. 1987. 'Honour and Shame: The Control of Women's Sexuality and Group Identity in Naples' in: Patricia Caplan (ed.). *The Cultural Construction of Sexuality* London, Tavistock Publications: 166-192.
Good, Byron. 1977. 'The Heart of What's the Matter the Semantics of Illness in Iran' *Culture, Medicine and Psychiatry* 1 (1): 25-58.
Good, Byron, and Mary-Jo del Vecchio Good. 1994. 'In the Subjunctive Mode: Epilepsy Narratives in Turkey' *Social Science & Medicine* 38 (6): 835-842.
Grosz-Ngate, Maria. 1989. 'Hidden Meanings: Explorations into a Bamanan Construction of Gender' *Ethnology* 28 (2): 167-183.
Hampshire, Katherine, Rachel Casiday, Kate Kilpatrick, and Catherine Panter-Brick. 2009. 'The Social Context of Childcare Practices and Child Malnutrition in Niger's Recent Food Crisis' *Disasters* 33 (1): 132-151.
Herzfeld, Michael. 1980. 'Honour and Shame: Problems in the Comparative Analysis of Moral Systems' *Man* 15 (2): 339-351.
———. 1988. *The Poetics of Manhood: Contest and Identity in a Cretan Mountain Village* Guilford, Princeton University Press.
Hof, Caroline, and Annemiek Richters. 2004. 'Exploring Intersections between Teenage Pregnancy and Gender Violence: Lessons from Zimbabwe' *African Journal of Reproductive Health* 3 (1): 51-65.

Holten, Lianne. 2010. *Pregnancy Strategies in the Mande Mountains of Mali* Amsterdam, Vrije Universiteit Press.
Howell, Signe (ed.). 1997. *The Ethnography of Moralities* London, Routledge.
Hunt, Linda. 2000. 'Strategic Suffering: Illness Narratives as Social Empowerment among Mexican Cancer Patients' in: Cheryl Mattingly, and Linda Garro (eds.). *Narrative and the Cultural Construction of Illness and Healing* Berkeley, University of California Press: 88-108.
Hunt, Nancy. 1999. *A Colonial Lexicon of Birth Ritual, Medicalization, and Mobility in the Congo* Durham, Duke University Press Books.
Hydén, Lars-Christer, and Elliot Mishler. 1999. 'Language and Medicine' *Annual Review of Applied Linguistics* 19 (1): 174-192.
Iliffe, John. 2005. *Honour in African History* Cambridge, Cambridge University Press.
Imperato, Pascal. 1977. *African Folk Medicine: Practices and Beliefs of the Bambara and Other Peoples* Baltimore, York Press Inc.
Jackson, Michael. 2005. *Existential Anthropology: Events, Exigencies and Effects* Oxford, Berghahn Books.
Jamieson, Mark. 2000. 'It's Shame that Makes Men and Women Enemies: The Politics of Intimacy among the Miskitu of Kakabila' *Journal of the Royal Anthropological Institute* 6 (2): 311-324.
Janes, Craig, and Kitty Corbett. 2009. 'Anthropology and Global Health' *Annual Review of Anthropology* 38: 167-183.
Jansen, Jan. 2000. *The Griot's Craft: An Essay on Oral Tradition and Diplomacy* Münster, Lit Verlag.
———. 2001. 'The Sunjata Epic: The Ultimate Version' *Research in African Literatures* 32 (1): 14-46.
———. 2005. 'Habitation and Warfare Strategies in 19th Century Mande – A View from the *Kafu*' in: Allen Howard and Richard M. Shain (eds.). *The Spatial Factor in African History: The Relationship of the Social, Material and Perceptual* Brill, Leiden: 261-290.
———. 2009. 'Framing Divination: A Mande Divination Expert and the Occult Economy' *Africa: The Journal of the International African Institute* 79 (1): 110-127.
———. 2010. 'What Gold Mining Means for the Malinké, and How it was Misunderstood by the French Colonial Administration' in: Cristiana Panella (ed.). *World of Debts: Interdisciplinary Perspectives on Gold Mining in West Africa* Amsterdam: Rozenberg: 95-110.
———. 2011 'Éducation arithmétique sous forme d'apprentissage. La géomancie dans les Monts Mandingues' *Cahiers d'Etudes Africaines* 51 (1): 9-49.
———, and Mountaga Diarra. 2006. *Entretiens avec Bala Kanté: Une Chronique du Manding du XXème Siècle* Leiden, Brill Academic Publishers.
Janzen, John. 1978. *The Quest for Therapy in Lower Zaire* Berkeley, University of California Press.
———. 1987. 'Therapy Management: Concept, Reality, Process' *Medical Anthropology Quarterly* 1 (1): 68-84.
Johnson-Hanks, Jennifer. 2006. *Uncertain Honor: Modern Motherhood in an African Crisis* Chicago, University of Chicago Press.
Jones, Heidi, Nafissatou Diop, Ian Askew, and Inoussa Kaboré. 1999. 'Female Genital Cutting Practices in Burkina Faso and Mali and their Negative Health Outcomes' *Studies in Family Planning* 30 (3): 219-230.
Jonkers, Marina, Annemiek Richters, Joost Zwart, Ferko Öry, and Jos van Roosmalen. 2011. 'Severe Maternal Morbidity among Immigrant Women in the Netherlands: Patients' Perspectives' *Reproductive Health Matters* 19 (37): 144-153.
Kamat, Vinay. 2008. 'Dying Under the Bird's Shadow: Narrative Representations of Degedege and Child Survival among the Zaramo of Tanzania' *Medical Anthropology Quarterly* 22 (1): 67-93.
Keita, Mahamadou Faganda. 2005. 'Le Mariage en Milieu Maninka: Représentations et Réalités des Chants Cérémoniels. Cas de la Commune Rurale de Siby' Master thesis, University of Bamako.

———. 2010. 'Sur les Sacrifices pour l'Orpaillage Artisanal dans le Manding' in : Cristiasna Panella (ed.). *World of Debts: Interdisciplinary Perspectives on Gold Mining in West Africa* Amsterdam, Rozenberg: 27-37.

Kleinman, Arthur. 1988. *The Illness Narratives: Suffering, Healing, and the Human Condition* New York, Basic Books (AZ).

———. 1999. 'Experience and its Moral Modes: Culture, Human Conditions, and Disorder' in: Grethe Peterson (ed.). *The Tanner Lectures on Human Values* Salt Lake City, University of Utah Press: 355-420.

———. 2006. *What really Matters: Living a Moral Life Amidst Uncertainty and Danger* Oxford, Oxford University Press.

Kleinman, Arthur, Veena Das, and Margaret Lock (eds.). 1997. *Social Suffering* Berkeley, University of California Press.

Kressel, Gideon. 1988. 'More on Honour and Shame' *Man* 23 (1): 167-170.

Laidlaw, James. 2002. 'For an Anthropology of Ethics and Freedom' *Journal of the Royal Anthropological Institute* 8 (2): 311-332.

Lauritzen, Sonja. 2004. 'Lay Voices on Allergic Conditions in Children: Parents' Narratives and the Negotiation of a Diagnosis' *Social Science & Medicine* 58 (7): 1299-1308.

LeGrand, Thomas, and Cheikh Mbacké. 1993. 'Teenage Pregnancy and Child Health in the Urban Sahel' *Studies in Family Planning*: 137-149.

Lock, Margaret. 2001. 'The Tempering of Medical Anthropology: Troubling Natural Categories' *Medical Anthropology Quarterly* 15 (4): 478-492.

———. 2002. *Twice Dead: Organ Transplants and the Reinvention of Death* Berkeley, University of California Press.

Mahmood, Saba. 2005. *Politics of Piety: The Islamic Revival and the Feminist Subject* Princeton, Princeton University Press.

Mann, Jonathan. 1997. 'Medicine and Public Health, Ethics and Human Rights' *The Hastings Center Report* 27 (3): 6-13.

Melhuus, Marit. 1997. 'The Troubles of Virtue: Values of Violence and Suffering in a Mexican Context' in: Signe Howell (ed.). *The Ethnography of Moralities*. London, Routledge: 178-202.

Menon, Usha. 2002. 'Making Śakti: Controlling (Natural) Impurity for Female (Cultural) Power' *Ethos* 30 (1-2): 140-157.

Messer, Ellen. 1997. 'Intra-Household Allocation of Food and Health Care: Current Findings and Understandings—Introduction' *Social Science & Medicine* 44 (11): 1675-1684.

Mezey, Nancy. 2000. 'Improving women's Health in Mali: Research, Policy Review, and Recommendations' in: James Bingen, David Robinson and John Staatz (eds.). *Democracy and Development in Mali* East Lansing MI, Michigan State University Press: 321-348.

Migliore, Sam. 2001. 'From Illness Narratives to Social Commentary: A Pirandellian Approach to "nerves"' *Medical Anthropology Quarterly* 15 (1): 100-125.

Millard, Ann. 1994. 'A Causal Model of High Rates of Child Mortality' *Social Science & Medicine* 38 (2): 253-268.

Moeller, Susan. 1999. *Compassion Fatigue: How the Media Sell Disease, Famine, War and Death* New York, Routledge.

Mohanty, Chandra. 2003. '"Under Western Eyes" Revisited: Feminist Solidarity through Anticapitalist Struggles' *Signs* 28 (2): 499-535.

Mosse, David. 2005. *Cultivating Development: An Ethnography of Aid Policy and Practice* London, Pluto Press.

Nader, Laura. 1995. 'Comment on Objectivity and Militancy: A Debate' *Current Anthropology* 36 (3): 426-427.

Narayan, Deepa, Robert Chambers, Meera Shah, and Patti Petesch. 2000. *Voices of the Poor: Crying Out for Change* New York, Oxford University Press for the World Bank.

Nguyen, Vinh-Kim, and Karine Peschard. 2003. 'Anthropology, Inequality, and Disease: A Review' *Annual Review of Anthropology* 32: 447-474.

Nichter, Mark. 2002. 'The Social Relations of Therapy Management' in: Mark Nichter, and Margareth Lock (eds.). *New Horizons in Medical Anthropology: Essays in Honour of Charles Leslie* London, Routledge: 81-110.

———.2008. *Global Health: Why Cultural Perceptions, Social Representations, and Biopolitics Matter* Tucson, University of Arizona Press.
Niehof, Anke. 2008. 'Introduction: Dimensions of Resilience in a Context of Health-Related Adversity' *Medische Antropologie* 20 (2): 217-226.
Ogden, Jessica. 1996. '"Producing" Respect: The "Proper Woman" in Postcolonial Kampala' in: Richard Werbner, and Terence Rasnger (eds.). *Postcolonial Identities in Africa* London, Zed Books: 165-192.
Okojie, Christiana. 1994. 'Gender Inequalities of Health in the Third World' *Social Science & Medicine* 39 (9): 1237-1247.
Olenja, Joyce. 1991. 'Factors which Influence Child Health with Specific Reference to Nutrition in Siaya District Western Kenya' *Journal of Tropical Pediatrics* 37 (3): 136-139.
Parpart, Jane, Shirin Rai, and Kathleen Staudt . 2002. *Rethinking Empowerment: Gender and Development in a Global/Local World* London, Routledge.
Peristiany, John George, and Julian Pitt-Rivers (eds.). 1992. *Honor and Grace in Anthropology* Cambridge, Cambridge University Press.
Peterson, Grethe (ed.). 2011. *The Tanner Lectures on Human Values* Salt Lake City, University of Utah Press.
Pietz, William. 1988. 'The problem of the Fetish. III. Bosman's Guinea and the Enlightenment Theory of Fetishism' *Res* 16: 105-123.
Pitt-Rivers, Julian. 1966. 'Honour and Social Status' in: John George Peristiany (ed.). *Honour and Shame: Values of Mediterranean Society* Chicago, University of Chicago Press: 19-79.
Pool, Robert. 2003. *Dialogue and the Interpretation of Illness: Conversations in a Cameroon Village* Oxford, Berg Publishers.
Porter, Roy. 2004. *Blood and Guts: A Short History of Medicine* London, Penguin Books.
Putnam, Robert. 1995. 'Bowling Alone: America's Declining Social Capital' *Journal of Democracy* 6 (1): 65-78.
Radley, Alan, and Michael Billig. 1996. 'Accounts of Health and Illness: Dilemmas and Representations' *Sociology of Health & Illness* 18 (2): 220-240.
Richardson, John (ed.). 1986. *Handbook of Theory and Research for the Sociology of Education* New York, Greenwood.
Richters, Annemiek. 1991. *De Medisch Antropoloog als Verteller en Vertaler* Heemstede, SMART.
———. 1994. *Women, Culture and Violence: A Development, Health and Human Rights Issue* Leiden, VENA publications.
———. 2004. 'Violence, Health and Human Rights: Challenges for Medical Anthropology' *Medische Antropologie,* 16 (1): 157-181.
———. 2011. 'Weer Mens Worden, over Geweld, Sociale Pijn en Gezondheid voor Iedereen' Leiden, Leiden University Medical Centre.
Richters, Annemiek, Theoneste Rutayisire, and Cora Dekker. 2010. 'Care as a Turning Point in Sociotherapy: Remaking the Moral World in Post-Genocide Rwanda' *Medische Antropologie* 22 (1): 93-108.
Riesman, Paul. 1977. *Freedom in Fulani Social Life: An Introspective Ethnography* Chicago, University of Chicago Press.
Riessman, Catherine. 1990. 'Strategic Uses of Narrative in the Presentation of Self and Illness: A Research Note' *Social Science & Medicine* 30 (11): 1195-1200.
———. 1993. *Narrative Analysis* Newbury Park CA, Sage Publications Inc.
———, and Jane Speedy. 2007. 'Narrative Inquiry in the Psychotherapy Professions' in: D. Jean Clandinin (ed.). *Handbook of Narrative Inquiry: Mapping a Methodology*. Thousand Oaks CA, Sage: 426-456.
Robbins, Joel. 2007. 'Between Reproduction and Freedom: Morality, Value, and Radical Cultural Change' *Ethnos* 72 (3): 293-314.
Romanucci-Ross, Lola. 1969. 'The Hierarchy of Resort in Curative Practices: The Admiralty Islands, Melanesia' *Journal of Health and Social Behavior* 10: 201-209.
Rydstrøm, Helle. 2003. *Embodying Morality: Growing Up in Rural Northern Vietnam* Honolulu, University of Hawaii Press.
Scheper-Hughes, Nancy. 1990. 'Three Propositions for a Critically Applied Medical Anthropology' *Social Science & Medicine* 30 (2): 189-197.

———. 1993. *Death without Weeping: The Violence of Everyday Life in Brazil* Berkeley, University of California Press.

———. 1995. 'The Primacy of the Ethical: Propositions for a Militant Anthropology' *Current Anthropology* 36 (3): 409-440.

———, and Philippe Bourgois (eds.). 2004. *Violence in War and Peace: An Anthology* Oxford, Blackwell Publishers.

Schulz, Dorothea. 2011. 'Renewal and Enlightenment: Muslim Women's Biographic Narratives of Personal Reform in Mali' *Journal of Religion in Africa* 41 (1): 93-123.

Shipton, Parker. 1990. 'How Gambians Save and What their Strategies Imply for International Aid' *The World Bank Policy Research Working Paper* 395.

Sidibé, Toumani, Hmamdoun Sangho, Mariam Sylla Traoré, Fatoumata Konaté, Haoua Keita, Baye Diakité, Hadizatou Coulibaly, and Broulaye Traoré. 2007. 'Management of Malnutrition in Rural Mali' *Journal of Tropical Pediatrics* 53 (2): 142-143.

Simon, Dominique, Alayne Adams, and Sangeetha Madhavan. 2002. 'Women's Social Power, Child Nutrition and Poverty in Mali' *Journal of Biosocial Science* 34 (2): 193-214.

Slobin, Kathleen. 1991. 'Family Mediation of Health Care in an African Community (Mali)' PhD thesis, University of California.

Soleman, Nadia, Daniel Chandramohan, and Kenji Shibuya. 2006. 'Verbal Autopsy: Current Practices and Challenges' *Bulletin of the World Health Organization* 84 (3): 239-245.

Squire, Corinne, Molly Andrews, and Maria Tamboukou. 2008. 'Introduction: What is Narrative Research?' in: Molly Andrews, Corinne Squire, and Maria Tamboukou (eds.). *Doing Narrative Research* London, Sage Publications Ltd.: 1-21.

Stoczkowski, Wiktor. 2008. 'The "Fourth Aim" of Anthropology' *Anthropological Theory* 8 (4): 345-356.

Strathern, Marilyn. 1987. 'An Awkward Relationship: The Case of Feminism and Anthropology' *Signs* 12 (2): 276-292.

Tefft, James, Valerie Kelly, Victor Wise, and John Staatz. 2003. 'Linkages between Child Nutrition and Agricultural Growth in Mali: A Summary of Preliminary Findings' *Food Security International Development Policy Syntheses* 64 (two pages).

Thorne, Sally. 2009. 'Is the Story Enough?' *Qualitative Health Research* 19 (9): 1183-1185.

Tolhurst, Rachel, Yaa Peprah Amekudzi, Frank Nyonator, S. Bertel Squire, and Sally Theobald. 2008. '"He Will Ask Why the Child Gets Sick so Often": The Gendered Dynamics of Intra-Household Bargaining over Health Care for Children with Fever in the Volta Region of Ghana' *Social Science & Medicine* 66 (5): 1106-1117.

Tolhurst, Rachel, and Frank Nyonator. 2006. 'Looking within the Household: Gender Roles and Responses to Malaria in Ghana' *Transactions of the Royal Society of Tropical Medicine and Hygiene* 100 (4): 321-326.

Tracy, Jessica, Richard Robins, and June Price Tangney (eds.). 2007. *The Self-Conscious Emotions: Theory and Research* New York, Guilford Press.

Traoré, Karim. 2000. *Le Jeu et le Sérieux: Essai d'Anthropologie Littéraire sur la Poésie Épique des Chasseurs du Mande (Afrique de l'Ouest)* Köln, Rüdiger Köppe.

Tsing, Anna L. 2005. *Friction: An Ethnography of Global Connection* Princeton, Princeton University Press.

United Nations (UN). 'The Millenium Development Goals Report 2011', accessed 5 March 2011, http://www.un.org/millenniumgoals/11_MDG%20Report_EN.pdf.

Van der Geest, Sjaak, Trudie Gerrits, and Flore Singer Aaslid. 2012. 'Introducing Ethnography and Self-Exploration' *Medische Antropologie* 24 (1): 5-22.

Van der Geest, Sjaak, and Susan Reynolds Whyte. 2003. 'Popularité et Scepticisme: Opinions Contrastées sur les Médicaments' *Anthropologie et Sociétés* 27 (2): 97-117.

Wacquant, Loïc. 2004. *Body & Soul: Notebooks of an Apprentice Boxer* New York, Oxford University Press.

Watts, Michael, and Hans Bohle. 1993. 'Hunger, Famine and the Space of Vulnerability' *GeoJournal* 30 (2): 117-125.

WHO (World Health Organization). 'Countries. Mali', accessed 18 December 2011, http://apps.who.int/countries/mli/en/.

Wikan, Unni. 1984. 'Shame and Honour: A Contestable Pair' *Man* 19: 635- 652.

Wilce, James. 2009. 'Medical Discourse' *Annual Review of Anthropology* 38: 199-215.

Williams, Cicely. 1935. 'Kwashiorkor: A Nutritional Disease of Children Associated with a Maize Diet' *Lancet* ii: 1151-1152.

Wilson, Richard, and Richard Brown (eds.). 2009. *Humanitarianism and Suffering: The Mobilization of Empathy* Cambridge, Cambridge University Press.

World Bank. 'Poverty headcount ratio at $2 a day (PPP) (% of population)', accessed 11 January 2012, http://data.worldbank.org/indicator/SI.POV.2DAY

Young, Helen, and Susanne Jaspars. 2006. *Meaning and Measurement of Acute Malnutrition, a Primer for Decision-Makers* London, Humanitarian Practice Network. Overseas Development Institute.

Zigon, Jarrett. 2007. 'Moral Breakdown and the Ethical Demand' *Anthropological Theory* 7 (2): 131-150.

———. 2008. *Morality: An Anthropological Perspective* Oxford, Berg Publishers.

———. 2009. 'Within a Range of Possibilities: Morality and Ethics in Social Life' *Ethnos* 74 (2): 251-276.

———. 2010. 'Moral and Ethical Assemblages: A Response to Fassin and Stoczkowski' *Anthropological Theory* 10 (1-2): 3-15.

Zobel, Clemens. 2006. 'Espaces Politiques Locaux, État et Représentation les Communes des Monts Mandingues et de la Haute Vallée du Niger' in : Claude Fay, Yaouaga Koné, and Catherine Quiminal (eds.). *Décentralisation et Pouvoirs en Afrique : En Contrepoint, Modèles Territoriaux Français* Paris, IRD: 263-278.

GLOSSARY OF BAMBARA WORDS

Note: all plural written with term + w
Pronunciation:
ɔ is pronounced as a 'oh' or 'ò'
ɛ is pronounced as 'eh' or 'è'
ɲ is pronounced as a French 'ny'

Badenya: harmony, lit.: children of the same mother
Basi: fetish, power object used by local medical expert
Bolokoli: circumcision
Bonda: patrilineal kin group
Boni korote: magical poison throwing
Bɔnya: respect
Buguda: temporarily inhabited hamlet close to fields
Dabali: evil
Dakɛsɛbu: tree, leaves used for medicinal purposes
Dalilu: personal secret knowledge
Danbe: honour
Dino: illness referred to as 'cold'
Dɔnso: hunter
Dugu: village
Dugutigi: village chief
Dugutigimuso: wife of the village chief
Dutigi: head of compound (with extended family)
Fadenya: conflict/rivalry; lit. children of the same father, but different mother
Fani: length of cloth worn as a skirt (in French: 'pagne')
Faramasifura: pharmacy (Western) medicine
Fasa (verb): loosing weight
Fura: medicine
Furatigi: healer/herbalist
Gɛlɛya: difficulty
Gwa: kitchen/household
Hinɛ: pity, compassion
Hɔrɔn: nobleman (male/female), a free person
Jamanatigi: regional chief
Jamu: patronymic
Jatigi: host
Jatigimuso: hostess
Jeli: bard

Jigilamɔgɔ: confidant
Jigin: hope
Jimakuma: water (amulet) with incantations
Jinɛ: spirit
Jinɛbana: illness caused by (evil) spirit(s)
Jinɛyɔrɔ: spirit dwelling
Jolitala: anaemia
Jɔn: slave
Juguya: evil
Ka malo(ya): to have shame
Kɛlɛya: jealousy/conflict
Kilisi: incantation
Kini: meal of rice or millet
Kolobɔbana: illness due to teething
Kɔnɔ: convulsions in children caused by infections such as malaria or tetanus and attributed to an evil-doing bird
Kɔnɔboli: diarrhoea
Kɔnɔ funteni: 'hot belly'
Kɔnɔrɔjoli: 'wounds in the belly' (blood in the stools)
Kungo: the bush
Kunkolodimi: headache
Malo: shame
Malobali: shameless
Maloya: (the discourse of) shame
Maninka: Malinke ethnicity
Maninkafura: indigenous/local (lit. Malinke) medicine
Mimi: illness of the throat
Misɛmani: medicine used to induce an abortion
Mugu: luxation, childhood illness caused by a fall
Musokɔrɔba: post-menopausal women specialized in attending births and treating young children
Numu: blacksmith (male)/potter (female) (social category within the *Ɲamakalaw*)
Ɲama: supernatural force (also sickness, refuse and dangerous energy)
Ɲamakala: craftsman/artisan, male or female (social category)
Ɲɛgoya: egoism
Peyiba (French): The Netherlands
Sandafɛ: ('close to heaven'?) a serious childhood illness with convulsions
Sayi: jaundice
Sede (Sere): malnutrition due to early weaning/pregnancies close together
Senankunya: joking relationship
Seretɔrɔ: tree, leaves used for medicinal purposes
Sɛbɛn: amulet, piece of writing

Sɛri: thin rice porridge
Sinkɔrɔntalen: pneumonia
Sinsin: twin fetish, power object
Siran: fear
Soma: local medical expert
Sotrama: minibus (abbreviation of: Société du Transport Malien)
Sɔgɔsɔgɔ: coughing
Sumaya: (uncomplicated) malaria
Surumugu: suru-powder, medicine used to induce an abortion or strengthen contractions during labour.
Tafo: a string with knots over which incantations have been said that is worn around the waist
Tɛgɛjɛ: white hand palms (anaemia)
Tɔrɔ: bad things / suffering

SAMENVATTING: MOEDERS, GENEESKUNDE EN MORALITEIT IN RURAAL MALI

Welke strategieën gebruiken zwangere vrouwen om een positieve obstetrische uitkomst te krijgen in Farabako, een afgelegen dorpje in zuid west Mali? Met deze vraag ging ik in 2007 als verloskundige en antropologe naar Farabako om een kraamkliniek op te zetten. Daar constateerde ik dat niet moedersterfte, maar juist hoge kindersterfte een probleem was. Het doel van mijn vervolgonderzoek in Farabako was om de factoren die tot deze hoge kindersterfte leiden te onderzoeken, en tevens te onderzoeken waarom moeders soms terughoudend waren in het nemen van actie als hun kind ernstig ziek was.

Het hoofddoel van dit onderzoek was om te achterhalen hoe in huishoudens in Farabako de diagnose van ziekte, de selectie en evaluatie van de behandeling, alsmede de steun voor de zieke plaatsvindt (*therapy management*). De focus lag op therapie management van zwangerschap en ziekte-episodes van kinderen. Ik heb een *grounded theory* benadering gebruikt, hetgeen inhield dat ik telkens terug ging naar het veld om thema's te onderzoeken die ik had aangetroffen in de daaraan voorafgaande data. Na vijf veldwerkperiodes had ik verzadiging in de data bereikt. Dit was een traject dat ik begon met een focus op de biomedische factoren die van invloed waren op moedersterfte en kindersterfte en dat eindigde met een focus op morele factoren als significante factoren in therapie management. Dit traject wordt beschreven in hoofdstuk 1 van het boek.

In hoofdstukken 2 en 3 geef ik een korte, historische en socio-economische schets van het dorp Farabako. Ik beschrijf de opties die de bewoners binnen de gezondheidszorg hadden voor de opening van de kraamkliniek in 2007. In alle latere hoofdstukken is het terugkerende thema: lokale moraliteiten als bepalende factoren in verschillende aspecten van therapie management.

In hoofdstuk 4 focus ik op de vulnerabiliteitscontext (*vulnerability context*) van kindersterfte in Farabako, te weten de mate van fysiek risico, de capaciteit om daarmee om te gaan en de potentiele gevolgen daarvan. Factoren die de kinderen van Farabako blootstelden aan het fysieke risico op morbiditeit en mortaliteit waren armoede, endemische ziekten, gebrek aan reproductieve keuze, en moeilijkheden in het toegang krijgen tot adequate biomedische zorg. De capaciteit van vrouwen om met fysiek risico om te gaan werd bemoeilijkt door hun beperkte sociaal kapitaal en door het morele discours over schaamte (*maloya*) die hen belemmerden in het vragen om hulp. Voor vrouwen was schaamte een wezenlijk onderdeel van de identiteitsconstructie als 'goede vrouw' waardoor hun reputatie (symbolisch kapitaal) versterkt werd. In dit hoofdstuk beschrijf ik hoe vrouwen door deze respons op gezondheidsproblemen weliswaar slagen in het vermijden van sociaal risico, maar dat deze respons (nog) niet is aangepast op de nieuwe biomedische mogelijkheden om fysiek risico te vermijden voor hen en voor hun kinderen.

In hoofdstuk 5 ga ik dieper in op het concept van schaamte (*maloya*). Ik benader schaamte als een geïnstitutionaliseerde moraliteit, een belichaamde dispositie en een publiek discours. Vrouwen in Farabako wegen het sociale risico om schaamteloos genoemd te worden af tegen het fysieke risico op morbiditeit en moraliteit. Deze ethische afweging wordt aan het licht gebracht door sociale veranderingen zoals de toenemende individualisering en de introductie van biomedische zorg. In dit hoofdstuk geeft ik voorbeelden van 'ethische momenten' in en rond de kraamkliniek in Farabako, waarin, binnen de context van therapie management, iets plaatsvindt waardoor vrouwen gedwongen werden om te reflecteren op de juiste ethische respons. Ik kijk naar de manieren waarop vrouwen zich bewegen binnen het morele discours over schaamte. Het 'hebben van schaamte', en dus de onderwerping aan de regels van het discours over schaamte, kan een noodzakelijke voorwaarde zijn voor de persoonlijke ontwikkeling van een vrouw in het worden van een 'goede vrouw' (een *technology of the self*).

In hoofdstuk 6 laat ik zien hoe het discours over schaamte bijdraagt aan de frictie tussen het biomedische en het lokaal medische discours. Ik onderzoek of de aanname standhoudt dat biomedische zorg alsmede zijn morele discours universeel toepasbaar zijn in de context van het opzetten van een kraamkliniek in Farabako. Ik betoog dat van een (Nederlands) verloskundig perspectief de kliniek gezien kan worden als een plaats waar de zogenoemde universaliteit van biomedische zorg en de particulariteit van het lokale gezondheidsdiscours en genderdiscours 'ongemakkelijk samenkomen' (*a zone of awkward engagement*). Een nieuwe vorm van biomedische zorg werd gecreëerd die paste binnen de lokale context met zijn specifieke moraliteiten. Morele vraagstukken, zoals wat het betekent om een 'goede genezer' of een 'goede vrouw' te zijn, lagen ten grondslag aan de frictie waaruit deze nieuwe vorm van biomedische zorg geboren werd. Ik beschrijf de ethische dilemma's die zijn ontstaan in deze nieuwe biomedische praktijk, en de rol van het morele discours in het gebruik van en de toegang tot biomedische zorg.

In hoofdstuk 7 onderzoek ik de invloed van het morele discours en het gender discours op de representatie van ziekte in Farabako. Onder de aanname dat een gezondheidsenquête mij de informatie zou verschaffen die ik nodig had om de hoge kindersterfte in Farabako te begrijpen, heb ik ouders en andere leden van het huishouden geïnterviewd over de ziekte-episodes van hun kind. Ik hoorde vaak zeer verschillende versies van één en dezelfde ziekte episode. De manier waarop ouders spraken over de ziekte-episode van hun kind vertelde mij vaak meer over hoe zij zich wilden positioneren binnen het medisch pluralisme en over hoe zij zich wilden presenteren naar mij toe (en mijn ontwikkelingsproject van de kraamkliniek) dan over hoe therapie management werkelijk plaatsvond. Daardoor kreeg ik niet de informatie die ik nodig achtte om de biomedische zorg aan kinderen in Farabako te verbeteren, namelijk informatie over klinische symptomen, diagnoses en behandelingen. De 'werkelijke ziekte episode' was vaak verborgen in hetgeen de ouders over de ziekte vertelden. Deze ziektegeschiedenissen bleken echter wel een goed instrument te zijn om binnen de context van therapie management inzicht te krijgen in genderconstructies en machtsverhoudingen binnen het huishouden.

In hoofdstuk 8 laat ik zien hoe moraliteiten niet alleen een rol spelen in de representatie van ziekten, maar ook in de constructie van ziektecategorieën. Ik laat zien dat het begrijpen van het lokale medische en morele discours een voorwaarde is om therapie management van ziekte-episodes van kinderen te begrijpen. Ik focus hierbij op het specifieke geval van ernstige ondervoeding. Vanuit biomedisch perspectief bezien wordt ernstige ondervoeding veroorzaakt door gebrek aan eten of een eenzijdig dieet. Vanuit een lokaal standpunt in Farabako bezien is ondervoeding daarentegen niet in de eerste plaats een probleem van eten. Het is een schaamtevolle ziekte veroorzaakt door een gebrek aan reproductieve keuze binnen de vulnerabiliteitscontext. Ik laat zien dat er binnen het biomedische en lokaal-medische discours een gemeenschappelijke noemer gezocht moet worden, een aspect derhalve dat past binnen beide discoursen. Alleen dan kan een medische interventie acceptabel en eventueel succesvol zijn.

In hoofdstuk 9 beschrijf ik hoe de vrouwen van Farabako spraken over hun gezondheid en over wat zij zagen als noodzakelijke voorwaarden om een toestand van welzijn te bereiken. Ik beschouw welzijn als een belangrijke factor in therapie management. Toen ik in levensgeschiedenisinterviews vrouwen vroeg om mij te vertellen over hun gezondheid, vertelden zij niet in de eerste plaats over hun fysieke gezondheid maar over hun sociale welzijn. Zij vertelden dat er 'niet goed voor ze gezorgd werd'. Zij spraken over het fysieke en emotionele geweld dat zij moesten gedogen om hun plaats binnen de familie te behouden. Voor de vrouwen van Farabako is de zekerheid dat er goed voor hen gezorgd wordt een voorwaarde voor fysiek en psychologisch welzijn. Centraal in dit hoofdstuk staat hoe de effecten van structureel geweld, in de vorm van armoede en een patriarchale samenleving, tot uiting komen in het articuleren en accepteren van lijden. Het accepteren van lijden bevestigt de patriarchale ideologie, maar kan tegelijkertijd ook deel uit maken van het ethisch project van het aan jezelf werken om een 'goede vrouw' en deugdzaam lid van de gemeenschap te worden. Daardoor kan het accepteren van lijden niet alleen beschouwd worden als een vorm van passiviteit maar juist ook als een vorm van *agency*.

In hoofdstuk 10 reflecteer ik op hoe tijdens dit onderzoek mijn klinisch toegepaste medisch antropologische benadering veranderde in een kritische medisch antropologische benadering. Ik verlegde mijn focus van de lokale gezondheidstheorieën en de toegankelijkheid van de gezondheidszorg in Farabako naar de moraliteiten van mijn respondenten en die van mijzelf als westerse, feministische antropoloog en biomedisch getrainde verloskundige. Mijn onderzoek veranderde van een morele antropologie naar een antropologie van moraliteiten. Ik beschrijf hoe deze stap nodig was om therapie management in Farabako te begrijpen.

In het laatste hoofdstuk beschrijf ik de mechanismen en factoren die er voor zorgden dat moeders soms niet bij machte waren om in actie te komen als zij of een van hun kinderen ziek werd. Ik onderzoek de verbanden tussen gezondheid, moraliteit, gender en armoede. Dit doe ik door de relatie tussen de belangrijke thema's van dit onderzoek, namelijk schaamte, lijden en het 'niet voor gezorgd worden' te analyseren. Ik betoog dat het lijden van vrouwen een uiting is van ontologische onzekerheid in de context van kwetsbaarheid (*vulnerability*). Het hebben van schaamte is een uiting van de belichaming van structurele ongelijkheid. Door het tonen van schaamte hebben vrouwen in Farabako een manier gecreëerd om te leven en samen te leven in een context van patriarchaat en *vulnerability*. Mijn stelling is dat in therapie management in Farabako schaamte werkt als een intersubjectieve logica in het omgaan met het potentiële risico op morbiditeit en mortaliteit onder kinderen. Gezondheidswerkers en beleidsmakers moeten de taal en de logica van de therapie management van hun patiënten begrijpen als een eerste stap om gezondheidsinterventies succesvol te maken.

Begrip van de rol van lokale moraliteiten in de benadering van gezondheid is cruciaal voor de implementatie van de biomedische zorg en het verlagen van morbiditeit en mortaliteit in geïsoleerde gebieden zoals Farabako. Deze etnografie kan bijdragen tot het ontwikkelen van een nieuwe taal voor klinische zorg en public health beleid, gericht op het spreken over gezondheid en welzijn met inachtneming van gevoelens van onzekerheid en machteloosheid als indicatoren van gebrek-aan-welbevinden (*ill-being*).

APPENDIX 1

Methodology Overview

This research was primarily qualitative, however, in fieldwork periods 1-3 an interpretative and concurrent mixed methods approach was used. A concurrent triangulation strategy was applied for data collection and analysis.

1st Fieldwork period

January-April 2007

Sample 1

This sample of informants was a non-probability, purposive and snowball sample.

- 54 women living in Farabako (83% of the total female population in the village).
- 10 *musokɔrɔbaw* (older women specialized in attending births and treating sick children).
- 5 *somaw* (male local medical experts specialized in sand divination).
- 5 midwives.
- 2 doctors.

Data collection 1

The fieldwork was divided into three interview phases:

1. *Survey phase:* to give an indication of the magnitude and social distribution of maternal and neonatal morbidity and mortality (quantitative and qualitative data).
   - A census of the village (356 inhabitants, including the children).
   - 54 reproductive life histories of women aged 18-60 yrs, using a semi-structured questionnaire.
2. *Exploratory phase:* to become familiar with socio-cultural and health service context.
   - 5 interviews with midwives (in Farabako, 3 other villages in the region and in Bamako) using a semi structured questionnaire.
   - 10 interviews with *musokɔrɔbaw* using a semi-structured questionnaires, vignettes, topic lists and free-listing.
   - 5 interviews with *somaw* using free-listing, vignettes and topic lists.
   - 1 interview of the only woman in the village who had no children.
   - 2 interviews with doctors in the region using topic lists.
   - Fieldnotes of observations and informal conversations.

3. *The Participatory phase:* to validate explorative and survey data.
   - 7 feedback focus group discussions with young women, men and *musokɔrɔbaw*.
   - Training and working with local midwives (75 prenatal check-ups and 10 deliveries).

Data analysis 1
A grounded theory approach was used to identify categories and concepts that emerged from the fieldwork notes. The data from the reproductive life histories was coded and analysed using CATPCA (Categorical Principal Components Analysis) in SPSS (a multivariate analysis). Further statistics (univariate and bivariate analysis) were used to analyse and visualize the quantitative data from the reproductive life histories. Qualitative and quantitative data were triangulated during data collection and analysis.

2nd Fieldwork period
January-February 2009

Sample 2
- 24 mothers of children under five years of age.
- 3 local medical experts (2 *somaw*, 1 herbalist, 5 *musokɔrɔbaw*).

Data collection 2
- Free-listing interviews with healers, (*musokɔrɔbaw*, *somaw* and herbalists) and parents asking them to name the children's illnesses they knew.
- Semi-structured interviews on therapy management. I asked 24 mothers to recount an illness episode of one of their children.
- 24 verbal autopsies.
- 24 name generator interviews. I asked the same 24 mothers to name the people whom they could ask for help if they or their children became ill and who had they asked for financial aid, advice or practical support in the past year.
- 24 support transaction interviews. I asked the same respondents to name the people who they themselves had recently helped who were ill.
- Open interviews and focus group discussions on the subject of shame (*maloya*) with mothers, fathers, *musokɔrɔbaw* and *somaw*.

Data analysis 2
Data from the illness episode interviews, verbal autopsies and name generator and support transaction interviews was analysed using CATPCA in SPSS. The name generator and support transaction interviews were further analysed using a network analysis (Netdraw), thereby showing the ties between individuals and families in the context of health (see Appendix 3). All the data was also analysed using a grounded theory method.

3rd Fieldwork period
October-December 2009

Sample 3
- 18 mothers.
- 12 fathers.
- 9 mothers-in-law.
- 7 healers (*musokɔrɔbaw*, *somaw* and herbalists).

Data collection 3
- 46 in-depth interviews, in Farabako (28) and Bamako (18), with mothers (some for the second time), fathers and mothers-in-law, and healers about the same illness episode of a child in the household.
- 46 verbal autopsies.
- 46 name generator interviews.
- 46 support transaction interviews.

Data analysis 3
Data was analysed using CATPCA in SPSS and Netdraw. All the data was also analysed using a grounded theory method.

4th Fieldwork period
February 2011

Sample 4
- 10 mothers living in Farabako.
- 4 healers (*somaw* and herbalists).

Data collection 4
- 10 life history interviews: Open, taped interviews with ten women whom I knew well. I asked them to tell me their life history and to tell me about their health.
- In-depth interviews with herbalists and *somaw* on the local ideas on medical ethics.

Data analysis 4
The interviews were transcribed and translated. The transcripts were analysed using a narrative analysis and a grounded theory method.

5th Fieldwork period
January 2012

Sample 5
- 28 mothers.
- 8 fathers.
- 6 *musokɔrɔbaw*.

Data collection 5
- 10 open and taped interviews with women on the significance of the discourse of shame (*maloya*).
- 4 feedback focus group discussions, with a group of six *musokɔrɔbaw*, a group of four young mothers, a group of four men in their forties and a group of young fathers.
- 18 informal interviews with mothers on the outcome of their first pregnancy.

Data analysis 5
The interviews were transcribed and translated. The transcripts were analysed using a grounded theory method.

APPENDIX 2

Table 1. Explanation of terms for free-listing children's illnesses in Farabako

Illness term in Farabako	Corresponding term in English	Symptoms details	Can be treated by	Number of times named
Damajalan		Blood in the urine Sickness in the belly	Soma	1
Disidimi	Chest pain	Pain in the chest Difficulty breathing Coughing	Herbalist	1
Farilafabana		Oedema belly, feet and face	Soma	1
Fɔɔnɔ	Vomiting	Vomiting	Doctor	2
Jinɛbana	Jinn-disease	Child sees a *jinɛ* or a *subaga* (witch) in dreams Cannot sleep	*Soma* (maybe *musokɔrɔba*, but definitely not doctor)	1
Jŭbɔ	Haemorrhoids	Haemorrhoids	Only *musokɔrɔba*	1
Kaliyabonbon	Itchy rash	Dark spots over all of the body, diarrhoea (said to be an 'illness in the belly')	Doctor can treat with injections	1
Kɔgɔdimi	Chest pain	Pain in the chest	*Musokɔrɔba* Doctor	1
Kolobɔbana	Fever due to teething	Vomiting Diarrhoea Pain in the eyes Fever Not drinking Inside of the mouth is warm (said to be a dangerous illness: many children die)	*Musokɔrɔba* *Soma* Herbalist Doctor	7

Illness term in Farabako	Corresponding term in English	Symptoms details	Can be treated by	Number of times named
Kɔnɔ	Convulsions in children, caused by tetanus or cerebral malaria, attributed to an evil bird.	Clenched fists Eyes rolling upwards Child trembles Spasms (~serious *sumaya*) (*Sɔgɔɲama* and *sandafɛ* used synonymously with *kɔnɔ* or as various forms of *kɔnɔ*)	*Soma, musokɔrɔba* and *dɔnso* (can cure faster than doctor) Doctor (can treat with antibiotics)	9
Kɔnɔbɔli	Diarrhoea Dysentery	Diarrhoea	*Soma* *Musokɔrɔba* Doctor Pharmacy medicine*	4
Kɔnɔdimi	Abdominal pain	Abdominal pain	*Musokɔrɔba* *Soma* Herbalist Doctor	2
Kundakulaye sɔgɔsɔgɔ		Serious cough Vomiting bile (Different from regular *sɔgɔsɔgɔ*)	*Musokɔrɔba* (Doctor does not recognize this disease and modern medicine does not work)	1
Kunkolodimi	Headache	Headache	Herbalist Doctor	1
Mimi	Throat infection	Throat ache Swollen glands Dirty mucus	Herbalist	3
Mugu	Luxation	Fever Difficulty breathing Child cries when chest is touched	Herbalist Doctor	1
Nàgàlojoli		Blood in the mouth and throat	*Musokɔrɔba* Herbalist	1
Nɛgɛtigɛbana	Tetanus	Wound from dirty knife Child trembles, has fear (~*kɔnɔ*)	Herbalist Doctor	1
Ntùmu	Worms	Worms	*Musokɔrɔba* Doctor	1
Ŋunajɔla	Fontanel 'stops'	Fontanel 'stops'	*Musokɔrɔba*	2

Illness term in Farabako	Corresponding term in English	Symptoms details	Can be treated by	Number of times named
Sandafɛ		Spasms (~*kɔnɔ*) Mouth waters ('Only *musokɔrɔbaw* can recognize this illness')	*Musokɔrɔba* Herbalist	4
Sayi	Jaundice, icterus	Complication of malaria Two types: 1. *Sayibilen* red eyes, constipation, weak body, muscle ache 2. *Sayijɛ* (anaemia) white eyes, swollen body, oedema also feet and belly	Herbalist (Biomedical treatment thought to be dangerous: if doctor gives an IV the child will die)	1
Sinkɔrɔtalen	Pneumonia	Pain in the chest Difficulty breathing Coughing Child cannot sleep on its side ('When there is much *sumaya*')	Doctor	4
Sɔgɔɲama	~cerebral malaria	Contractures Red skin Swollen belly ('Looks like *kɔnɔ* but is different')	Dɔnso	3
Sɔgɔsɔgɔ	Coughing	Cough Fever ('Goes together with other illnesses')	Doctor (is best because 'modern medicine works faster') Herbalist *Musokɔrɔba*	4
Sumaya	Malaria	Vomiting Diarrhoea Urine and vomit are yellow Fever Can become *kɔnɔ* Two kinds: 'ordinary *sumaya*' and '*sayi*' (jaundice)	*Soma* *Musokɔrɔba* Doctor Pharmacy medicine Herbalist	10
Tɛgɛjɛ	Anaemia	White palms and foot soles Child sleeps a lot ('Not enough blood')	*Musokɔrɔba*	1
Tɔgɔtɔgɔnin	Dysentery	Diarrhoea with blood Pain in the belly	Herbalist Doctor	1
Tulodimi	Ear pain	Ear infection	*Soma*	1

A *musokɔrɔba* is an elder women specialised in attending births and treating young children; a *soma* is a local medical experts specialized in divination and amulet making; a *dɔnso* is a hunter.

*Self-medication with medicine bought at a pharmacy or from a travelling (iilegal) commercial drug seller.

Table 2. Free-listing of children's illnesses in Bamako

Explanation of free-listing terms

Illness term named	Corresponding term in English	Can be treated by	Number of times named
Angine	Throat infection	Doctor	3
Farigan	Fever	Doctor Pharmacy medicine*	2
Fɔɔnɔ	Vomiting	Doctor Pharmacy medicine *Musokɔrɔba*	3
Kɛtɛkɛtɛnin	Whooping cough	Doctor	1
Kɔnɔ	Convulsions due to severe infection	Doctor	2
Kɔnɔbɔli	Diarrhoea	Doctor Pharmacy medicine *Musokɔrɔba*	4
Kɔnɔdimi	Stomach ache	Pharmacy medicine	3
Kɔnɔrɔjoli	Blood in stool	Doctor	1
Kùnfilàtu	Cholera	Doctor	1
Mura	Cold	Pharmacy medicine	4
Palu (French)	Malaria	Doctor Pharmacy medicine *Musokɔrɔba*	12
Nyɔni	Measles	Doctor	1
Sayi	Jaundice	Doctor	1
Sede (sere)	Malnutrition	Doctor	1
Sɔgɔsɔgɔ	Cough	Doctor Pharmacy medicine *Musokɔrɔba*	6
Tétanos	Tetanus	Doctor	1

* Self-medication with medicine bought at a pharmacy or from a travelling (illegal) commercial drug seller.

13 respondents (4 men and 9 women, all parents, all living in Bamako).

APPENDIX 3

Women's social networks in Farabako

This is a spatial visualization of women's social networks within the village of Farabako (a bird's eye view). The software program Netdraw was used to analyse the data from name generator interviews and support transaction interviews. Squares indicate individual women and men in the village of Farabako. The ties represent people who women could ask for advice, practical support or money when they or one of their children was ill. The ties also indicate the people women had given support to.

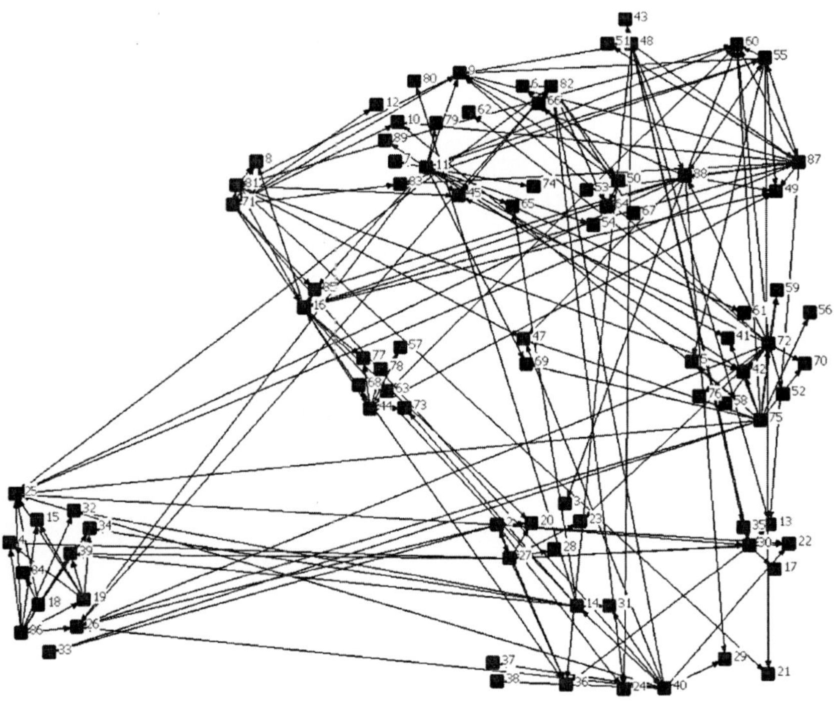

Women's social networks in the context of health

This figure is the visualization of people women could ask for money if a child was ill. The large squares are my respondents. The smaller squares are the people my respondents could ask for money.

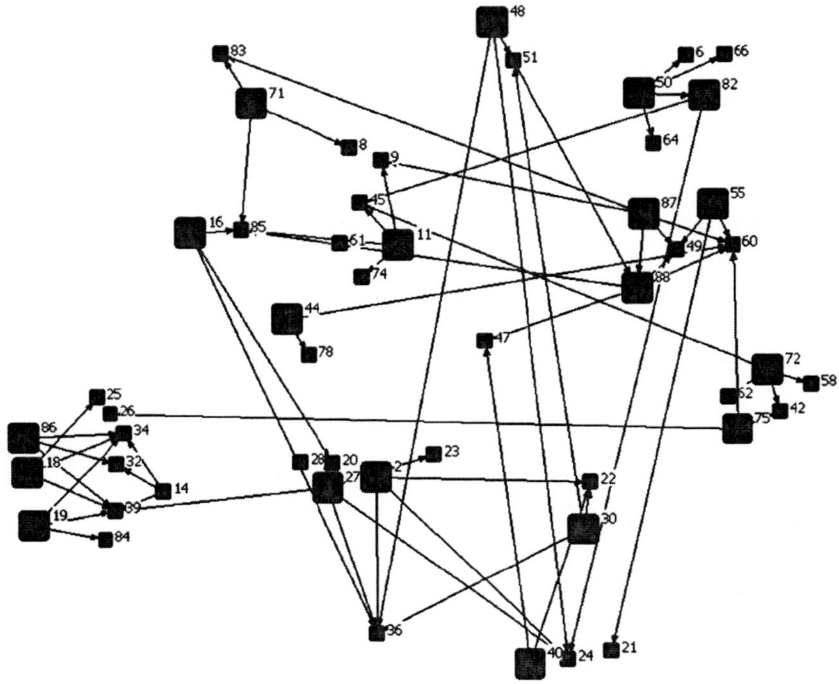

Women's money network in the context of health

APPENDIX 4

Map of Mali

Farabako

http://www.un.org/Depts/Cartographic/map/profile/mali.pdf
(accessed 24 July 2012)

APPENDIX 5

Table 3. Household Therapy Management of Children's Illness Episodes

Household #, name and age of child	**Therapy Group Member**	**Symptoms**	**Diagnosis**
1. **Baba Kante ♂** (1 yr) Farabako	Mother	Vomiting Fever	*Sumaya* (uncomplicated malaria)
	Father *Soma*	Fever	*Siran* (fear caused by sorcery)
	Musokɔrɔba	Crying when picked up Fever Pain in the chest	1. *Mugu* (sprain caused by falling) 2. *Sandafɛ* (serious illness with convulsions)
2. **Modibo Keita ♂** (age 3 yrs) Farabako	Mother	Fever Yellow urine	*Sumaya* (uncomplicated malaria)
	Father	Fever Swollen belly	*Sumaya* (uncomplicated malaria)
	Musokɔrɔba	Cold	*Sumaya* (malaria)
3. **Samba Kante ♂** (age 1,5 yrs) Foster child Farabako	Grandmother	Swollen hands and feet White palms Fever	1. *Dino* (cold) 2. *Tɛgɛjɛ* (white palms) 3. *Jolitala* ('no blood', anaemia) 4. *Tɛgɛjɛ* 5. *Sede (Sere)* (kwashiorkor)
	Father	Swollen hands and feet	?
	Great-grandmother *Musokɔrɔba*	Emaciation Fever	*Sede (Sere)* (kwashiorkor)

Person Consulted	Therapy	Duration of Illness
Doctor (day 1)	Pharmacy medicine	4 days
1. Sand divination by father 2. Doctor (day 1)	1. Traditional medicine 2. Pharmacy medicine.	2 days
1. Herself 2. Doctor (day 3)	1. Traditional medicine 2. Pharmacy medicine	3 days
1. Herbalist, 2. *Musokɔrɔba* 3. Doctor (day 4)	1.Traditional medicine 2. Pharmacy medicine bought by herself 3. Pharmacy medicine bought with prescription	4 days
1. Herbalist 2. Doctor (day 2)	1. Traditional medicine (does not mention medicine bought by his wife) 2. Pharmacy medicine prescribed by doctor	5 days
1. Only the doctor	1. Pharmacy medicine	3 days
1. *Musokɔrɔba* 2. *Musokɔrɔba* 3. Doctor (day 14) 4. Local midwife 5. Dutch midwife [LH] (day 30) 6. Doctor (day 31)	1. Traditional medicine 2. Traditional medicine and *kilisiw* 3. Medicine prescribed by doctor (iron, antibiotics, anti-malarial) 4. Traditional medicine 5. Fortified milk, antibiotics, quinine 6. Special milk-feed	31 days
1. *Musokɔrɔba*	1. Traditional medicine	? (was mostly absent)
1. Herself (*musokɔrɔba*) 2. Doctor	1. Various kinds of Traditional medicine 2. Pharmacy medicine	90 days

Household #, name and age of child	**Therapy Group Member**	**Symptoms**	**Diagnosis**
4. **Faseme Kante ♂** (age 2 yrs) Farabako	Mother	*Kɔnɔbɔli* (diarrhoea) *Disidimi* (pain in the chest)	*Kolobɔbana* (fever of the teeth) *Disidimi* (chest pain) Pneumonia
	Father	Dirty eyes Diarrhoea, Coughing	*Sɔgɔsɔgɔ* (coughing)
	Musokɔrɔba	Diarrhoea	*Kɔnɔbɔli* (diarrhoea) *Sumaya* (malaria)
5. **Sayon Kante ♂** (age 1yr) Farabako	Mother	Vomiting Jaundice Fever Difficulty breathing	*Sumaya* (malaria)
	Musokɔrɔba	Fever Swollen face	*Kolobɔbana* (fever of the teeth)
6. **Bakari Keita ♂** (age 3 months) Farabako	Mother	Fever Difficulty breathing Coughing Pustule in armpit	*Sufɛ farigan* (fever in the night) Pustule
	Father	Crying Not sleeping, coughing Pustule	*Sɔgɔsɔgɔ* (coughing)
	Grandmother *Musokɔrɔba*	Coughing Fever Clenched fists Upturned eyes	*Disidimi* (chest pain) *Kɔnɔ* (serious illness with convulsions) *Kolobɔbana* (fever of the teeth)

Person Consulted	**Therapy**	**Duration of Illness**
1. Grandmother in Guinea 2. Midwife	1. Traditional medicine 2. Injections and tablets	4 days
1. Midwife	1.Traditional medicine 2. Injections and tablets	27days
1. Drug-seller 2. People from vaccination campaign 3. Herself (*musokɔrɔba*)	1. Yellow tablets 2. None 3. Traditional medicine	28 days
1. *Soma* and head of the extended family	1. Traditional medicine	5 days
1. *Musokɔrɔba*	1. Traditional medicine	?
1. *Musokɔrɔba* 2. *Musokɔrɔba* 3. Male family elder 4. Clinic Farabako 5. Pharmacy Nioumamakana	1. Traditional medicine 2. Traditional medicine 3. Petroleum & *kilisiw* (incantations) on pustule 4. Paracetamol and antibiotics 5. Cough syrup	12 days
1. *Musokɔrɔba* 2. Pharmacy Nioumamakana day 5 3. Clinic Farabako (day 8)	1. Traditional medicine 2. Cough syrup antibiotics 3. Antibiotics and Paracetamol	15 days
1. Grandmother herself 2. Neighbour told her to buy antibiotics at clinic Farabako (day 3) 3. Pharmacy Nioumamakana 4. *Musokɔrɔba* 5. Her husband, a *Dɔnso* (hunter)	1. Traditional medicine 2. Antibiotics in clinic Farabako 3. Cough syrup 4. No treatment 5. *Kilisiw* (incantations)	12 days

Household #, name and age of child	Therapy Group Member	Symptoms	Diagnosis
7. **Fasuru Keita ♂** (age 10 months) Farabako	Mother	Fever Something in the throat	*Mimi* (throat infection)
	Father	Not sleeping Not drinking	*Kɔnɔdimi* (belly ache) *Farigan* (fever)
	Musokɔrɔba	Diarrhoea Sore throat	*Kolobɔbana* (lump in the throat)
	Herbalist	Lump in the neck (size of a bean)	*Mimi* (throat infection due to sorcery)
8. **Bobo Kante ♂** (2 yrs) Farabako	Mother	Diarrhoea	*Kɔnɔrɔjoli* (wounds in the belly, blood in the stools) *Kɔnɔbɔli* (diarrhoea) *Sede (Sere)* (kwashiorkor)
	Mother-in-law	Skin lesions	*Kɔnɔrɔjoli* (wounds in the belly' blood in the stools) *Sede (Sere)* (kwashiorkor)
	First *Musokɔrɔba*	Swollen feet Emaciated	*Sede (Sere)* (kwashiorkor)
	Second *Musokɔrɔba*	Skin lesions	
	Soma	Vomiting Skin lesions Diarrhoea	*Dabali* (evil, done by mother's old boyfriend)

Person Consulted	Therapy	Duration of Illness
1. *Musokɔrɔba* 2. Drug-seller 3. Clinic Farabako 4. Herbalist	1. Traditional medicine 2. 10 tablets Nivaquine 3. Paracetamol syrup 4. *Kilisiw* (incantations) on oil	15 days
1. *Musokɔrɔba* 2. Herbalist 3. Clinic Farabako	1. Traditional medicine 2. *Kilisiw* and oil 3. Antibiotics	6 days
1. Herself *(musokɔrɔba)* 2. Her son (has knowledge of traditional medicine)	1. Traditional medicine, *kilisiw* (incantations) on the belly 2. *Kilisiw* (incantations) on the throat	5 days
1. Himself (herbalist)	*Kilisiw* Incantations on oil, massage of the neck	?
1. *Musokɔrɔba* 2. Her husband 3. Travelling salesman 4. *Musokɔrɔba* in other village (day 15) 5. Dutch midwife [LH]	1. Traditional medicine 2. Traditional medicine 3. 4 tablets 4. Traditional medicine 5. Antibiotics, quinine	20 days
1. *Soma* 2. Local midwife 3. *Musokɔrɔba* a 4. *Musokɔrɔba* b 5. *Soma* 6. Visitor from Guinea	1. Sand divination and sacrifice 2. Advised to go to doctor 3. Traditional medicine 4. Traditional medicine 5. Traditional medicine 6. Traditional medicine	5 days
1. Herself (*musokɔrɔba*)	1. Traditional medicine	
1. Herself *(musokɔrɔba)*	1. Traditional medicine	
1. Himself (*soma*)	1. Sand divination (two chickens needed for sacrifice)	?

Household #, name and age of child	Therapy Group Member	Symptoms	Diagnosis
9. **Mambi Kante** ♂ (5 yrs old) village on outskirts of Bamako	Mother	Fear	*Siran* (fear)
	Father *soma*	Fear, crying	*Jinɛbana* (jinn-disease) *Sumaya* (uncomplicated malaria)
	Musokɔrɔba	Fever	
10. **Jean Traore** ♂ (age 4yrs) Bamako	Mother	Vomiting, Diarrhoea Fever	*Kolobɔbana* (fever of the teeth)
	Father	Fever	*Palu* (malaria)
11. **Nahan Keita** ♀ (age 8 months) village on outskirts of Bamako	Mother	Coughing Sputum	Born with a 'deformation of the lungs'
	Father	Difficulty breathing	*Kɔnɔrɔjoli* (wounds in the belly) Pneumonia
	Grandmother *Musokɔrɔba*	Child was not totally better after the visit to the doctor	

Person Consulted	Therapy	Duration of Illness
1. Old man living close by	1. Traditional medicine and oil to rub on the skin	60 days (until husband returned)
1. Himself (*soma*) 2. Specialist in curing illnesses caused by jinn, consulted through a messenger 3. Doctor friend who lives in the village 4. Second consultation doctor	1. Traditonal medicine 2. Traditional medicine from town at border of Guinea 3. Injections 4. Syrup and tablets	75 days (after returning to village)
1. Herself *(musokɔrɔba)* (after doctor's treatment was not totally effective)	Traditional medicine	?
1. Traditional healer at the market	1. Traditional medicine	3 days
1. His older sister	1. Pharmacy medicine	
1. Her husband		
1. His mother 2. Doctor friend 3. Second consultation doctor friend 4. Hospital	1. Traditional medicine 2. Syrup 3. Referral hospital 4. X-ray, injections syrup	20 days
1. Healer at the market	1. *Kilisiw* (incantations) on chest of the child and in water and oil to rub chest with	